DISEMBODIED SOULS

THE *NEFESH* IN ISRAEL AND KINDRED SPIRITS IN THE ANCIENT NEAR EAST, WITH AN APPENDIX ON THE KATUMUWA INSCRIPTION

SBL

Society of Biblical Literature

Ancient Near East Monographs

General Editors
Ehud Ben Zvi
Roxana Flammini

Editorial Board
Reinhard Achenbach
Esther J. Hamori
Steven W. Holloway
René Krüger
Alan Lenzi
Steven L. McKenzie
Martti Nissinen
Graciela Gestoso Singer
Juan Manuel Tebes

Volume Editor
Ehud Ben Zvi

Number 11

DISEMBODIED SOULS

THE *NEFESH* IN ISRAEL AND KINDRED SPIRITS IN THE ANCIENT NEAR EAST, WITH AN APPENDIX ON THE KATUMUWA INSCRIPTION

DISEMBODIED SOULS

THE *NEFESH* IN ISRAEL AND KINDRED SPIRITS IN THE ANCIENT NEAR EAST, WITH AN APPENDIX ON THE KATUMUWA INSCRIPTION

Richard C. Steiner

SBL Press
Atlanta

DISEMBODIED SOULS

THE *NEFESH* IN ISRAEL AND KINDRED SPIRITS IN THE ANCIENT NEAR EAST, WITH AN APPENDIX ON THE KATUMUWA INSCRIPTION

Library of Congress Cataloging-in-Publication Data

Steiner, Richard C., author.
Disembodied souls : the Nefesh in Israel and kindred spirits in the ancient Near East, with an appendix on the Katumuwa Inscription / by Richard C. Steiner.
pages cm. — (Society of Biblical Literature ancient Near East monographs ; 11)
Includes bibliographical references and indexes.
ISBN 978-1-62837-076-8 (paper binding : alk. paper) — ISBN 978-1-62837-077-5 (electronic format) — ISBN 978-1-62837-078-2 (hardcover binding : alk. paper) 1. Nefesh (The Hebrew word) 2. Inscriptions, Aramaic—Turkey—Zincirli (Gaziantep Ili) 3. Bible. Old Testament—Language, style. 4. Bible. Old Testament—Criticism, interpretation, etc., Jewish. I. Title.
PJ4819.N44S74 2015
492›.29—dc23

2014039318

Printed on acid-free, recycled paper conforming to ANSI /NISO Z39.48–1992 (R1997) and ISO 9706:1994 standards for paper permanence.

לזכר נשמות סבי אשתי:

ר׳ נתן נטע בן ר׳ ראובן ורחל

שרה בת ר׳ יעקב וחנה

ר׳ יצחק יעקב בן ר׳ יוסף וואלף

חנה בת ר׳ ברוך יוסל

עברו באש התופת, ולא ידע איש את קבורתם.

ועל כגון זה אמרו:

אין עושין נפשות לצדיקים; דבריהן הן הן זכרונן.

Contents

Preface and Acknowledgments ix
Abbreviations xiii
Introduction 1
1. A Disembodied נבש at Samal and Its Ancient Near Eastern Kinfolk 10
2. Women Trapping Souls 23
3. Pillows and Pillow Casings 28
4. Cloth Patches as Pillow Filling 38
5. Souls in Bags 43
6. Pillow-Traps for Dream-Souls 46
7. From Dream-Souls to Bird-Souls 55
8. Disembodied נפשות Elsewhere in the Hebrew Bible 68
9. The רוח 81
10. The Reunion of the Disembodied Soul with Its Kinsmen 93
11. Afterthoughts on the Afterlife of the Soul 101
12. Semantic Structure 115
13. Alleged Evidence against the Existence of Disembodied נפשות 119
14. Conclusions 124
Appendix 1: The Katumuwa Inscription from Zincirli 128
Appendix 2: The Meaning of לְצוֹדֵד 163
Bibliography 167
Index of Ancient Texts 199
Index of Subjects 205

Preface and Acknowledgments

This monograph has a long and convoluted history. Its original kernel—a discussion of the biblical term כסת in the light of its Mishnaic Hebrew counterpart (chapter 3)—emerged from a course on biblical semantics and lexicology first offered at the Bernard Revel Graduate School of Yeshiva University in 1976. From the very beginning, the course had a unit on the importance of Mishnaic Hebrew for biblical lexicology, and, after teaching the course for a number of years, I added the discussion of כסת to that unit. Decades later, when I offered the course in the spring of 2011, it dawned on me that, in shedding light on the meaning of Biblical Hebrew כסת in Ezek 13:18 and 20—verses that deal with women who pretend to trap נפשות in כסתות—Mishnaic Hebrew had illuminated the meaning of Biblical Hebrew נפש as well.

I wrote an essay on the subject and, in January of 2012, I submitted it to two SBL editors, one after the other. I sent it first to James C. VanderKam, the editor of *JBL*, who responded virtually immediately. Then I sent it to Ehud Ben Zvi, the editor of Ancient Near Eastern Monographs (ANEM). He, too, responded virtually immediately. Their responses were remarkably similar in other respects as well. They both informed me, in the nicest way possible, that my essay did not conform to the length restrictions that they were sworn to uphold. In addition, they both encouraged me to fix the problem by changing the length—albeit in opposite directions. Their kindness helped to alleviate my frustration at finding that my essay on the trapping of souls had itself become trapped in an academic limbo, a sort of no-publish zone. It was, in the eyes of SBL, much too long for an article and much too short for a monograph.

At the time, shortening the essay seemed like a daunting task, and so I decided to expand it into a monograph, under the guidance of Prof. Ben Zvi and his anonymous referees. That course turned out to be far from easy. It took an additional three years of intensive work just to gain a passing familiarity with the seemingly bottomless pit of Sheol and the afterlife. It is my pleasant duty to thank Prof. Ben Zvi for his encouragement and advice and for honoring the end product with a place in the ANEM series.

Beginning in January of 2014, two years after contacting the SBL editors, I presented the then-current draft of this monograph to a doctoral seminar in the Bernard Revel Graduate School. I am deeply indebted to Prof. Aaron Koller, my colleague and former student, for volunteering to assist me in the running of that seminar and for reading and commenting on the monograph at two different stages. It was he who persuaded me that I could not avoid grappling with the problems surrounding the afterlife of the נפש (chapter 11)—hellish problems whose snares I had hoped to avoid. Another participant in the seminar deserving of special thanks is Rabbi Shaul Seidler-Feller. After subjecting the draft that I circulated to painstaking scrutiny, he sent me no fewer than fourteen pages of corrections and queries.

Two other colleagues at the Bernard Revel Graduate School, Dean David Berger and Prof. S. Z. Leiman, contributed to this work in ways great and small. Dean Berger managed to scrape together a subsidy for the typesetting of this work at a time of serious financial deficits; Prof. Leiman provided invaluable bibliographic assistance with his well-known generosity. In addition, both of them were of great help in formulating the title of the monograph and—together with Prof. Joshua Blau—the Hebrew dedication. I would also like to thank my brother, Prof. Mark Steiner, who commented on several philosophical matters, and Prof. John Huehnergard, who helped with a cuneiform matter relevant to the Katumuwa inscription.

I am extremely grateful to four bibliophiles whose cheerful, patient assistance went far beyond the call of duty: Mary Ann Linahan and Zvi Erenyi of the Yeshiva University libraries, Maurya Horgan and Paul Kobelski of the HK Scriptorium. They took countless burdens off of my shoulders and countless hours off of the time needed to bring this work to completion. Indeed, it is no exaggeration to say that Ms. Linahan was a major benefactor of this research project.

As always, my dear, devoted wife Sara has been my chief source of support. It is with profound gratitude that I dedicate this book to her grandparents ז"ל: Nosen Nute and Sure Rosenschein; Yitzchok

Yankev and Chane Weisz. If only they had survived Auschwitz, "their נפש would have been bound up with her נפש," to paraphrase Gen 44:30 and 1 Sam 18:1.

Last but not least, I take this opportunity to thank those who helped me remain a נפש חיה, a "living soul," in the face of health problems that coincided with the writing of this book. One of them is Dr. Stephen R. Karbowitz, my pulmonologist, who cared for my נשמת חיים as if it were his own. Another is Dr. Rivka S. Horowitz, my cousin and private "concierge doctor," whose deep love for her family makes her a worthy heir of her mother, Irene (Chaya) ז"ל. She richly deserves the title נפש חיה, in the postbiblical sense of "Chaya's monument." And, above all:

מודה אני לפניך, מלך חי וקיים, שהחזרת בי נשמתי וכו׳

Abbreviations

AASF	Annales Academiae Scientiarum Fennicae
AB	Anchor Bible
AGJU	Arbeiten zur Geschichte des antiken Judentums und des Urchristentums
AHw	Wolfram von Soden. *Akkadisches Handwörterbuch.* 3 vols. Wiesbaden: Harrassowitz, 1965–1981.
ALASP	Abhandlungen zur Literatur alt-Syrien-Palästinas
ANET	J. B. Pritchard, ed. *Ancient Near Eastern Texts Relating to the Old Testament.* 3rd ed. Princeton: Princeton University Press, 1969.
AnOr	Analecta Orientalia
AOAT	Alter Orient und Altes Testament
AR	*Archiv für Religionswissenschaft*
ATD	Das Alte Testament deutsch
BA	*Biblical Archaeologist*
BAR	*Biblical Archaeology Review*
BASOR	*Bulletin of the American Schools of Oriental Research*
BDB	F. Brown, S. R. Driver, and C. A. Briggs. *A Hebrew and English Lexicon of the Old Testament.* Oxford: Clarendon, 1907.
BH	Biblical Hebrew
Bib	*Biblica*
BibOr	Biblica et Orientalia
CAD	*The Assyrian Dictionary of the Oriental Institute of the University of Chicago.* Chicago: Oriental Institute, 1956.
CANE	Jack M. Sasson, ed. *Civilizations of the Ancient Near East.* 4 vols. New York: Scribner, 1995.
CAT	Manfried Dietrich, Oswald Loretz, and Joaquín Sanmartín, eds. *The Cuneiform Alphabetic Texts from Ugarit, Ras Ibn Hani, and Other Places.* AOAT 360. Münster: Ugarit-Verlag, 1995.

CHANE	Culture and History of the Ancient Near East
COS	William W. Hallo, ed. *The Context of Scripture.* 3 vols. Leiden: Brill, 1997–2002.
Cowley	A. Cowley, ed. *Aramaic Papyri of the Fifth Century B.C.* Oxford: Clarendon, 1923.
DBY	Darby Bible
DDD	Karel van der Toorn, Bob Becking, and Pieter W. van der Horst, eds. *Dictionary of Deities and Demons in the Bible.* 2nd rev. ed. Grand Rapids: Eerdmans, 1999.
DISO	Charles-F. Jean and Jacob Hoftijzer. *Dictionnaire des inscriptions sémitiques de l'ouest.* New ed. Leiden: Brill, 1965.
DNWSI	J. Hoftijzer and K. Jongeling. *Dictionary of the North-West Semitic Inscriptions.* 2 vols. Handbook of Oriental Studies, The Near and Middle East 21. Leiden: Brill, 1995.
FAT	Forschungen zum Alten Testament
GWT	God's Word Translation
HALAT	L. Koehler, W. Baumgartner, and J. J. Stamm, *Hebräisches und aramäisches Lexikon zum Alten Testament.* Leiden: Brill, 1967–1996.
HALOT	L. Koehler, W. Baumgartner, and J. J. Stamm. *The Hebrew and Aramaic Lexicon of the Old Testament.* Translated and edited under the supervision of M. E. J. Richardson. 5 vols. Leiden: Brill, 1994–2000.
HAT	Handbuch zum Alten Testament
HKAT	Handkommentar zum Alten Testament
HO	Handbuch der Orientalistik = Handbuch of Oriental Studies
HSM	Harvard Semitic Monographs
HSS	Harvard Semitic Studies
HTR	*Harvard Theological Review*
IBC	Interpretation: A Bible Commentary for Teaching and Preaching
ICC	International Critical Commentary
IDB	G. A. Buttrick, ed. *The Interpreter's Dictionary of the Bible.* 4 vols. Nashville: Abingdon, 1962.
IEJ	*Israel Exploration Journal*
JANES	*Journal of the Ancient Near Eastern Society*
JBL	*Journal of Biblical Literature*

JJS	*Journal of Jewish Studies*
JNES	*Journal of Near Eastern Studies*
Josephus	
Ant.	*Antiquities of the Jews*
J.W.	*Jewish War*
JQR	*Jewish Quarterly Review*
JSS	*Journal of Semitic Studies*
JSSSup	Journal of Semitic Studies Supplement
KAI	H. Donner and W. Röllig, eds. *Kanaanäische und aramäische Inschriften.* 3 vols. in 1. Wiesbaden: Harrassowitz, 1966–1969.
KAT	Kommentar zum Alten Testament
KHC	Kurzer Hand-Commentar zum Alten Testament
KTU	M. Dietrich, O. Loretz, and J. Sanmartín, eds. *Die keilalphabetischen Texte aus Ugarit.* AOAT 24.1. Neukirchen-Vluyn: Neukirchener Verlag, 1976.
JNES	*Journal of Near Eastern Studies*
JSS	*Journal of Semitic Studies*
LCL	Loeb Classical Library
Ma'agarim.	Electronic Resource. *Historical Dictionary of the Academy of the Hebrew Language.* Jerusalem: Academy of the Hebrew Language. Online, http://maagarim.hebrew-academy.org.il/
MGWJ	*Monatsschrift für Geschichte und Wissenschaft des Judentums*
MH	Mishnaic Hebrew
NIDB	Katharine Doob Sakenfeld, ed. *The New Interpreter's Dictionary of the Bible.* 5 vols. Nashville: Abingdon, 2006–2009.
NJPS	New Jewish Publication Society Version
NRSV	New Revised Standard Version
OBO	Orbis biblicus et orientalis
OTL	Old Testament Library
OTS	*Oudtestamentische Studiën*
RB	*Revue biblique*
RHPR	*Revue d'histoire et de philosophie religieuses*
RSV	Revised Standard Version
SAA	State Archives of Assyria
SAOC	Studies in Ancient Oriental Civilizations
SBLDS	Society of Biblical Literature Dissertation Series

SC	Sources chrétiennes
SEL	*Studi epigrafici e linguistici*
SHCANE	Studies in the History and Culture of the Ancient Near East
SHR	Studies in the History of Religions (supplements to *Numen*)
SNTSMS	Society for New Testament Studies Monograph Series
STDJ	Studies on the Texts of the Desert of Judah
TADAE	Bezalel Porten and Ada Yardeni. *Textbook of Aramaic Documents from Ancient Egypt.* 4 vols. Texts and Studies for Students. Jerusalem: Hebrew University of Jerusalem, 1986–1999.
TDNT	G. Kittel and G. Friedrich, eds. *Theological Dictionary of the New Testament.* Translated by G. W. Bromiley. 15 vols. Grand Rapids: Eerdmans, 1964–1976.
TDOT	Johannes Botterweck and H. Ringgren eds. *Theological Dictionary of the Old Testament.* Translated by J. T. Willis, G. W. Bromiley, and D. E. Green. 8 vols. Grand Rapids: Eerdmans, 1974–.
TSAJ	Texte und Studien zum antiken Judentum
TSSI	John C. L. Gibson. *Textbook of Syrian Semitic Inscriptions.* 4 vols. Oxford: Clarendon, 1971–2009.
UF	*Ugarit-Forschungen*
VTSup	Supplements to Vetus Testamentum
WBC	Word Biblical Commentary
WO	*Die Welt des Orients*
WUNT	Wissenschaftliche Untersuchungen zum Neuen Testament
ZAW	*Zeitschrift für die alttestamentliche Wissenschaft*

Introduction

For over a century, the Israelite נפש has fought a losing battle for the hearts and minds of biblical scholars, seeking to retain its traditional status as an entity separate from the body and capable of existing outside of it. During the early decades of the twentieth century, the outcome still seemed uncertain. At that time, it was still possible to assert that "*nefesh* is used as the name of the disembodied spirit";[1] that "the Hebrews apparently retained down to historical times the conception of the soul as a separable thing, which can be removed from a man's body in his lifetime, either by the wicked art of witches, or by the owner's voluntary act in order to deposit it for a longer or shorter time in a place of safety";[2] that "like many other peoples of antiquity, the ancient Israelites believed that the soul could slip in and out of the body at will."[3] In retrospect, however, it is clear that even then biblical scholarship was in the process of abandoning the disembodied נפש—"giving up the ghost," so to speak.[4] Already in 1913, we find H. Wheeler Robinson transporting the ancient Israelite נפש (according to the modern scholarly view) to

---

[1] Lewis B. Paton, "The Hebrew Idea of the Future Life. I. Earliest Conceptions of the Soul," *Biblical World* 35 (1910): 10.

[2] James G. Frazer, *Folk-lore in the Old Testament: Studies in Comparative Religion, Legend and Law* (3 vols.; London: Macmillan, 1918–1919), 2:513.

[3] W. O. E. Oesterley, *Immortality and the Unseen World: A Study in Old Testament Religion* (London: Society for Promoting Christian Knowledge, 1921), 15.

[4] See Joel B. Green, "Soul," *NIDB* 5:359: "Biblical studies . . . since the early 20th century almost unanimously supported a unitary account of the human person." Intellectual historians may be interested in the use of the word *unanimously* (< *unus animus* "one soul") in a statement denying that the traditional concept of the soul has any scriptural basis!

the Roman period and attributing it to Paul: "A true Jew, he shrinks from the idea of a disembodied spirit."[5]

The process was, of course, a gradual one. An article in the *Journal of Biblical Literature* from 1916 straddles the fence, as though the traditional view were compatible with the modern one: "The nature of the disembodied soul was never conceived by the ancient Semites as apart from the body which it once animated."[6] This transitional phase did not last long. It soon became widely accepted that "the *nephesh* cannot be separated from the body"[7] and that "the Hebrew could not conceive of a disembodied נפש."[8] This view of Israelite thought is very much alive in contemporary scholarship.[9] In an article published in 2011, we read that "there is little or no evidence that belief in a soul existed, at least in the sense of a soul as a disembodied entity entirely discrete from the body."[10] An article from 2013 asserts that "in the 756 instances of . . . *nefeš* in the Hebrew Bible" it does not "ever clearly appear in disembodied form, apart from a physical object (always human in the Bible . . .). After death, the Biblical Hebrew *nefeš* has no separate existence; when it departs, it ceases to exist and . . . 'goes out (*yṣʾ*)' like a light."[11]

The modern view of the word נפש is not new. It is found already in John Parkhurst's *Hebrew and English Lexicon* (1762):

---

[5] H. Wheeler Robinson, *The Christian Doctrine of Man* (2nd ed.; Edinburgh: T&T Clark, 1913), 131.

[6] W. Carleton Wood, "The Religion of Canaan: From the Earliest Times to the Hebrew Conquest," *JBL* 35 (1916): 124.

[7] Robert Laurin, "The Concept of Man as a Soul," *ExpTim* 72 (1960–1961): 132.

[8] N. W. Porteous, "Soul," *IDB* 4:428b.

[9] For a rare exception, see Stephen L. Cook, "Death, Kinship, and Community: Afterlife and the חסד Ideal in Israel," in *The Family in Life and in Death: The Family in Ancient Israel. Sociological and Archaeological Perspectives* (ed. Patricia Dutcher-Walls; New York: T&T Clark International, 2009), 107: "The soul (נפש) is separable from the body in biblical faith, as in ancient Near Eastern culture in general. . . ."

[10] James F. Osborne, "Secondary Mortuary Practice and the Bench Tomb: Structure and Practice in Iron Age Judah," *JNES* 70 (2011): 42 n. 48.

[11] Seth L. Sanders, "The Appetites of the Dead: West Semitic Linguistic and Ritual Aspects of the Katumuwa Stele," *BASOR* 369 (2013): 44.

> נפש hath been supposed to signify the *spiritual part* of man or what we commonly call his *soul*, I must for myself confess, that I can find no passage where it hath *undoubtedly* this meaning. Gen. xxxv. 18. Ps. xvi. 10. seem fairest for this signification, but may not נפש in the former passage be most properly rendered *breath*, and in the latter a *breathing* or *animal frame*?[12]

In Thomas Hobbes's *Leviathan* (1651), we find an earlier and fuller exposition:

> The Soule in Scripture, signifieth always, either the Life, or the Living Creature; and the Body and Soule jointly, the *Body alive*. In the fift day of the Creation, God said, Let the waters produce *Reptile animæ viventis*, the creeping thing that hath in it a Living Soule; the English translate it, *that hath life*: And again, God created Whales, *& omnem animam viventem*; which in the English is, *every Living Creature*: And likewise of Man, God made him of the dust of the earth, and breathed in his face the breath of Life, *& factus est Homo in animam viventem*, that is, *and Man was made a Living Creature*. And after *Noah* came out of the Arke, God saith, hee will no more smite *omnem animam viventem*, that is, *every Living Creature*: And Deut. 12. 23. *Eate not the Bloud, for the Bloud is the Soule*; that is, *the Life*. From which places, if by *Soule* were meant a *Substance Incorporeall*, with an existence separated from the Body, it might as well be inferred of any other living Creature, as of Man.[13]

This exposition comes in a chapter (44) entitled "Of Spirituall Darknesse from MISINTERPRETATION of Scripture."[14]

---

[12] John Parkhurst, *An Hebrew and English Lexicon without Points* (London: W. Faden, 1762), 203.

[13] Thomas Hobbes, *Leviathan or the Matter, Forme, and Power of a Common-wealth Ecclesiasticall and Civil* (London: Andrew Crooke, 1651), 339–40 = *Hobbes's Leviathan: Reprinted from the Edition of 1651 with an Essay by the Late W. G. Pogson Smith* (Oxford: Oxford University Press, 1909), 481.

[14] Ibid., 333=472. Already in this title, it is clear that Hobbes rejected the traditional view of the soul in the Bible. For this and other challenges to Christian anthropological dualism, see John W. Cooper, *Body, Soul, and Life Everlasting: Biblical Anthropology and the Monism–Dualism Debate* (Grand Rapids: Eerdmans, 1989).

An even earlier source is the commentary of a major Jewish exegete in thirteenth-century Italy, Isaiah of Trani. In commenting on 1 Sam 25:29, he writes:

> כל מקום שאומר הַנֶּפֶשׁ, הוא הגוף והנשמה ולא הנשמה לבד, דכתיב וְהַנֶּפֶשׁ אֲשֶׁר־תֹּאכַל וכתיב עַל־נֶפֶשׁ מֵת, ואין לומר על הנשמה נֶפֶשׁ מֵת.[15]

> Wherever it says הנפש, it refers to the body and the soul (הנשמה)—not to the soul alone, for it is written וְהַנֶּפֶשׁ אֲשֶׁר־תֹּאכַל (Lev 7:20), and it is written עַל־נֶפֶשׁ מֵת (Num 6:6), where the phrase נֶפֶשׁ מֵת cannot be used of the soul.[16]

It is clear from this discussion that the author's agreement with modern scholars is limited to the meaning of the word נפש. He does not deny that the Bible recognizes the existence of a soul separate from the body. For that, however, he believes that the correct term is נשמה, not נפש.

The philosophical component of the modern view is even older than the philological component. In his treatise on the soul, Aristotle writes: *ὅτι μὲν οὖν οὐκ ἔστιν ἡ ψυχὴ χωριστὴ τοῦ σώματος, ἢ μέρη τινὰ αὐτῆς, εἰ μεριστὴ πέφυκεν, οὐκ ἄδηλον*, "That, therefore, the soul (or certain parts of it, if it is divisible) cannot be separated from the body is quite clear."[17] Further: *καὶ διὰ τοῦτο καλῶς ὑπολαμβάνουσιν οἷς δοκεῖ μήτ' ἄνευ σώματος εἶναι μήτε σῶμά τι ἡ ψυχή*, "And for this reason those have the right conception who believe that the soul does not exist without a body and yet is not itself a kind of body."[18]

---

[15] See מקראות גדולות הכתר — ספר שמואל (ed. Menachem Cohen; Ramat Gan: Bar-Ilan University Press, 1993), 133b, s.v. והיתה נפש אדני צרורה בצרור החיים.

[16] This argument appears to assume that the use of Hebrew נפש in some passages in the sense of "person" somehow precludes its use in other passages in the medieval sense of נשמה, that is, "soul." It may even assume that נפש had only one meaning. If so, it seems likely that Isaiah of Trani, who refers to Rashi as המורה "the teacher," was influenced by the latter's revolutionary approach to lexicology. Rashi, unlike his predecessors, felt that words often have a single underlying meaning; see Richard C. Steiner, "Saadia vs. Rashi: On the Shift from Meaning-Maximalism to Meaning-Minimalism in Medieval Biblical Lexicology," *JQR* 88 (1998): 213–58.

[17] Aristotle, *De Anima* (trans. D. W. Hamlyn; Oxford: Oxford University Press, 1993), 10 (2.1.12 413a) with changes in punctuation.

[18] Aristotle, *De Anima*, 14 (2.2.14 414a).

There are many passages in the Hebrew Bible where it is possible to see a reference to the soul as traditionally understood. Such *possible* references to the soul, cited with confidence by earlier generations, may still be worth discussing. It may be possible to elevate them to the level of *probable* through the use of new evidence or the like. The problem with them, however, is that they can be (and have been) explained away through various exegetical maneuvers by those inclined to do so. The meaning "soul" is easy to dismiss because the plethora of other meanings that have been proposed for נפש ("person," "life," "life-force," "breath," "gullet," etc.) virtually guarantees that there will be one among them to fit any given context. If not, figurative interpretation is always available as a last resort.

It is clear, therefore, that our initial focus must be on passages in the Hebrew Bible where נפש not only *may* mean "soul" but, in Parkhurst's words, "hath *undoubtedly* this meaning"—passages in which it is *necessary* to see a soul separate from the body. From my perspective, only one of the passages cited by previous defenders of the disembodied נפש has the potential to be such a "smoking gun," and I believe that it is worthy of special attention. We need to see whether the evidence can withstand intense scrutiny.

The passage in question is in Ezekiel 13:17–21:

17. וְאַתָּה בֶן־אָדָם שִׂים פָּנֶיךָ אֶל־בְּנוֹת עַמְּךָ הַמִּתְנַבְּאוֹת מִלִּבְּהֶן וְהִנָּבֵא עֲלֵיהֶן׃
18. . . . הוֹי לִמְתַפְּרוֹת כְּסָתוֹת עַל כָּל־אַצִּילֵי יָדַי וְעֹשׂוֹת הַמִּסְפָּחוֹת עַל־רֹאשׁ כָּל־
קוֹמָה לְצוֹדֵד נְפָשׁוֹת הַנְּפָשׁוֹת תְּצוֹדֵדְנָה לְעַמִּי וּנְפָשׁוֹת לָכֶנָה תְחַיֶּינָה׃
19. וַתְּחַלֶּלְנָה אֹתִי אֶל־עַמִּי בְּשַׁעֲלֵי שְׂעֹרִים וּבִפְתוֹתֵי לֶחֶם לְהָמִית נְפָשׁוֹת אֲשֶׁר לֹא־
תְמוּתֶנָה וּלְחַיּוֹת נְפָשׁוֹת אֲשֶׁר לֹא־תִחְיֶינָה בְּכַזֶּבְכֶם לְעַמִּי שֹׁמְעֵי כָזָב׃
20. . . . הִנְנִי אֶל־כִּסְּתוֹתֵיכֶנָה אֲשֶׁר אַתֵּנָה מְצֹדְדוֹת שָׁם אֶת־הַנְּפָשׁוֹת
לְפֹרְחוֹת וְקָרַעְתִּי אֹתָם מֵעַל זְרוֹעֹתֵיכֶם וְשִׁלַּחְתִּי אֶת־הַנְּפָשׁוֹת אֲשֶׁר אַתֶּם מְצֹדְדוֹת
אֶת־נְפָשִׁים לְפֹרְחֹת׃
21. וְקָרַעְתִּי אֶת־מִסְפְּחֹתֵיכֶם וְהִצַּלְתִּי אֶת־עַמִּי מִיֶּדְכֶן וְלֹא־יִהְיוּ עוֹד בְּיֶדְכֶן
לִמְצוּדָה . . . ׃

In this monograph, I shall argue that the passage means something like the following:

> 17. And you, man, set your face toward the women of your people who pose as prophetesses, (prophesying) out of their own minds, and prophesy against them.
>
> 18. . . . Woe unto those (women posing as prophetesses) who sew (fabric to make empty) pillow casings (and sew them) onto

> the joints of every arm, and who make the cloth patches (for pillow filling, and put them) on the head of every (woman among them of tall) stature, in order to trap (dream-)souls. Can you (really) trap souls belonging to My people while keeping your own souls alive?
>
> 19. You have profaned Me [= My name] among My people for/with handfuls of barley and morsels of bread, proclaiming the death of souls that will/should not die and the survival of souls that will/should not live—lying to My people, who listen to (your) lies.
>
> 20. . . . I am going to deal with your (empty) pillow casings in which you (pretend to) trap (dream-)souls (and turn them) into bird-souls. And I shall free (from your clutches) the souls (of those who listen to your lies), for you (are pretending to) trap dream-souls (and turn them) into bird-souls.
>
> 21. And I shall tear your cloth patches (from your heads) and rescue my people from your clutches [lit., hands], and they will no longer become prey in your clutches [lit., hands]. . . .

At the end of the nineteenth century, it was suggested that the phrase לְצוֹדֵד נְפָשׁוֹת referred to a magical trapping of souls. James G. Frazer dealt with this subject already in 1890:

> Souls may be extracted from their bodies or detained on their wanderings not only by ghosts and demons but also by men, especially by sorcerers. In Fiji if a criminal refused to confess, the chief sent for a scarf with which to "catch away the soul of the rogue." At the sight, or even at the mention of the scarf the culprit generally made a clean breast. For if he did not, the scarf would be waved over his head till his soul was caught in it, when it would be carefully folded up and nailed to the end of a chief's canoe; and for want of his soul the criminal would pine and die. The sorcerers of Danger Island used to set snares for souls. . . .[19]

After pages of such examples, Frazer remarked in a footnote, "Some time ago my friend Professor W. Robertson Smith suggested to me that the practice of hunting souls, which is denounced in Ezekiel xiii. 17 sqq. must have been akin to those described in the text."[20]

---

[19] James G. Frazer, *The Golden Bough: A Study in Comparative Religion* (1st ed.; 2 vols.; London: Macmillan, 1890), 117.

[20] Ibid., 120 n. 1.

Like Frazer, Alfred Bertholet took it for granted that the trapped souls were from living people,[21] while Richard Kraetzschmar asserted that at least some of them (the ones referred to in the phrase לְחַיּוֹת נְפָשׁוֹת אֲשֶׁר לֹא־תִחְיֶינָה) were spirits of the dead in the underworld, roused from their rest through necromancy.[22] Kraetzschmar's necromantic interpretation, after being consigned to the "land of oblivion" for a good part of the twentieth century, was brought back to life in modified form by Karel van der Toorn and Marjo C. A. Korpel:

> In my opinion the key expression 'hunt for souls' must be understood as an allusion to necromancy. The description transports us to a seance, in which a group of female diviners, by means of mysterious cords and veils, tries to communicate with the 'spirits of the dead.' The latter are called 'souls' by Ezekiel.[23]

> The prophetesses killed the souls of good people, condemning them to eternal emprisonment in Sheol, the second death from which even the inhabitants of the hereafter were not exempt. . . . But they kept alive the souls of evil people to invoke them from the Nether World whenever they wanted to make use of their nefarious powers.[24]

At the beginning of the twentieth century, the suggestion that Frazer published in William Robertson Smith's name was developed by Adolphe Lods, citing many parallels from Frazer's work, and subsequently by Frazer himself.[25] To Frazer it seemed obvious that the

---

[21] Alfred Bertholet, *Das Buch Hesekiel* (KHC 12; Freiburg i. B.: J. C. B. Mohr, 1897), 72.

[22] Richard Kraetzschmar, *Das Buch Ezechiel* (HKAT; Göttingen: Vandenhoeck & Ruprecht, 1900), 135. So, too, Sigmund Mowinckel, *Psalmenstudien* (6 vols.; Kristiania: J. Dybwad, 1921–1924), 1:65 (very briefly).

[23] Karel van der Toorn, *From Her Cradle to Her Grave: The Role of Religion in the Life of the Israelite and the Babylonian Woman* (trans. Sara J. Denning-Bolle; Biblical Seminar 23; Sheffield: JSOT Press, 1994), 123.

[24] Marjo C. A. Korpel, "Avian Spirits in Ugarit and in Ezekiel 13," in *Ugarit, Religion and Culture: Proceedings of the International Colloquium on Ugarit, Religion and Culture, Edinburgh, July 1994. Essays Presented in Honour of Professor John C. L. Gibson* (ed. N. Wyatt, W. G. E. Watson, and J. B. Lloyd; Ugaritisch-biblische Literatur 12; Münster: Ugarit-Verlag, 1996), 105.

[25] Adolphe Lods, *La croyance à la vie future et le culte des morts dans*

נפשות being trapped were disembodied souls of living people, no different from the ones he had studied in cultures all over the world. His interpretation of the magical aspect, far more developed than Bertholet's, is not without its advocates,[26] but the latter are outnumbered by those who reject it.[27] Some studies devoted to the term נפש do not mention this critical passage from Ezekiel at all.[28]

l'antiquité israélite (2 vols.; Paris: Fischbacher, 1906), 1:46–48; James G. Frazer, "Hunting for Souls," *AR* 11 (1908): 197–99; idem, *Folk-lore in the Old Testament*, 2:510–13.

[26] Oesterley, *Immortality*, 16; Henry P. Smith, "Frazer's 'Folk-lore in the Old Testament,'" *HTR* 17 (1924): 74–75; Adolphe Lods, "Magie hébraïque et magie cananéenne," *RHPR* 7 (1927): 13; Daniel Lys, *Nèphèsh: Histoire de l'âme dans la révélation d'Israël au sein des religions proche-orientales* (Études d'histoire et de philosophie religieuses 50; Paris: Presses Universitaires de France, 1959), 161, cf. 179; H. W. F. Saggs, "'External Souls' in the Old Testament," *JSS* 19 (1974): 1–12; and Ziony Zevit, *The Religions of Ancient Israel: A Synthesis of Parallactic Approaches* (London: Continuum, 2001), 562; not to mention Theodor H. Gaster, *Myth, Legend, and Custom in the Old Testament: A Comparative Study with Chapters from Sir James G. Frazer's* Folklore in the Old Testament (New York: Harper & Row, 1969), 615–17.

[27] See, for example, J. A. Selbie, "Ezekiel xiii. 18-21," *ExpTim* 15 (1903–1904): 75; Paul Torge, *Seelenglaube und Unsterblichkeitshoffnung im Alten Testament* (Leipzig: J. C. Hinrichs, 1909), 27 n. 2; Johann Schwab, *Der Begriff der nefeš in den heiligen Schriften des Alten Testamentes: Ein Beitrag zur altjüdischen Religionsgeschichte* (Borna-Leipzig: R. Noske, 1913), 40; G. A. Cooke, *A Critical and Exegetical Commentary on the Book of Ezekiel* (ICC 21; Edinburgh: T&T Clark, 1936), 146; Johannes Hendrik Becker, *Het Begrip nefesj in het Oude Testament* (Amsterdam: Maatschappij, 1942), 91–92; A. Murtonen, *The Living Soul: A Study of the Meaning of the Word næfæš in the Old Testament Hebrew Language* (StudOr 23.1; Helsinki: Societas Orientalis Fennica, 1958), 55–56; Walther Zimmerli, *Ezekiel 1: A Commentary on the Book of the Prophet Ezekiel, Chapters 1–24* (trans. Ronald E. Clements; Hermeneia; Philadelphia: Fortress Press, 1979), 297; Moshe Greenberg, *Ezekiel 1–20: A New Translation with Introduction and Commentary* (AB 22; Garden City, N.Y.: Doubleday, 1983), 240; William H. Brownlee, *Ezekiel 1–19* (WBC 28; Waco, Tex.: Word Books, 1986), 195; Leslie C. Allen, *Ezekiel 1–19* (WBC 28; Dallas: Word Books, 1994), 204; Rüdiger Schmitt, *Magie im Alten Testament* (AOAT 313; Münster: Ugarit-Verlag, 2004), 285; and Jonathan Stökl, "The מתנבאות in Ezekiel 13 Reconsidered," *JBL* 132 (2013): 73 n. 45. This list includes only works that deal explicitly with the meaning of נְפָשׁוֹת in Ezek 13:18–20.

[28] Max Lichtenstein, *Das Wort* נפש *in der Bibel: Eine Untersuchung über die historischen Grundlagen der Anschauung von der Seele und die Entwickelung*

In addition to this anthropological controversy, there are philological controversies surrounding our passage. Are כְּסָתוֹת and מִסְפָּחוֹת (Ezek 13:18) short-lived Akkadianisms that disappeared after the exilic period, or are they native Hebrew words known also from tannaitic literature? Does לְפֹרְחוֹת (13:20) mean "like birds," "as birds," "of birds," "into birds," or something else? To these, I shall add a third lexical question: Is נְפָשִׁים an error for נְפָשׁוֹת or a rare technical term, distinct from נְפָשׁוֹת in the singular as well? I shall argue that resolution of these lexical questions has much to contribute to the resolution of the theological controversy. Through study of the words כְּסָתוֹת, מִסְפָּחוֹת, פֹּרְחוֹת, and נְפָשִׁים and comparison with ancient Near Eastern material, I shall attempt to demonstrate that the passage in Ezekiel refers quite clearly to disembodied souls.

Success in this area will provide us with an incentive to search for other disembodied נפשות (as well as רוחות) in the Hebrew Bible and to investigate what happens to them after death. I shall try to show that the fragmentary and seemingly contradictory biblical evidence concerning the afterlife of the נפש can be elucidated by evidence from archaeological sources, rabbinic sources (concerning Jewish funerary practice and the beliefs associated with it), and ancient Near Eastern literary sources—all converging to produce a coherent and plausible picture.

Before dealing with the passage from Ezekiel, I shall discuss the ancient Near Eastern context of our problem.[29] I shall attempt to show that, if "the Hebrew could not conceive of a disembodied נפש," he must have been a rather sheltered soul, oblivious to beliefs and practices found all over the ancient Near East. I shall begin with the new evidence bearing on our question that was discovered only six years ago in excavations at Zincirli, ancient Samal, in southeastern Turkey, near the Syrian border. This discovery alone is reason enough to reopen the question, for it, too, is potentially a "smoking gun."

---

der Bedeutung des Wortes נפש (Berlin: Mayer & Müller, 1920); Risto Lauha, *Psychophysischer Sprachgebrauch im Alten Testament: Eine struktursemantische Analyse von* לב, נפש *und* רוח (AASF, Dissertationes Humanarum Litterarum 35; Helsinki: Suomalainen tiedeakatemia, 1983).

[29] Cf. Cook, "Death," 106: "A comparative approach is particularly helpful in interpreting death and afterlife in Israel, because the Hebrew Bible leaves a lot unsaid about this subject. . . ."

1

A Disembodied נבש at Samal and Its Ancient Near Eastern Kinfolk

What does it mean to say that "the Hebrew could not conceive of a disembodied נפש"?[1] The most obvious interpretation is that the Hebrew could not conceive of a נפש freed from the body. Can it also mean that the Hebrew could not conceive of a נפש in the shape of anything but a body? If it could, I would have no objection to it.[2] However, this interpretation of the claim is not compatible with the dictionary definition of the English verb *disembody*.[3]

In this monograph, the term *disembodied souls* (or *external souls*) will be used to refer to human souls that are located, at least temporarily, outside of (corporeal) human bodies.[4] Hence, in order to establish that the noun נפש can *sometimes*[5] refer to a disembodied

---

[1] Porteous, "Soul," 428.

[2] I shall return to this point in ch. 13 below.

[3] See *The American Heritage Dictionary of the English Language* (4th ed.; Boston: Houghton Mifflin, 2000), 517, s.v.: "1. To free (the soul or spirit) from the body. 2. To divest of material existence or substance."

[4] Souls that are *able* to leave the body during life are called "free souls" (or "separable souls") by anthropologists, in contrast to "body souls." For the distinction, see Hermann Hochegger, "Die Vorstellungen von 'Seele' und Totengeist bei afrikanischen Völkern," *Anthropos* 60 (1965): 279–81, 327–31. The belief that the soul can exist outside the body is not identical to the belief that it is separate and distinct from the body, but the latter belief is probably a necessary condition for the former.

[5] It must be stressed that I do not intend to deal with the entire

soul, whether in Israel or one of its neighbors, one need only find a single prooftext that describes a person's נפש as being *in* something *other than* a human body.[6]

The new evidence from Zincirli mentioned above is of precisely this type. It appears in the Aramaic funerary monument of an official named Katumuwa, a servant of King Panamuwa II (died ca. 733/732 B.C.E.).[7] In the inscription, the term נבש = נפש[8] ocurs twice, both times with a 1cs suffixed pronoun referring to Katumuwa. The most important occurrence is in line 5, where the phrase נבשי זי בנצב זן implies that Katumuwa's נבש is—or will be—in the stele.[9] In my view, this does not mean that the stele is the eternal resting place of his נבש; it is merely a pied-à-terre for visits from the netherworld.[10] Be that as it may, it is clear that this phrase describes Katumuwa's נבש as being in something other than a human body. During the time that Katumuwa's נבש is in the stele, it is, by definition, a dis-

---

semantic range of נפש, which is quite broad (see the introduction above and ch. 12 below). My goal is merely to establish the existence of a single disputed meaning, and I shall make little mention of contexts that are irrelevant to that goal.

[6] The description, of course, must be manifestly literal. A description that can be dismissed as figurative, such as the idiom commonly rendered as "put/take one's life (נפש) in one's hands" (Judg 12:3; 1 Sam 19:5; 28:21; Job 13:14), is not a compelling prooftext.

[7] A new translation, commentary, and analysis of the text appear in Appendix 1 below. For the vocalization *Katumuwa* used here (instead of *Kuttamuwa*, accepted earlier by scholars), see K. Lawson Younger, "Two Epigraphic Notes on the New Katumuwa Inscription from Zincirli," *Maarav* 16 (2009): 159–66; and add the following note by Jay Jasanoff (e-mail communication): "*Katumuwa* looks a lot more plausible to me. **katu-* 'battle' (vel sim.) is the kind of element, semantically speaking, that Indo-European types liked to put in their names, and it actually is so employed in Germanic and Celtic (cf. Ger. *Hedwig*, OHG *Hadubrand*; Welsh *Cadwalader*, *Cadfael*)."

[8] For the spelling of this word with *bet* instead of *pe*ʾ, see Appendix 1 below.

[9] Dennis Pardee, "A New Aramaic Inscription from Zincirli," *BASOR* 356 (2009): 62–63.

[10] See the parallels cited below. Contrast Pardee, "New Aramaic Inscription," 62–63.

embodied soul.[11] This soul is by no means a mere figure of speech; it is to receive a ram every year as a funerary offering.

In this case, we have evidence that corroborates this conclusion, giving us confidence that our method is sound. The evidence comes from a slightly earlier Aramaic inscription from the same site, an inscription of King Panamuwa I (died ca. 745 B.C.E.) engraved on a colossal statue of the god Hadad (*KAI* no. 214). In this inscription, the king commands his descendants to invite him to partake of any sacrifice that they offer to his statue of Hadad, mentioning his name together with that of Hadad, and he curses those who do not do so:

ומנמנ. בני. יאחז[. חט]ה. וישב. על. משבי. ... ויזבח. הדד. זנ[.] ... ויזכר. אשמ.
הדד ... פא. יאמר. [תאכל. נ]בש. פנמו. עמכ. ותש[תי.] נבש. פנמו. עמכ. עד.
יזכר. נבש. פנמו. עמ[. הד]ד.

. . .

מ[נמנ.] בני. יאחז. חטר. וישב. על. משבי. ו[י]מלכ. על. יא[די]. ... ויז[בח. הדד.
זנ. ולא. יזכ]ר. אשמ. פנמו. יאמר. ת[א]כל. נבש. פנ[מו.] עמ. הדד. תשתי. נבש.
פנמו. עמ. ה[ד]ד. ... זבחה. ואל[.] ירקי. בה[.] ומז. ישאל. אל. יתנ. לה. הדד. ...
[וא]ל. יתנ. לה. לאכל. ברגז. ושנה. למנע. מנה. בלילא.

Whoever from among my descendants shall grasp the scepter and sit on my throne . . . and sacrifice to this Hadad . . . and mention the name of Hadad, let him then say, "May the נבש of Panamuwa eat with you [= Hadad], and may the נבש of Panamuwa drink with you." Let him keep mentioning the נבש of Panamuwa with Hadad.

. . .

[11] So, too, Virginia R. Herrmann, "Introduction: The Katumuwa Stele and the Commemoration of the Dead in the Ancient Middle East," in *In Remembrance of Me: Feasting with the Dead in the Ancient Middle East* (ed. Virginia Rimmer Herrmann and J. David Schloen; Chicago: Oriental Institute of the University of Chicago, 2014), 17: "this is the first mention in a West Semitic context of the concept of a soul that was separable from the body"; eadem, "The Katumuwa Stele in Archaeological Context," in *In Remembrance of Me*, 52: "excavation beneath the floors of this room has turned up no trace of human remains. It seems that Katumuwa's 'soul' could inhabit this place quite apart from his body, which presumably lay in a necropolis elsewhere. . . ." For a contrary view, based on a different definition of *disembodied* ("outside of a body or object"), see Sanders, "Appetites of the Dead," 44, 50.

> Whoever from among my descendants shall grasp the scepter and sit on my throne and reign over Y'DY . . . and sacrifice to this Hadad without mentioning the name of Panamuwa (and) saying, "May the נבש of Panamuwa eat with Hadad, and may the נבש of Panamuwa drink with Hadad"— . . . his sacrifice, and may he [= Hadad] not look favorably upon it [= the sacrifice], and whatever he [= the sacrificer] asks, may Hadad not give him . . . and may he not allow him to eat, in (his) agitation, and may he withhold sleep from him at night.[12]

The word נבש in this passage has long been taken to mean "soul" or the like, even by those who deny that meaning to BH נפש.[13] Already at the beginning of the twentieth century, the passage was considered clear enough to be used as evidence for disembodied נפשות in Israel.[14] The reason for this is obvious. The inscription can hardly have been intended solely for that short period after Panamuwa's death when his organs of ingestion were still intact. That is why the inscription refers to Panamuwa's נבש—rather than Panamuwa himself—as eating and drinking with his god. Moreover, the god in question is not a god of the netherworld. Thus, the assumption appears to be that, even after Panamuwa's body decays, his נבש will live on, with the ability to eat and drink above ground. The same is true of Katumuwa's נבש, whose eating and drinking were thought to take place inside the funerary monument. It is no wonder, then,

---

[12] Josef Tropper, *Die Inschriften von Zincirli: Neue Edition und vergleichende Grammatik des phönizischen, sam'alischen und aramäischen Textkorpus* (Abhandlungen zur Literatur Alt-Syrien-Palästinas 6; Münster: Ugarit-Verlag, 1993), 76–84, lines 15–18, 20–24, with minor changes.

[13] In addition to Tropper's translation, see *DISO*, 183, s.v. נפש; *KAI* 2:215; *TSSI* 2:67, 69; *DNWSI* 2:747, s.v. נפש; and Edmond Jacob, Albert Dihle, et al., "ψυχή κτλ," *TDNT* 9:621 n. 61: "A view that differs from that of Israel may be found in the inscr. of King Panammuwa of Samʾal. . . . " By contrast, Herbert Niehr ("Zum Totenkult der Könige von Samʾal im 9. und 8. Jh. v. Chr.," *SEL* 11 [1994]: 63–65) has rejected the meaning "soul" for נבש in *KAI* no. 214 on the grounds that the meaning is unattested outside of that text, arguing instead for the meaning "spirit of the dead" (*Totengeist*). However, this meaning, too, was unattested outside of *KAI* no. 214 at the time when he wrote his article.

[14] Lods, *La croyance,* 1:62 with n. 2. See, more recently, Cook, "Death," 107.

that the Samalian noun נבש, unlike the Hebrew noun נפש, is commonly understood to refer at times to disembodied souls.

Also worthy of mention is the funerary inscription of Posidonius from Halikarnassos dated to between ca. 350 and 250 B.C.E.[15] This Greek inscription parallels Katumuwa's funerary inscription in a number of respects. Like the נבש of Katumuwa, the Δαίμων of Posidonius is to receive a ram as a funerary offering. According to a recent study, the term Δαίμων is used here to designate "the immortal 'guiding spirit' of an individual."[16]

This evidence shows that Samalian נבש could be used of a disembodied soul. Does this conclusion have any relevance for the meaning of BH נפש? Does it reflect a widespread ancient Near Eastern conception that might have been familiar to the Israelites and accepted by at least some of them? Should we expect to find a reflection of this conception somewhere in the Bible?

According to the members of the Oriental Institute team that discovered and published the Katumuwa inscription, the answer to all of these questions would seem to be negative. In the view of J. David Schloen and Amir S. Fink, the phrase "a ram for my soul, which is/will be in this stele" must be interpreted based on the assumption (for which direct evidence is lacking) that Katumuwa was cremated. According to them, the conception reflected in that phrase stands "in contrast to the traditional West Semitic conception that one's soul resides in one's bones after death, but it is in keeping with Hittite/Luwian (and more generally 'Indo-European') conceptions of the afterlife, in which the soul is released from the body by means of cremation."[17] Similarly, Dennis Pardee believes that "the ongoing presence of the *nbš* within the stele . . . is plausibly an aspect of cremation as practiced in this area by populations with both Luwian and Aramaean antecedents, and, in such a context, it appears to reflect the belief that the *nbš* found its dwelling in the stele after the body had gone up in smoke."[18] In short, these scholars believe that the Samalian conception of the soul reflected

[15] See Appendix 1 below.

[16] Ibid.

[17] J. David Schloen and Amir S. Fink, "New Excavations at Zincirli Höyük in Turkey (Ancient Samʾal) and the Discovery of an Inscribed Mortuary Stele," *BASOR* 356 (2009): 11.

[18] Pardee, "New Aramaic Inscription," 62.

in the two Aramaic inscriptions has an Anatolian origin and may thus be irrelevant to the Israelites.

H. Craig Melchert disagrees with this view, based on Manfred Hutter's work on cult steles. According to Hutter, "the notion that the deity is present in the stele clearly had its origin in Syria, whence this religious phenomenon spread to Anatolia as well as Israel."[19] Melchert adduces linguistic evidence to prove that the same must be true of the notion of the *soul* residing in the *funerary* stele.[20]

In addition, we may note that the view of Schloen and Fink and Pardee does not seem fully consonant with another view held by them:

> It is now clear why in later West Semitic contexts from the latter part of the first millennium B.C. the word *NBŠ* comes to denote the mortuary monument itself.[21]

> It appears not unlikely that it was the fusing of the old Semitic concepts regarding the stele as important in the mortuary cult with later ones such as those expressed in *KAI* 214 and in the new inscription that led at a later time to identifying the *npš* with the funerary monument itself. . . .[22]

In other words, the semantic development by which Aramaic and Hebrew נפש/נבש came to refer to the funerary monument[23] can now be explained as a case of synecdoche (*pars pro toto*) or metonymy rooted in the belief that the soul resides in its funerary monument.

---

[19] Manfred Hutter, "Kultstelen und Baityloi: Die Ausstrahlung eines syrischen religiösen Phänomens nach Kleinasien und Israel," in *Religiongeschichtliche Beziehungen zwischen Kleinasien, Nordsyrien, und dem Alten Testament: Internationales Symposion Hamburg, 17.–21. März 1990* (ed. Bernd Janowski, Klaus Koch and Gernot Wilhelm; OBO 129; Göttingen: Vandenhoeck & Ruprecht, 1993), 105.

[20] H. Craig Melchert, "Remarks on the Kuttamuwa Inscription," *Kubaba* 1 (2010): 9, http://www.fcsh.unl.pt/kubaba/KUBABA/Melchert_2010__Remarks_on_the_Kuttamuwa_Stele.pdf.

[21] Schloen and Fink, "New Excavations," 11.

[22] Pardee, "New Aramaic Inscription," 63.

[23] See the literature cited by Pardee, "New Aramaic Inscription," 62 n. 14, and by *DNWSI* 2:748–49, s.v. נפש; and add Jacob S. Licht, נפש in אנציקלופדיה מקראית, 5:903–4. This semantic change is paralleled in Egypt, where "Old Kingdom pyramids were often called the *ba*s of their owners"; see James P. Allen, "Ba," *The Oxford Encyclopedia of Ancient Egypt*, 1:161. For more on the *ba*, usually translated "soul," see at n. 40 below and passim.

It is not known when and where this semantic development first took place,[24] but the fact that it is attested among Jews, Arabs (Taima) and South Arabians suggests that it resonated with people who did not practice cremation. Perhaps even more telling is the failure of this semantic development to spread to Phoenician until the Roman era,[25] despite the fact that "cremation burial was introduced into the region by the Phoenicians."[26] The theory of Schloen and Fink and Pardee[27] would have led us to expect a strong correlation between cremation and the use of נפש/נבש to refer to the funerary monument, but, if anything, we find the opposite correlation.

All of this points up the need for an alternative explanation, and, as it happens, Pardee hints at one himself:

> The abundant Mesopotamian evidence for free-moving ghosts is not to be ignored (for displacements and emplacements of various

---

[24] For possible Achaemenid attestations of the new meaning and a discussion of its origin, see Lothar Triebel, *Jenseitshoffnung in Wort und Stein: Nefesch und pyramidales Grabmal als Phänomene antiken jüdischen Bestattungswesens im Kontext der Nachbarkulturen* (AGJU 56; Leiden: Brill, 2004), 53–61, 243–45. For Epigraphic South Arabian *nfs*[1] with the meaning "funerary monument" (overlooked by Triebel), see A. F. L. Beeston, M. A. Ghul, W. W. Müller, and J. Ryckmans, *Sabaic Dictionary* (Louvain-la-Neuve: Peeters, 1982), 933, s.v.; and Stephen D. Ricks, *Lexicon of Inscriptional Qatabanian* (Studia Pohl 14; Rome: Pontificio Istituto Biblico, 1989), 109, s.v.

[25] Triebel, *Jenseitshoffnung*, 70 (with n. 35), 220–21 (with nn. 118–21). For the Neo-Punic examples from North Africa (ca. first century C.E.), see Ziony Zevit, "Phoenician NBŠ/NPŠ and Its Hebrew Semantic Equivalents," in *Maarav 5–6*, special issue, *Sopher Mahir: Northwest Semitic Studies Presented to Stanislav Segert* (ed. Edward M. Cook; Winona Lake, Ind.: Eisenbrauns, 1990), 337. Zevit (ibid., 337 n. 1) notes that "the more common Phoenician word is *mṣbt*."

[26] Elizabeth Bloch-Smith, *Judahite Burial Practices and Beliefs about the Dead* (JSOTSup 123; Sheffield: JSOT Press, 1992), 52. The region to which the author refers is the southern Levant.

[27] In the most recent collection of essays on the Katumuwa stele, *In Remembrance of Me: Feasting with the Dead in the Ancient Middle East* (see n. 11 above), there is no consensus concerning this theory. See, for example, Virginia R. Herrmann, "The Katumuwa Stele in Archaeological Context," 52; and Herbert Niehr, "The Katumuwa Stele in the Context of the Royal Mortuary Cult at Samʾal," 60—both in that volume.

> ghostly entities in Mesopotamia, see, e.g., Scurlock 1995; 2002). On the other hand, the old West Semitic vocabulary for such entities is much poorer than in Akkadian (there is, for example, no clear equivalent for Akkadian *eṭṭemu* [*sic*], "ghost"), and our textual resources are also much poorer; as a result we know comparatively little about such concepts from ancient Levantine sources.[28]

Pardee's opinion that there was no clear semantic equivalent of the Akkadian term *eṭemmu* in West Semitic is subject to dispute; other scholars hold that Samalian נבש was precisely such an equivalent.[29] Their view goes back to Jonas C. Greenfield, who showed that the treatment demanded by King Panamuwa I for his נבש is similar in several respects to the treatment of the *eṭemmu* in the Mesopotamian *kispu* ritual.[30] Additional parallels can easily be found in the articles by JoAnn Scurlock cited by Pardee:

---

[28] Pardee, "New Aramaic Inscription," 63 n. 18.

[29] See, for example, Tropper, *Die Inschriften*, 77: "The word *nbš* is used unambiguously, here and in what follows, in the sense of 'spirit of the dead' (*Totengeist*) and thus corresponds semantically to the Akkadian word *eṭemmu*." See also Karel van der Toorn, *Family Religion in Babylonia, Syria, and Israel: Continuity and Change in the Forms of Religious Life* (SHCANE 7; Leiden: Brill, 1996), 167; and, more hesitantly, Tzvi Abusch, "Ghost and God: Some Observations on a Babylonian Understanding of Human Nature," in *Self, Soul and Body in Religious Experience* (ed. A. I. Baumgarten, J. Assmann, G. G. Stroumsa; SHR 78; Leiden: Brill, 1998), 373 n. 23.

[30] Jonas C. Greenfield, "Un rite religieux araméen et ses parallèles," *RB* 80 (1973): 49–50. Among other parallels, Greenfield notes the obligation, at Samal and in Mesopotamia, to "mention the name" (זכר אשם, *šuma zakāru*) of deceased ancestors invited to partake of the funerary offerings. In addition to the Old Babylonian text that he cites, we may mention an Assyrian text: *šumka itti eṭemmē azkur šumka itti kispī azkur* "I have mentioned your name with the ghosts (of my family), I have mentioned your name with funerary offerings." For this text, see *CAD* E:399–400, s.v. *eṭemmu;* and Brian B. Schmidt, "The Gods and the Dead of the Domestic Cult at Emar: A Reassessment," in *Emar: The History, Religion, and Culture of a Syrian Town in the Late Bronze Age* (ed. Mark W. Chavalas; Bethesda, Md.: CDL, 1996), 150. These parallels are powerful evidence for a correspondence between the Samalian נבש and the Mesopotamian *eṭemmu*.

> There are two words used in ancient Mesopotamian texts to designate semi-divine, wind-like or shadow-like entities which exist in living beings, survive death, and subsequently receive offerings from the deceased's descendants at his tomb. One of these, the *zaqīqu*, seems to have been a dream soul.[[31]] The other, *eṭemmu*, which is conventionally translated as "ghost," seems to have been a body spirit. Both of these souls were believed to depart from the body at death and both souls eventually found their way to the Netherworld, where they were supposed to receive a continuous set of funerary offerings from the living.[32]

> In the royal cult, regular offerings were made individually to all ancestors of the reigning king.[33]

> In order to ensure that the ghosts actually received what was intended for them, it was customary to invoke their names while making offerings. A statue of the deceased could also serve to localize the spirit for funerary offerings. . . . Funerary-cult statues are best attested for kings, but important officials might also be permitted to have one as a sign of royal favor.
>
> For most of the year, ghosts were shut up behind the gates of the netherworld and quietly received what was laid out or poured out for them by relatives. Several times a year, however, they were allowed to leave their homes in the netherworld and to come back for short visits.[34]

These accounts of the mortuary cult in Mesopotamia—with its food offerings to the souls of the dead, its use of statues as emplacements for souls invited to a feast, and its invocation of the names of the

---

[31] For the dream-soul, see chapter 6 below.

[32] JoAnn Scurlock, "Soul Emplacements in Ancient Mesopotamian Funerary Rituals," in *Magic and Divination in the Ancient World* (ed. Leda Ciraolo and Jonathan Seidel; Ancient Magic and Divination 2; Leiden: Brill, 2002), 1. For a different interpretation of the evidence, see Josef Tropper, *Nekromantie: Totenbefragung im Alten Orient und im Alten Testament* (AOAT 223; Neukirchen-Vluyn: Neukirchener Verlag, 1989), 47–56. For more on the *eṭemmu* as an immortal soul, see at chapter 12, nn. 13–14 below.

[33] JoAnn Scurlock, "Death and the Afterlife in Ancient Mesopotamian Thought," in *CANE* 3:1888.

[34] Ibid., 1889.

invited souls—explain most of the important details of the Samalian inscriptions.[35]

Clearly, the Samalian conception of the soul was not by any means foreign to the rest of the ancient Near East. Moreover, the question of Hittite influence becomes moot if the Hittite traditions in question ultimately derive from Syro-Mesopotamian traditions, as at least some Hittitologists believe. Thus, in discussing the Syro-Hittite funerary monuments, Dominik Bonatz writes:

> Such conceptions testify that the separation between the living and the dead was overcome in an intermediate zone, a sacred area, where social interaction with the dead took place. Funerary monuments functioned as marks of this place. The dead could have been evoked there from the netherworld by the invocation of his name and an invitation for a meal. . . .
>
> Before discussing the historical context of the erection of these funerary monuments, an attempt should be made to sketch the process of their emergence beginning with their antecedents in the second millennium B.C.
>
> The family ritual for the dead, the *kispu*, was established at the time of the emergence of the Amorite dynasties at the beginning of the second millennium B.C. The social interaction with the dead, his invocation by name, the offering of food and drink, and the citation of the genealogies of his ancestors constitute the framework for an essential form of collective memory.[36]

A similar point is made by Volkert Haas in discussing the origin of the use of statues in the Hittite funerary cult: "A distinct cult for dead rulers is attested by offering lists setting forth food rations

---

[35] See also André Lemaire, "Rites des vivants pour les morts dans le royaume de Sam'al (VIIIe siècle av. n. è.)," in *Les vivants et leurs morts: Actes du colloque organisé par le Collège de France, Paris, le 14–15 avril 2010* (OBO 257; Fribourg: Academic Press, 2012), 136; and idem, "Le dialecte araméen de l'inscription de Kuttamuwa (Zencirli, viiie s. av. n. è.)," in *In the Shadow of Bezalel: Aramaic, Biblical and Ancient Near Eastern Studies in Honor of Bezalel Porten* (ed. Alejandro F. Botta; CHANE 60; Leiden: Brill, 2013), 149. I am indebted to Maurya Horgan for the former reference.

[36] Dominik Bonatz, "Syro-Hittite Funerary Monuments: A Phenomenon of Tradition or Innovation?" in *Essays on Syria in the Iron Age* (ed. Guy Bunnens; Ancient Near Eastern Studies, Supplement 7; Louvain: Peeters, 2000), 191–93.

for kings present in the form of statues. This type of cult for the ancestral dead derives from the Syro-Mesopotamian traditions of the third millennium."[37]

This cult may be attested at Ugarit, too. According to Paolo Xella's interpretation, *KTU* 1.161 describes a "ritual in honor of deceased kings of Ugarit," a "sacrificial meal of the Shadows" which was "tied to the Mesopotamian and Mari tradition of the *kispu*."[38] In any event, evidence for disembodied souls at Ugarit is not hard to find. One need only open the standard Ugaritic dictionaries to the entry for *npš* to find renderings such as "may his soul [*npšh*] go out like a breath."[39]

Last but not least, we may mention the various Egyptian counterparts of the Samalian נבש:

> For the Egyptians a complete person was composed of various physical and spiritual parts. The body itself was considered an essential element that was animated by a soul, or *ba*. The *ba* was represented as a bird that flew off or departed at a person's death or burial. It would generally stay near the body but could also leave the tomb to assume other forms. These transformations were not permanent and were apparently not transmigrations.
>
> A second spiritual element of any person was his *akh*, a term that is often left untranslated but could be rendered "spirit." This spirit, like the *ba*, is an element that survives after death.

---

[37] Volkert Haas, "Death and the Afterlife in Hittite Thought," in *CANE* 3:2029.

[38] Paolo Xella, "Death and the Afterlife in Canaanite and Hebrew Thought," in *CANE* 3:2062; cf. Richard Elliott Friedman and Shawna Dolansky Overton, "Death and Afterlife: The Biblical Silence," in *Judaism in Late Antiquity* (ed. Jacob Neusner; 5 vols.; Leiden: Brill, 1995–2001), 4:38. For other views and literature, see Theodore J. Lewis, *Cults of the Dead in Ancient Israel and Ugarit* (HSM 39; Atlanta: Scholars Press, 1989), 5–46; Oswald Loretz, "Nekromantie und Totenvokation in Mesopotamien, Ugarit und Israel," in *Religionsgeschichtliche Beziehungen zwischen Kleinasien, Nordsyrien, und dem Alten Testament* (ed. Bernd Janowski, Klaus Koch, and Gernot Wilhelm; OBO 129; Göttingen: Vandenhoeck & Ruprecht, 1993), 296–97; Baruch A. Levine, Jean-Michel de Tarragon, and Anne Robertson, "The Patrons of the Ugaritic Dynasty (KTU 1.161)," in Hallo, William W., and K. Lawson Younger, eds., *The Context of Scripture* (3 vols.; Leiden: Brill, 1997–2002), 1:357–58.

[39] See at chapter 8, nn. 16–18 below.

> The Egyptian notion of the *ka*, another spiritual component, is more difficult to comprehend. . . .
>
> The *ka* was important to a person's survival in the afterlife. Should the corpse perish, the survival of the *ka* could still guarantee continued existence. . . . *Ka* servants were priests in charge of administering the endowments connected with a burial, which were ordinarily spent for the offerings to be provided over a long period of time. . . .
>
> Another aspect of an individual that deserves mention is the person's shadow or shade (*šuyt*), which has a parallel in the Latin *umbra*. This is both mentioned in the funerary literature (*Book of the Dead*, chap. 92) and depicted in tomb paintings.[40]

In short, belief in the existence—and afterlife—of disembodied souls was extremely widespread in the ancient Near East. It was current in Mesopotamia and Syria (Samal and Ugarit), not to mention Egypt. It is possible that the Semites inherited the belief in question from their common ancestors, the speakers of Proto-Semitic. That language is believed to have had a term **nap(i)š* with the meaning "soul," in addition to the meanings "vitality, life," "person, personality," and "self."[41] In at least some of the daughter languages, the reflex of **nap(i)š* denotes a soul that exits the body at death, a free soul capable of existing without a body. We have already seen that this is true of Samalian נבש and Ugaritic *npš*. That it is also true of Arabic *nafs* is clear from the Quran (39:42): اللهُ يَتَوَفَّى الأَنْفُسَ حِينَ مَوْتِهَا وَالَّتِي لَمْ تَمُتْ فِي مَنَامِهَا "It is Allah that takes the souls at the time of their death, and (as for) those (souls) that have not died, (it is Allah that takes them) in their sleep." It may, therefore, be legitimate to reconstruct that denotation for **nap(i)š*, at least in Proto-West Semitic.

Even earlier evidence comes from paleoarchaeological findings in Iraq. In the foreword to the most recent publication inspired by the discovery of the Katumuwa inscription, Gil J. Stein writes:

> Even as early as 50,000 years ago, in the depths of the Ice Age, we know that Neanderthals believed that there was some kind of continuing existence of the human spirit even after death, so that burials in Shanidar Cave in Iraq contained offerings of flowers

---

[40] Leonard H. Lesko, "Death and the Afterlife in Ancient Egyptian Thought," in *CANE* 3:1763–64.

[41] Alexander Militarev and Leonid Kogan, *Semitic Etymological Dictionary* (Münster: Ugarit-Verlag, 2000), 1:308. See also chapter 12 below.

> and other grave goods meant for the departed person's spirit in the afterlife.[42]

Now, a belief that humans have a soul that survives death is not the same as a belief in disembodied souls.[43] Nevertheless, it seems clear that the two beliefs often go together.

All in all, the evidence presented in this chapter suggests that a belief in the existence of disembodied souls was part of the common religious heritage of the peoples of the ancient Near East. This is sufficient to cast serious doubt on the assertion that "the Hebrew could not conceive of a disembodied נפש," but it is not sufficient to refute it. For that, we must delve into Ezekiel's prophecy, attempting to understand it as fully as possible. In my view, this prophecy has been misinterpreted in a number of ways. A great deal of philological spadework will be needed to correct the various misinterpretations. Only then will it be possible to prove my thesis, viz., that this passage provides compelling evidence for a belief in disembodied souls.

The next six chapters are devoted to a detailed analysis of Ezekiel's prophecy. I shall attempt to show that the women whom Ezekiel condemned were sewing pillow casings (כְּסָתוֹת) and cutting up clothing—possibly stolen from their intended victims—into the cloth patches (הַמִּסְפָּחוֹת) that served as pillow filling in ancient Israel. They were using these to attract and trap dream-souls, which would wither away unless their owners redeemed (read: ransomed) them.

---

[42] Gil J. Stein, "Foreword," in Herrmann and Schloen, *In Remembrance of Me*, 9. Cf. Ralph S. Solecki, Rose L. Solecki, Anagnostis P. Agelarakis, *The Proto-Neolithic Cemetery in Shanidar Cave* (College Station: Texas A & M University Press, 2004), 109 (dealing with later burials, from the eleventh millennium B.P.).

[43] See Klaas Spronk, *Beatific Afterlife in Ancient Israel and in the Ancient Near East* (AOAT 219; Neukirchen-Vluyn: Neukirchener Verlag, 1986), 32–33.

2

Women Trapping Souls

It has long been recognized that the techniques for trapping נפשות described in Ezekiel's prophecy involved magic,[1] perhaps even witchcraft.[2] G. A. Cooke, for example, writes:

> Prophetesses is too good a name for them; witches or sorceresses would suit the description better. They played upon the credulity of the people by magic arts.[3]

---

[1] Rudolf Smend, *Der Prophet Ezechiel* (2nd ed.; Kurzgefasstes exegetisches Handbuch zum Alten Testament 8; Leipzig: S. Hirzel, 1880), 76–77; Friedrich Delitzsch, "Glossario Ezechielico-Babylonico," in *Liber Ezechielis* (ed. S. Baer; Leipzig: B. Tauchnitz, 1884), xii (bottom); Bertholet, *Das Buch Hesekiel,* 71; Walther Eichrodt, *Ezekiel: A Commentary* (trans. Cosslett Quin; OTL; Philadelphia: Westminster, 1970), 169–70; Zimmerli, *Ezekiel 1,* 296–97; Greenberg, *Ezekiel 1–20,* 239–40; Peter C. Craigie, *Ezekiel* (Daily Study Bible Series; Philadelphia: Westminster, 1983), 93–94; Brownlee, *Ezekiel 1–19,* 196; Joseph Blenkinsopp, *Ezekiel* (IBC; Louisville: John Knox, 1990), 70.

[2] Heinrich Ewald, *Die Propheten des Alten Bundes* (2nd ed.; 3 vols.; Göttingen: Vandenhoeck & Ruprecht, 1867–1868), 2:400; Selbie, "Ezekiel xiii. 18-21," 75; J. Barth, "Notiz: Zu dem Zauber des Umnähens der Gelenke," *MGWJ* 57 (1913): 235; Lods, "Magie," 12; Cooke, *Book of Ezekiel,* 145–46; Georg Fohrer, *Ezechiel* (HAT 1/13; Tübingen: Mohr Siebeck, 1955), 74–75; John William Wevers, *Ezekiel* (Century Bible, New Series; London: Nelson, 1969), 87–88; Leslie C. Allen, *Ezekiel 1–19,* 204; Graham I. Davies, "An Archaeological Commentary on Ezekiel 13," in *Scripture and Other Artifacts: Essays on the Bible and Archaeology in Honor of Philip J. King* (ed. Michael D. Coogan, J. Cheryl Exum, and Lawrence E. Stager; Louisville: Westminster John Knox, 1994), 121–22; Ann Jeffers, *Magic and Divination in Ancient Palestine and Syria* (SHCANE 8; Leiden: Brill, 1996), 94; Daniel I. Block, *The Book of Ezekiel,* vol. 1, *Chapters 1–24* (NICOT; Grand Rapids: Eerdmans, 1997), 412, 416–17; Schmitt, *Magie,* 284.

[3] Cooke, *Book of Ezekiel,* 144.

This view, nearly unanimous since the nineteenth century,[4] was prevalent among the medieval Jewish exegetes as well.[5] It is based on the plain sense of the phrase מְתַפְּרוֹת כְּסָתוֹת עַל כָּל־אַצִּילֵי יָדַי וְעֹשׂוֹת הַמִּסְפָּחוֹת עַל־רֹאשׁ כָּל־קוֹמָה לְצוֹדֵד נְפָשׁוֹת (Ezek 13:18), irrespective of whether the נפשות in question are people or souls. It is only in the realm of magic that people are trapped by sewing things on arms—or that souls are trapped at all. Additional evidence for this view will be adduced below.

The prophecy itself, however, does not call the women sorceresses or witches. Instead, it refers to them as בְּנוֹת עַמְּךָ הַמִּתְנַבְּאוֹת מִלִּבְּהֶן (13:17).[6] The adverbial מִלִּבְּהֶן "out of their own minds" (with parallels in Num 16:28; 1 Kgs 12:33; and Neh 6:8) implies that these women are engaging in some sort of fabrication. Now, a very similar adverbial can be seen in the phrase נְבִיאֵי מִלִּבָּם, used of the false prophets in 13:2, but there is a crucial difference. That phrase and נְבִיאֵי יִשְׂרָאֵל הַנִּבָּאִים, also in 13:2, contain the word for "prophets," while in 13:17, the word for "prophetesses" (נביאות) is noticeably absent. The contrast may well be deliberate.[7]

Another contrast between 13:2 and 13:7 concerns the verb stem used with the participle of the root נ-ב-א. The former has הַנִּבָּאִים

---

[4] For femininist defenses of these women aimed at elevating their professional status, see Renate Jost, "Die Töchter deines Volkes prophezeien," in *Für Gerechtigkeit streiten: Theologie im Alltag einer bedrohten Welt. Für Luise Schottroff zum 60. Geburtstag* (ed. Dorothee Sölle; Gütersloh: Kaiser, 1994), 59–65; Nancy R. Bowen, "The Daughters of Your People: Female Prophets in Ezekiel 13:17–23," *JBL* 118 (1999): 417–33; Irmtraud Fischer, *Gotteskünderinnen: Zu einer geschlechterfairen Deutung des Phänomens der Prophetie und der Prophetinnen in der Hebräischen Bibel* (Stuttgart: Kohlhammer, 2002), 227–30; Angelika Berlejung, "Falsche Prophetinnen: Zur Dämonisierung der Frauen von Ez 13:17-21," in *Theologie des AT aus der Perspektive von Frauen* (ed. Manfred Oeming; Münster: Lit, 2003), 179–210; Wilda Gafney, *Daughters of Miriam: Women Prophets in Ancient Israel* (Minneapolis: Fortress, 2008), 107–9; and Stökl, "The מתנבאות," 66. For a discussion of one aspect of Bowen's article, see Appendix 2 below.

[5] Isaiah of Trani, for example, speaks of "the women who practiced witchcraft and sorcery" (הנשים הכשפניות והקוסמות), and he takes לְצוֹדֵד נְפָשׁוֹת to mean "to destroy their נפש with your spells" (לאבד נפשם בקסמיכם).

[6] For the expression בְּנוֹת עַמְּךָ, see Moshe Eisemann, *Yechezkel/The Book of Ezekiel* (New York: Mesorah, 1977), 222–23.

[7] Berlejung, "Falsche Prophetinnen," 187.

in the *nifʿal* stem, the one normally used by Ezekiel with this root (thirty-five times), while the latter has הַמִּתְנַבְּאוֹת in the *hitpaʿel*. The stem of הַמִּתְנַבְּאוֹת contrasts also with the stem of the immediately following imperative הִנָּבֵא, addressed to Ezekiel. Many commentators have argued that these contrasts are deliberate.

In accordance with a well-known meaning of the *hitpaʿel*, several medieval Jewish exegetes took הַמִּתְנַבְּאוֹת to mean "who pose as prophetesses."[8] Many modern scholars agree. G. A. Cooke, for example, translates הַמִּתְנַבְּאוֹת as "who play the prophetess,"[9] and he asserts that its verb stem "gives a touch of contempt, cp. I K. 22^{10}, Jer. 14^{14} 29^{26}."[10] Daniel I. Block expands on this idea: "While the expression *nĕbîʾâ*, 'prophetess,' is applied to at least five women in

---

[8] Joseph Ibn Kaspi in מקראות גדולות הכתר — ספר יחזקאל (ed. Menachem Cohen; Ramat Gan: Bar-Ilan University Press, 2000), 67a (to 13:19): עושות עצמם נביאות; Isaac Abravanel, פירוש הנביאים לרבינו יצחק אברבנאל (ed. Yehudah Shaviv; Jerusalem: Chorev, 2009–), 6:140 (to 13:17): מראות עצמן נביאות. For the *hitpaʿel* used to express pretense, see, for example, Paul Joüon, *A Grammar of Biblical Hebrew* (trans. and rev. T. Muraoka; 2 vols.; Subsidia Biblica 14.1–2; Rome: Pontificio Istituto Biblico, 1991), 1:159 §53i. For Arabic *tanabbaʾa*, see Edward W. Lane, *Arabic-English Lexicon* (London: Williams & Norgate, 1863–1877), 2753 col. a: "*He arrogated to himself the gift of prophecy*, or *office of a prophet*." This is the only meaning listed there.

[9] Cooke, *Book of Ezekiel*, 145. Similar views of the verb are expressed by Wevers (*Ezekiel*, 87), Zimmerli (*Ezekiel 1*, 296), Greenberg (*Ezekiel 1–20*, 239, with discussion and literature), Klaus-Peter Adam ("'And he behaved like a prophet among them' [1 Sam 10:11b]: The Depreciative Use of נבא and the Comparative Evidence of Ecstatic Prophecy," *WO* 39 [2009]: 19), and others. Jost ("Die Töchter," 59) and Stökl ("The מתנבאות," 66) attempt to refute the aforementioned interpretation based on the form וְהִנַּבֵּאתִי (*hippaʿel* < *hitpaʿel*), used by Ezekiel in reference to himself in 37:10. Fischer (*Gotteskünderinnen*, 227) goes further, claiming that, in light of Jost's argument, the depreciative interpretation of הַמִּתְנַבְּאוֹת is "to be unmasked as gender-bias." However, the use of the nonstandard form וְהִנַּבֵּאתִי is not compelling evidence against the depreciative interpretation, because it may well be a deliberate echo of הִנָּבֵא אֶל־הָרוּחַ הִנָּבֵא בֶן־אָדָם in v. 9, as suggested by Walther Zimmerli, *Ezekiel 2: A Commentary on the Book of the Prophet Ezekiel, Chapters 25–48* (trans. James D. Martin; Hermeneia; Philadelphia: Fortress, 1983), 256; and Moshe Greenberg, *Ezekiel 21–37: A New Translation with Introduction and Commentary* (AB 22A; Garden City, N.Y.: Doubleday, 1997), 744.

[10] Cooke, *Book of Ezekiel*, 145.

the OT, Ezekiel refuses to dignify his target audience with the title. At best, he allows that they 'acted like prophets,' but like the false prophets in the previous oracle these women are frauds."[11]

In what sense were these women acting like prophets? It appears from v. 23 (לָכֵן שָׁוְא לֹא תֶחֱזֶינָה וְקֶסֶם לֹא־תִקְסַמְנָה עוֹד "therefore you shall see/utter no more false visions nor divine any more divination") that they were claiming to see/divine the future, but what were they predicting? The answer may lie in v. 19, where the phrase לְהָמִית נְפָשׁוֹת probably refers to a prediction that a certain person would die without the help of the women (cf. Jer 28:16: הַשָּׁנָה אַתָּה מֵת "this year you are going to die"), and the phrase בְּשַׁעֲלֵי שְׂעֹרִים וּבִפְתוֹתֵי לֶחֶם probably refers to the fee demanded for their help (cf. Mic 3:5: וַאֲשֶׁר לֹא־יִתֵּן עַל־פִּיהֶם וְקִדְּשׁוּ עָלָיו מִלְחָמָה "they declare war against him that does not put [anything] in their mouths").[12]

If this interpretation is correct, the offer of the women to help avert the tragedy for a fee is tantamount to a ransom demand. Like the witches of West Africa,[13] the women claim to have trapped their victim's soul, and they are demanding payment for its safe return; otherwise, they "prophesy," the victim will wither away and die.

In this reading, the causative terms לְהָמִית and לְחַיּוֹת have a declarative nuance.[14] But even if לְהָמִית is causative in the narrow sense, it would be odd to conclude that Ezekiel is ascribing the power of life and death to women whom he repeatedly brands as liars (cf. מִלִּבְּהֶן in v. 17, בְּכַזֶּבְכֶם in v. 19, שֶׁקֶר in v. 22, שָׁוְא in v. 23). One early Jewish exegete from Byzantium by the name of Reuel argued that the fear aroused by the black magic could be lethal: ולהמית נפ(שות) אש(ר) לא תמו(תנה) — כי אם נמצאו צדיקים לא היו נותנים להן מאכל מאומה כי היו יראים מפני ייי . . . , היו קוסמות ואומרות להם כי את[ם] תמותו

---

[11] Block, *Book of Ezekiel, Chapters 1–24*, 413.

[12] The latter parallel was pointed out by Eliezer of Beaugency (twelfth century); see מקראות גדולות הכתר — ספר תרי עשר (ed. Menachem Cohen; Ramat Gan: Bar-Ilan University Press, 2012), 179b, s.v. ואשר לא יתן.

[13] See at chapter 6, nn. 11–14 below.

[14] So NJPS: "you have announced the death of persons who will not die"; and Greenberg, *Ezekiel 1–20*, 234: "sentencing to death persons who should not die." Cf. וְטִהֲרוֹ/וְטִמְּאוֹ הַכֹּהֵן "and the priest shall declare him pure/impure" (Lev 13:6, 8); וְהִצְדִּיקוּ אֶת־הַצַּדִּיק וְהִרְשִׁיעוּ אֶת־הָרָשָׁע "and they shall declare the innocent party innocent and the guilty party guilty" (Deut 25:1); etc.

בשנה זאת. והם היו דואגים המות ומהם היו מתים מן הדאגה "And *to kill souls that should not die*—for if there were some righteous men who did not give them [= the women] any food because they were afraid of the Lord . . . , they [= the women] would practise divination and say to them, 'You will die within this year,' and they [= the righteous men] were worried about dying, and some of them died of worry."[15] A similar point was made by Walther Eichrodt: "Often, too, they were seriously harmed by the paralysing fear induced by the dark doings of the witches."[16]

[15] Nicholas de Lange, *Greek Jewish Texts from the Cairo Genizah* (TSAJ 51; Tübingen: Mohr Siebeck, 1996), 190–91, lines 234–37. The commentary is preserved on scrolls (*rotuli*) dated to ca. 1000.

[16] Eichrodt, *Ezekiel*, 170.

3

Pillows and Pillow Casings

In order to clarify Ezekiel's use of the word נפשות, we must first establish the meaning of the word כְּסָתוֹת. The latter comes close to being a *hapax legomenon* in the Bible, with two occurrences (one of them with a suffixed pronoun: כִּסְּתוֹתֵיכֶנָה) in a single passage (Ezek 13:18, 20). The information provided by the biblical contexts is far from adequate.

In the nineteenth century, scholars rejected the traditional interpretation of כסתות (see below) and began to discuss alternative interpretations. Rudolf Smend conjectured that the כסתות in question were magical bands.[1] Friedrich Delitzsch developed this conjecture, comparing the Hebrew word to Akkadian *kasītu* and assigning to the latter the concrete sense of "bond, fetter" on the basis of a single cuneiform context.[2] Biblical scholars quickly seized on this interpretation, and, for the most part, they have remained faithful to it to this day.[3] They paid little attention when the modern

---

[1] Smend, *Ezechiel,* 76–77.

[2] Delitzsch, "Glossario Ezechielico-Babylonico," xii; idem, *Assyrisches Handwörterbuch* (Leipzig: J. C. Hinrichs, 1896), 342 (in the phrase *kasīti lirmu,* interpreted as "may my bond be loosened").

[3] Bertholet, *Das Buch Hesekiel,* 71; Kraetzschmar, *Das Buch Ezechiel,* 135; BDB, 492b, s.v. כסה II; Barth, "Notiz," 235; Johannes Herrmann, *Ezechiel* (KAT 11; Leipzig: A. Deichert, 1924), 81; Lods, "Magie," 13; Cooke, *Book of Ezekiel,* 148; Fritz Dumermuth, "Zu Ez. XIII 18–21," *VT* 13 (1963): 228–29; Wevers, *Ezekiel,* 87; Eichrodt, *Ezekiel,* 169; *HALAT,* 467b, s.v. כֶּסֶת; Zimmerli, *Ezekiel 1,* 297; Stephen P. Garfinkel, "Studies in Akkadian Influences in the Book of Ezekiel" (Ph.D. diss., Columbia University, 1983), 94; Brownlee, *Ezekiel 1–19,* 193; Blenkinsopp, *Ezekiel,* 70; Davies, "Archaeological Com-

Akkadian dictionaries undermined this interpretation of כסתות by rejecting the concrete sense of *kasītu* suggested by Delitzsch, in the context known to him and in similar ones published later.[4] Another problem that scholars chose to ignore was the form: *kasītu* should have been borrowed as כְּסִית* (cf. שְׁבִית, חֲנִית, בְּכִית, not to mention כְּסוּת), appearing in v. 18 as כְּסִיתוֹת* and in v. 20 as כְּסִיתוֹתֵיכֶנָה* (cf. חֲנִיתוֹתֵיהֶם in Isa 2:4, etc.; and שְׁחִיתוֹתָם in Lam 4:20, etc.).[5] Several problems with the context were glossed over, as well: fetters are not sewn (מְתַפְּרוֹת in v. 18); they are not worn by the captor (זְרוֹעֹתֵיכֶם in v. 20);[6] and people cannot be hunted or trapped[7] in them (מְצֹדְדוֹת שָׁם in v. 20) or with them. The cumulative weight of these problems did not prompt scholars to rethink the Akkadian etymology and look for a single solution to all of them. Instead, those problems that were noted were eliminated in an ad hoc fashion through emendation or the like.

The Akkadian etymology must be evaluated in the light of what we know about the sociolinguistic situation in Judah and Mesopotamia. In Judah, government officials were able to converse in Aramaic at the end of the eighth century B.C.E., but the common people were not (Isa 36:11). In Mesopotamia, the encroachment of Aramaic was far more advanced. In Babylonia, the countryside was dominated by Aramaic-speaking tribes, and even in the cities "many scribes and other people" were bilingual.[8] Thus, in ca. 710 B.C.E., Sargon II felt compelled to rebuke an official from Ur for request-

---

mentary on Ezekiel 13," 121; Toorn, *From Her Cradle*, 123; Jeffers, *Magic*, 94; Block, *Book of Ezekiel, Chapters 1–24*, 413; Bowen, "Daughters," 424 n. 31; Armin Lange, *Vom prophetischen Wort zur prophetischen Tradition: Studien zur Traditions- und Redaktionsgeschichte innerprophetischer Konflikte in der Hebräischen Bibel* (Tübingen: Mohr Siebeck, 2002), 147; and Stökl, "The מתנ־באות," 64.

[4] *CAD* K:243–44, s.v. *kasītu*: "binding magic," "state of being bound"; *AHw*, 453b, s.v. *kasītu*: "Gebundenheit."

[5] Also possible: כְּסִיּוֹת*.

[6] Saggs, "'External Souls,'" 5.

[7] For a different interpretation of מְצֹדְדוֹת, see Appendix 2 below.

[8] Michael P. Streck, "Akkadian and Aramaic Language Contact," in *The Semitic Languages: An International Handbook* (ed. Stefan Weninger; Handbücher zur Sprach- und Kommunikationswissenschaft 36; Berlin: De Gruyter Mouton, 2012), 418.

ing permission to write to him in Aramaic rather than Akkadian.[9] In Assyria, the entire population spoke Aramaic by the beginning of the seventh century, the speakers of Akkadian being bilingual.[10]

It is probable, therefore, that the Judean exiles communicated with their Babylonian captors and neighbors in Aramaic,[11] and that they never felt the need to learn Akkadian. This would have been true even if Akkadian had been in its prime in Ezekiel's time (fl. 593–571 B.C.E.).[12] In fact, most scholars believe that Akkadian was either dead or dying by the beginning of the Late Babylonian period (625/600 B.C.E.).[13] Akkadian was, of course, still being written then, but

---

[9] *CAD* S:225, s.v. *sepēru*; M. Dietrich, *The Neo-Babylonian Correspondence of Sargon and Sennacherib* (SAA 17; Helsinki: Helsinki University Press, 2003), no. 2 lines 15–22; Streck, "Akkadian and Aramaic," 416.

[10] See S. Parpola, "National and Ethnic Identity in the Neo-Assyrian Empire and Assyrian Identity in Post-Empire Times," *Journal of Assyrian Academic Studies* 18, no. 2 (2004): 5–49, and the literature cited there.

[11] For evidence that the scribes assigned to deal with the prisoners from Judah were native speakers of Aramaic, see Richard C. Steiner, "Variation, Simplifying Assumptions and the History of Spirantization in Aramaic and Hebrew," in שערי לשון: מחקרים בלשון העברית, בארמית ובלשונות היהודים מוגשים למשה בר־אשר (ed. A. Maman, S. E. Fassberg, and Y. Breuer; 3 vols.; Jerusalem: Bialik, 2007), 1:*62 with n. 36.

[12] These are the dates of the contents of the book, according to Greenberg, *Ezekiel 1–20*, 12, 15.

[13] Wolfram von Soden, *Grundriss der akkadischen Grammatik* (3rd ed.; AnOr 33; Rome: Pontificium Institutum Biblicum, 1995), 299 §193a: "probably only a written language"; Giorgio Buccellati, *A Structural Grammar of Babylonian* (Wiesbaden: Harrassowitz, 1996), 2: "no longer a spoken language"; Stephen A. Kaufman, *The Akkadian Influences on Aramaic* (Assyriological Studies 19; Chicago: University of Chicago Press, 1974), 169: "an imperfectly learned, dying language"; Andrew George, "Babylonian and Assyrian: A History of Akkadian," in *Languages of Iraq, Ancient and Modern* (ed. J. N. Postgate; London: British School of Archaeology in Iraq, 2007), 60: "steadily losing ground as a vernacular, spoken language when Nebuchadnezzar II (604–562) made Babylon great again." (I am indebted to John Huehnergard for this last reference.) For a dissenting view and additional references, see Johannes Hackl, "Language Death and Dying Reconsidered: The Rôle of Late Babylonian as a Vernacular Language," *Imperium and Officium Working Papers*, July 2011, http://iowp.univie.ac.at/sites/default/files/IOWP_RAI_Hackl.pdf. Streck ("Akkadian and Aramaic," 418), too, objects to "the often repeated simple view that . . . Neo-

"it is quite probable that in the LB period, and perhaps even earlier, the great majority of those writing Akkadian documents were native Aramaic speakers."[14] Thus, any words of Akkadian origin borrowed by the exiles would *not* have come directly from Akkadian.[15] They would have been words used so commonly in Babylonian Aramaic that the exiles might have begun to use them in their own Aramaic speech and in Hebrew. No wonder, then, that almost all of the well-established Babylonian loanwords collected by Paul V. Mankowski from Ezekiel are attested in Aramaic as well.[16] Akkadian *kasītu*, by contrast, is unknown in Aramaic. Even in Akkadian, *CAD* lists only four attestations of the word, all in virtually identical requests or instructions to release someone from his/her bound state.

All of this makes a borrowing from Akkadian unlikely; it suggests that the comparison of כסתות to Akkadian *kasītu* should be viewed as a relic of the pan-Babylonian period of Hebrew lexicography. Fortunately, there is an excellent alternative—the traditional interpretation based on Mishnaic Hebrew.

Tannaitic literature is a gold mine of information about the term כֶּסֶת.[17] Examination of the contexts in which it occurs reveals that (1) a כסת was not considered a garment, and hence was not subject to the laws of fringes[18] and of mixtures;[19] (2) it was often made of

---

and even more Late Babylonian were only written languages," but see also at n. 8 above.

14 Kaufman, *Akkadian Influences*, 169.

15 Contra Isaac Gluska, "Akkadian Influences on the Book of Ezekiel," in *"An Experienced Scribe Who Neglects Nothing": Ancient Near Eastern Studies in Honor of Jacob Klein* (ed. Yitschak Sefati et al.; Bethesda, Md.: CDL, 2005), 718–37. I am indebted to Aaron Koller for this reference.

16 Paul V. Mankowski, *Akkadian Loanwords in Biblical Hebrew* (HSS 47; Winona Lake, Ind.: Eisenbrauns, 2000). The only exception, unattested in Aramaic, is שָׁשַׁר (Ezek 23:14). It should be noted that Mankowski's Aramaic documentation is incomplete for some of the borrowings and that he discusses neither כסתות nor מספחות in his book.

17 For a discussion of this term, see now Karen Kirshenbaum, ריהוט הבית במשנה (Ramat Gan: Bar-Ilan University Press, 2013), 243–49. I am indebted to Aaron Koller for this reference.

18 ספרי על ספר במדבר (ed. H. S. Horovitz; Leipzig: Gustav Fock, 1917), 125, §115 lines 1–2.

19 *M. Kil.* 9:2.

leather,[20] but wool or flax could also be used;[21] (3) it sometimes had a round shape;[22] (4) it could be made out of a scarf (מִטְפַּחַת),[23] presumably by folding it in half, rounding the corners (when desired), and sewing the borders, leaving a temporary opening of less than five handbreadths to allow for insertion of the filling;[24] (5) it was very similar to a כַּר,[25] differing primarily in size;[26] (6) it was normally filled with soft material[27] for use as a cushion, as padding[28] or as an insulator.[29]

Wilhelm Gesenius, too, looked at some of the contexts in the Mishnah, but he seems to have relied primarily on two dictionaries of Rabbinic Hebrew: the *ʿArukh* of Nathan b. Jehiel of Rome and *Sefer ha-tishbi* of Elijah Levita. From the description of the former (כסת הוא קטן שמשים תחת מראשותיו "the כסת is small, that which one places under the head")[30] and the Western Yiddish glosses of the latter (פְּפוּלְבֶן = *Pfulben*, פּוּלְשְׁטֶר = *Pulster*),[31] Gesenius learned that *pul-*

---

[20] *M. Kelim* 16:4, *m. Miqw.* 7:6; 10:2.

[21] *M. Kelim* 29:2.

[22] *M. Miqw.* 10:2.

[23] *M. Kelim* 28:5 (cf. 26:9); see below.

[24] *M. Kelim* 16:4; see below. In the modern manufacturing process, the temporary opening is six inches in length.

[25] The two nouns are frequently conjoined in rabbinic literature; from the Bible, one would never have guessed that they denoted similar objects.

[26] The relative sizes of the כר and the כסת can be deduced from *m. Kelim* 28–29. From *m. Kelim* 28:5, we learn that a כר could be made out of a סדין and that a כסת could be made out of a מטפחת; and from 29:2, it appears that a סדין was roughly four times the size of a מטפחת. Despite this, some medieval and post-medieval scholars believed that כר was the smaller one, placed under the head. This belief is called a common mistake in Tosafot to *b. ʿAbod. Zar.* 65a and is refuted there.

[27] *T. B. Qam.* 11:12; *t. Ohol.* 12:2.

[28] מכילתא דרבי ישמעאל (ed. H. S. Horovitz and I. A. Rabin; Frankfurt am Main: J. Kauffmann, 1931), 180 lines 12–14 = Menahem I. Kahana, המכילות לפרשת עמלק: לראשוניותה של המסורת במכילתא דרבי ישמעאל בהשוואה למקבילתה במכילתא דרבי שמעון בן יוחי (Jerusalem: Magnes, 1999), 168–69, lines 148–51; *m. Kelim* 28:9.

[29] *M. Šabb.* 4:2.

[30] Nathan b. Jehiel, ספר ערוך השלם (8 vols.; Vienna: n.p., 1878–1892), 4:309b bot., s.v. כַּר; cf. 280b, s.v. כֶּסֶת. The latter entry, ignored by Gesenius (see n. 32 below), is somewhat less clear than the former.

[31] Elijah Levita, ספר התשבי (Basel: Conrad Waldkirch, 1601), 45a. The

vini "pillows, cushions" was the meaning of the word in Rabbinic Hebrew.[32] He noted that the rabbinic evidence agreed perfectly with the evidence of the versions, which render כסתות with words meaning "pillows, cushions" (LXX *προσκεφάλαια*; Symmachus *ὑπαγκώνια*; Peshiṭta בסדותא; Vulgate *pulvilli*).[33] Only one thing was missing: a plausible explanation of the function of the pillows.[34] They seemed incongruous in the context.[35]

One scholar made a valiant attempt to explain the pillows. Adolphe Lods asserted that "the cushion was a receptacle 'where they trapped souls.'"[36] He suggested that it might be comparable to one of the receptacles that, according to Frazer's survey, were used for holding souls by tribes around the world. But how can a pillow be a receptacle? Lods was silent about this problem.

It was no doubt this problem that led, in the nineteenth century, to the abandonment of the traditional interpretation—the interpretation based on postbiblical Hebrew and most of the versions. It was not realized that a minor modification is all that is needed to make that interpretation fit the context like a glove.

---

vocalization (including the third *shewa* of פְּפוּלְבְּן) is that of the author; see S. Z. Leiman, "Abarbanel and the Censor," *JJS* 19 (1968): 49 n. 1.

[32] Wilhelm Gesenius, *Thesaurus philologicus linguae Hebraeae et Chaldaeae Veteris Testamenti* (3 vols. in 1; Leipzig: F. C. W. Vogel, 1835–1853), 700b, s.v. כֶּסֶת.

[33] Cf. the rendering *cervicalia* "pillows" in Jerome's Latin translation of Origen's homily on our passage; see Origen, *Homélies sur Ézéchiel* (ed. Marcel Borret; SC 352; Paris: Cerf, 1989), 126 §2 line 9; 130 §3 line 25; 134 §4 lines 4, 6, 9, 10, 15.

[34] A few of the Church Fathers had grappled with this problem. Pope Gregory the Great understood the pillows/cushions as a metaphor for the coddling of the souls of sinners by the prophetesses, who flattered them instead of rebuking them; see *Ancient Christian Commentary on Scripture, Old Testament*, vol. 13, *Ezekiel, Daniel* (ed. Kenneth Stevenson and Michael Glerup; Downers Grove, Ill.: InterVarsity, 2008), 49: "It is as if a person reclined with a cushion under the elbow or a pillow under his head, is not reproved severely when he sins but is treated with enervating favoritism, in order that he may recline at ease in his error, the while no asperity of reproof assails him."

[35] The point is made explicitly by modern scholars, e.g., Saggs, "'External Souls,'" 2; Korpel, "Avian Spirits," 103; and Berlejung, "Falsche Prophetinnen," 193.

[36] Lods, *La croyance*, 1:47.

Two crucial postbiblical passages show that the word כסת can refer to the pillow casing alone, without any filling. In both of them, the Mishnah (*m. Kelim* 20:1 and 25:1) gives the following list: הַכָּרִים וְהַכְּסָתוֹת (וְ)הַשַּׂקִּין וְהַמַּרְצָפִּים.[37] The fact that the third and fourth items are sacks and packing bags, respectively, hints that the first and second items were also (or, at least, could also be used as) bags. In fact, one of these passages (*m. Kelim* 20:1), taken together with the corresponding passage in the Tosefta (*t. Kelim BM* 10:2/3), makes it clear that all four items had two functions: (1) one could keep/carry things *in* them, and (2) one could sit/lie *on* them.[38] In the words of Maimonides:

> קאל אן הד׳ה אלכלים אד׳ וקד יג׳לס עליהא והי סאלמה דון ת׳קב פכאנהא עמלת מן אוליה׳ חאלהא ללשיאין ג׳מיעא, לתכון מן כְּלֵי קִבּוּל וליג׳לס עליהא.[39]
>
> It says that these *utensilia*[40]—inasmuch as one sometimes sits on them when they are intact, without perforation—are considered as though they were made from the very beginning for both things, to be receptacles and to be sat on.

Several medieval exegetes understood Ezekiel's כסתות as having the first function. Menaḥem b. Saruq's gloss for כסתות is

[37] I have reproduced the vocalized text of Codex Kaufmann to the extent that the pointing is visible in the online photographs (http://kaufmann.mtak.hu/en/ms50/ms50-coll6.htm). The conjunction in parentheses was added by a later hand. The last word, vocalized מַרְצָפִּים in Codex Parma (see n. 45 below), is derived from μάρσυπ(π)ος ~ μάρσιππος "bag, pouch." See the discussion of this passage in Kirshenbaum, ריהוט הבית, 248–49.

[38] The point of the passages is that the two functions were independent. The second function (and the type of ritual impurity associated with it) remained even when the כסת was torn and thus lost the first function.

[39] משנה עם פירוש רבינו משה בן מימון (ed. Yosef Qafiḥ; 7 vols.; Jerusalem: Mossad Harav Kook, 1963–1968), 6:179b–180b. The translation from the Judeo-Arabic is mine. So, too, in his *Mishneh Torah*, Hilkhot Kelim 24:11: כלים שעיקר עשייתן לקבלה ולמשכב כאחד כגון הכרים והכסתות והשקין והמרצופין "*utensilia* made from the very beginning for both receiving/containing and lying, e.g., mattress casings, pillow casings, sacks and packing bags." Cf. Asher b. Jehiel, פירוש הרא״ש השלם לרבינו אשר ב״ר יחיאל זצ״ל על מסכת כלים (ed. Y. Goldshtof; Jerusalem: Diqduq Halakhah, 1993), 245.

[40] I.e., functional artifacts.

שקים ואמתחות "sacks and bags";[41] Joseph Qara's is כיסין "pouches"; Menaḥem b. Simeon's is השקים אשר ישימו בהן הקסמים "the sacks in which they place the instruments of divination."[42] Reuel's gloss for כִּסְּתוֹתֵיכֶנָה is סַקוֹפַּתְנִיאָה אִישׁוֹן סַקוּלִיאָה = σακκοπάθνια ἴσον σακκούλια "large bags = sacks."[43]

The view of Ezekiel's כסתות as pillow casings (rather than pillows) yields an etymology far better than the ones suggested by modern biblical scholars.[44] The etymology is hinted at by Joseph Qara's gloss, cited above, and by the suffixed form כִּיסָתוֹ (rather than the expected כִּסְתוֹ) that appears in one early vocalized manuscript of the Mishnah.[45] These two pieces of evidence suggest that כֶּסֶת < *kistu* is nothing other than the feminine form of כִּיס < *kīsu*,[46] with the expected vowel shortening in a closed syllable.[47] In other words, the vowel alternation in כֶּסֶת ~ כִּיס has the same origin as that in שַׁחַת ~ שִׁיחָה, in מַזְכֶּרֶת ~ מַזְכִּיר, in גְּבֶרֶת ~ גְּבִיר (pausal גְּבָרֶת), in אַדִּיר ~

---

[41] Menaḥem b. Saruq, *Maḥberet* (ed. Angel Sáenz-Badillos; Granada: Universidad de Granada, 1986), 219*.

[42] For the last two, see מקראות גדולות הכתר — ספר יחזקאל, 66b, 67b. Some modern Hebrew dictionaries also cite כיס in connection with כסת, either as a gloss or as one possible etymology; see Kirshenbaum, ריהוט הבית, 246.

[43] De Lange, *Greek Jewish Texts*, 190–91 line 239 with n. 239: "σακκοπάθνια are large bags (Diocletian, *Edict on Princes*, ed. Lauffer, 11.8). . . .ἴσον: 'equals'. . . . It is possible that σακκούλια is an explanation of σακκοπάθνια, an old translation that was no longer understood."

[44] For an alternative to the Akkadian etymology discussed above in this chapter, see Korpel, "Avian Spirits," 103; Block, *Book of Ezekiel, Chapters 1–24*, 413. Both scholars assume that, if כסת is a native Hebrew word, its root is כ-ס-ה "cover." So, too, Gesenius, cited in n. 46 below. However, the expected noun from that root is כְּסוּת or כְּסִית*—not כֶּסֶת.

[45] *Mishna Codex Parma (De Rossi 138): An Early Vowelized Manuscript of the Complete Mishna Text* (Jerusalem: Kedem, 1970), 290, col. a line 3 (*m. Mid.* 1:8).

[46] Gesenius, too, saw that the final *t* of כסת was the feminine ending, but he failed to see the connection with כיס. Instead, he put כסת under the root כ-ס-ה in his *Thesaurus* (p. 700).

[47] For this sound change, see Richard C. Steiner, "Vowel Syncope and Syllable Repair Processes in Proto-Semitic Construct Forms: A New Reconstruction Based on the Law of Diminishing Conditioning," in *Language and Nature: Papers Presented to John Huehnergard on the Occasion of His 60th Birthday* (ed. Rebecca Hasselbach and Naʿama Pat-El; SAOC 67; Chicago: Oriental Institute, 2012), 379 n. 77, 381–82.

אַדֶּרֶת* (pausal אַדָּרֶת), and probably in קִיר מוֹאָב ~ קֶרֶת* (pausal קָרֶת).[48] It is true that one would have expected the plural to be כִּיסוֹת (cf. שִׂיחוֹת and מַזְכִּירוֹת) instead of כְּסָתוֹת, but there are other examples of the feminine ending *-t* being incorporated into the root by metanalysis; Gesenius compares דְּלָתוֹת and קְשָׁתוֹת,[49] to which we may add -שִׁפְתוֹת. As for the *dagesh* in the *samekh* of כִּסְּתוֹתֵיכֶנָה, Menaḥem b. Simeon compares it to the one in עִקְּבוֹת (Ps 89:52; cf. also עִקְּבֵי in Gen 49:17 and Judg 5:22).[50] I would add עַצְּבוֹתָם (Ps 147:3) and best of all קַשְּׁתֹתֵיהֶם (Neh 4:7), קַשְּׁתוֹתָם (Jer 51:56, Ps 37:15), קַשְּׁתֹתָיו (Isa 5:28) with *dagesh* in a sibilant preceding feminine *t*. This very plausible etymology implies that the list in *m. Kelim* is an ancient one, preserving the original meaning of the word.

The phrase מְתַפְּרוֹת כְּסָתוֹת makes perfect sense in this interpretation.[51] It probably refers to two activities. First, since it is parallel to עֹשׂוֹת הַמִּסְפָּחוֹת, it refers to the making of pillow casings by sewing the borders of folded pieces of fabric or leather. In this reading, it should be compared to the descriptions in *m. Kelim* 28:5: כֶּסֶת שֶׁעֲשָׂאָהּ מִטְפַּחַת וּמִטְפַּחַת שֶׁעֲשָׂאָהּ כֶּסֶת טָמֵא "a (ritually impure) pillow casing that one made into a scarf or a (ritually impure) scarf that one made into a pillow casing remains impure" and in *m. Kelim* 16:4: הַכַּר וְהַכֶּסֶת שֶׁלָּעוֹר . . . מִשֶּׁיִּתְפְּרֵם וְיִשַׁיֵּיר בָּהֶן פָּחוּת מֵחֲמִשָּׁה טְפָחִים "mattress casings and pillow casings of leather (become functional and, hence, susceptible to ritual impurity) . . . from the time that one sews them, leaving (an opening of) less than five handbreadths."[52] Thus, the women are sewing folded pieces of fabric or leather to make pillow casings[53] that will be used to trap and/or store the

[48] For the last example, cf. Moabite קר "city." The Moabite meaning of קִיר מוֹאָב (Isa 15:1), "city of Moab," is recognized by *Targum Jonathan*. For the connection between the meanings "city" and "wall," cf. Greek τεῖχος, which has the meaning "walled city" in addition to the meaning "wall." For the relationship between קִיר and קִרְיָה, see Steiner, "Vowel Syncope," 379 n. 77.

[49] Gesenius, *Thesaurus*, 700.

[50] See Cohen, מקראות גדולות הכתר — ספר יחזקאל, 67.

[51] For the use of the *piʿel*-stem here, see Appendix 2 below.

[52] Here, again, I have reproduced the vocalized text of Codex Kaufmann to the extent that the pointing is visible in the online photographs (http://kaufmann.mtak.hu/en/ms50/ms50-coll6.htm).

[53] In this reading, כסתות is the so-called "accusative of product"; cf.

souls of their victims. At the same time, they are sewing the pillow casings onto their arms, that is, their sleeves—presumably in order to free their hands for the capture of additional souls. The reason for the use of pillow casings instead of ordinary sacks will become apparent later.

Korpel, "Avian Spirits," 102: "it is manufactured by sewing." Contrast Carl F. Keil, *Biblical Commentary on the Prophecies of Ezekiel* (trans. James Martin; 2 vols.; Edinburgh: T. & T. Clark, 1876), 1:171: "the word תָּפַר (to sew together) is inapplicable to cushions"; and Vladimir Orel, "Textological Notes," *ZAW* 109 (1997): 412: "It seems, however, that such a translation ['cushions'] is incompatible with the verb *tāpar* used here."

4

Cloth Patches as Pillow Filling

Another rare word in this prophecy, possibly a *hapax legomenon*, is הַמִּסְפָּחוֹת. It refers to something that the women wore on their heads (עַל־רֹאשׁ כָּל־קוֹמָה). It goes without saying that anything placed on the head covers the head, at least in part. Exegetes from the Hellenistic era (LXX τὰ ἐπιβόλαια "the coverings") to the present have exploited that fact in interpreting הַמִּסְפָּחוֹת. Some of them have also been influenced, consciously or unconsciously, by the phonetically similar term הַמִּטְפָּחוֹת "shawls" in Isa 3:22. But this similarity is a purely random one; it has no etymological source and, hence, no evidentiary value.

Here again we are faced with a choice between Akkadian and Mishnaic Hebrew. And here again it was Friedrich Delitzsch who, for better or worse, brought Akkadian into the picture.[1] In this case, however, Bible scholars have invoked the alleged cognate, Akk. *sapāḫu* "scatter, disperse; spread, stretch," in support of a variety of meanings. Delitzsch himself assumed that מספחות were linen cloths. G. R. Driver conjectured that "מספחה denotes some kind of loose, flowing or spreading or all-enveloping, garment such as a 'shawl' or 'veil.'"[2] Other scholars claimed that *sapāḫu* is an antonym of *kasû* "bind" with the meaning "loose, untie,"[3] but that meaning is

[1] Friedrich Delitzsch, "Glossario Ezechielico-Babylonico," xiii.

[2] G. R. Driver, "Linguistic and Textual Problems: Ezekiel," *Bib* 19 (1938): 63–64.

[3] Johannes Herrmann, *Ezechiel*, 81; Cooke, *Book of Ezekiel*, 146; Davies, "Archaeological Commentary," 121.

not universally accepted today.[4] Moreover, "whilst the verb *sapāḫu* is found used with reference to magic, there appears to be no evidence in Akkadian for an amulet named from this root,"[5] and "it is more to the point to seek a meaning for *mispāḥôt* that would involve the notion of tightening or fastening, rather than one of loosening or scattering."[6] Finally, it has been proposed that מספחות is a metathesized borrowing of Akk. *musaḫḫiptu* "net."[7] This is a seductive suggestion; however, "since *musaḫḫiptu* is attested to only in lexical texts, and is restricted to hunting gazelles,[[8]] its use as an etymon for *mispāḥâ* is highly speculative at best, and cannot be accepted."[9]

As noted in the previous chapter, any words of Akkadian origin borrowed by the Judean exiles would have been Akkadian words in common use in Babylonian Aramaic. However, no borrowing of Akk. *musaḫḫiptu* is found in Aramaic. How likely is it that the Aramaic-speaking exiles borrowed an Akkadian term that modern scholars know only from lexical lists? Finally, we should note that Biblical Hebrew has a number of common terms for bird traps and nets: פַּח,[10] מוֹקֵשׁ, and רֶשֶׁת. It is legitimate to ask why the exiles would have borrowed another such term.

If we were forced to use a Semitic cognate to determine the meaning of מספחות, we could do a lot worse than Arabic *safīḥ* "(large) sack."[11] As I have already noted, Ezekiel's women are using כסתות as sacks to trap souls.[12] However, as it turns out, there is no

---

[4] No such meaning appears in *CAD* S:151, s.v. *sapāḫu*; *AHw*, 1024, does have "auflösen."

[5] Saggs, "'External Souls,'" 6.

[6] Garfinkel, "Studies," 104.

[7] Saggs, "'External Souls,'" 6–7; and Korpel, "Avian Spirits," 103.

[8] For an apparently different view, see Armas Salonen, *Vögel und Vogelfang im alten Mesopotamien* (Suomalaisen Tiedeakatemian toimituksia B180; Helsinki: Suomalainen Tiedeakatemia, 1973), 41: "$^{\tilde{g}iz}$s a – m a š – d a_3 = *musaḫḫiptu* 'Vogelfangnetz' eig. 'Gazellennetz.'"

[9] Garfinkel, "Studies," 105.

[10] A borrowing of Egyptian *pḫ3* "bird trap"; see Yoshiyuki Muchiki, *Egyptian Proper Names and Loanwords in North-West Semitic* (SBLDS 173; Atlanta: Society of Biblical Literature, 1999), 253.

[11] Lane, *Arabic-English Lexicon*, 1369, col. b, s.v.; and A. de Biberstein Kazimirski, *Dictionnaire arabe-français* (Beirut: Librairie du Liban, 1860), 1097, col. a, s.v.

[12] See chapter 3 above.

need to look outside of ancient Hebrew sources for the meaning of this word.

Here again Mishnaic Hebrew provides a compelling solution. A remarkably insightful article on the subject was published in 1895 by an obscure scholar, N. N. Tarashchansky, in an equally obscure Hebrew journal that ceased publication after only one year.[13] Tarashchansky pointed out that there is another attestation of מספחות, once again collocated with כסת "pillow," in the Tosefta (*B. Qam.* 11:12): כר מלא מוכין וכסת מלאה מספחות "a mattress full of מוכין and a pillow full of מספחות." This phrase, in turn, he compared with the phrase כר מלא מוכין וכסת מלאה מוכין "a mattress full of מוכין and a pillow full of מוכין" in *b. B. Qam.* 119b, concluding that מספחות = מוכין. Finally, he argued that the term מוכין, usually used of fuzzy, absorbent lumps of fibers, could also refer to small fragments or shreds of cloth, based on *m. Neg.* 11:12: קִיצְּצוֹ וַעֲשָׂאוֹ מוּכִּין[14] "if he cut it [= the garment] and made it into מוכין." He concluded that Ezekiel's מספחות were patches of cloth.[15] In support of the meaning "patch," he pointed to (1) *Targum Jonathan*'s rendering of מספחות as פַּתְכּוֹמָרִין, which seems to mean "patchwork covers";[16] (2) *Kalla Rab.* 6:4, which presents a halakhic argument based on the assumption that מִסְפָּחוֹת (Ezek 13:18) is the plural of מִסְפַּחַת "scab" (Lev 13:6, from the root ס-פ-ח "attach").

The critical importance of the toseftan parallel has been accepted by the handful of scholars aware of it.[17] Henoch Yalon, one of the founders of the Israeli school of Hebrew philology, commented that

---

[13] N. N. Tarashchansky, מִסְפָּחוֹת, *Talpiyyot* 1 (1895): 15–17 (in אוצר הספרות section).

[14] So in Codex Kaufmann (http://kaufmann.mtak.hu/en/ms50/ms50-coll6.htm).

[15] For a very similar interpretation, in a Judeo-Arabic commentary from the early eleventh century, see פירוש ר' יהודה אבן בלעם לספר יחזקאל (ed. Maʿaravi Perez; Ramat Gan: Bar-Ilan University Press, 2000), 46-47.

[16] This word occurs again in *Targum Jonathan* to Ezek 16:16, where טְלֻאוֹת "patched" is rendered by מְחַפְּיָן פַּתְכּוֹמָרִין, seemingly with the meaning "covered with patchwork covers."

[17] Saul Lieberman, תוספת ראשונים (4 vols.; Jerusalem: Bamberger & Wahrmann, 1937–1939), 2:104; idem, תוספתא כפשוטה: באור ארוך לתוספתא (10 vols.; New York: Jewish Theological Seminary of America, 1955–), 9:139; Henoch Yalon, review of Yehudah Grazovski (Goor), מלון השפה העברית, in Henoch Yalon, ed., קונטרסים לעניני הלשון העברית (Jerusalem: Wahrmann

"it is clear beyond any doubt that the מספחות in the Tosefta cannot be separated from the מספחות in Ezekiel."[18] Louis Ginzberg, who noted the toseftan parallel independently in 1934, wrote, "Thus, מספחות occurring with כסתות in Ezek 13:18 is not to be changed to מטפחות, and even less is כסתות to be interpreted as 'magic bands' based on the Assyrian."[19] Alluding to the medieval copyists who pointed out words in Latin texts that were not to be read because they were Greek (*Graeca sunt, non leguntur*), he concluded in exasperation that "modern commentators on the Bible seem to follow the rule *Hebraica sunt, non leguntur*!"[20]

Tarashchansky's argument is convincing by itself, but it is possible to add a few supporting comments. To מִסְפָּחוֹת as the plural of מִסְפַּחַת (rather than מִסְפָּחָה, the singular form generally reconstructed today),[21] we may compare מִטְפָּחוֹת (Isa 3:22) as the plural of מִטְפַּחַת (Ruth 3:15). Thus, מִסְפַּחַת (from the root ס-פ-ח "attach") originally referred to a small attachment used to cover and repair rent skin or clothing, that is, a scab or a patch. The use of מספחות to refer to any small pieces of cloth, whether used as patches or not, is a natural semantic development. A similar semantic widening is attested in Jewish Babylonian Aramaic, where רוקעתא from the root ר-ק-ע "patch" means "piece of cloth, rag."[22]

The realization that מספחות were cloth patches used as filling for pillows and cushions helps to explain the renderings of Symmachus and Jerome: ὑπαυχένια "pillows for the neck" and *cervica-*

Books, 1963), part 2 (= שנה שניה), 21–22; Greenberg, *Ezekiel 1–20*, 239; Rimon Kasher, יחזקאל (2 vols.; Tel-Aviv: Am Oved, 2004), 1:303.

[18] Yalon, קונטרסים, part 2, 22.

[19] Louis Ginzberg, "Beiträge zur Lexikographie des Jüdisch-Aramäischen," *MGWJ* 78 (1934): 28. Ginzberg correctly rules out the possibility that the toseftan parallel is based on the biblical verses. Such literary borrowings in Mishnaic Hebrew are not difficult to recognize; see Eduard Y. Kutscher, "Mittelhebräisch und Jüdisch-Aramäisch im neuen Köhler-Baumgartner," in *Hebräische Wortforschung: Festschrift zum 80. Geburtstag von Walter Baumgartner* (VTSup 16; Leiden: Brill, 1967), 160–61 = idem, *Hebrew and Aramaic Studies* (Jerusalem: Magnes, 1977), 158–59.

[20] Ginzberg, "Beiträge," 29.

[21] See, for example, BDB and *HALAT*, s.v. מִסְפָּחָה.

[22] See Michael Sokoloff, *A Dictionary of Jewish Babylonian Aramaic of the Talmudic and Geonic Periods* (Ramat Gan: Bar-Ilan University Press, 2002), 1067a-b, s.v.

lia "pillows." It even explains the shift in our verse from indefinite כסתות to definite המספחות. The women first make pillow casings, and then they make *the* filling needed to turn them into pillows. Once pillow casings are sewn, filling is expected and thus grammatically definite.

In my opinion, Tarashchansky did not grasp the full significance of his discovery. For him, עֹשׂוֹת הַמִּסְפָּחוֹת was a kind of poetic parallel of מְתַפְּרוֹת כְּסָתוֹת, equivalent to it in meaning.[23] I suggest that the phrases מְתַפְּרוֹת כְּסָתוֹת and עֹשׂוֹת הַמִּסְפָּחוֹת refer to distinct processes in the manufacture of pillows: the sewing of folded pieces of fabric or leather into pillow casings and the cutting up of old clothing to make pillow filling. In this case, however, the מספחות are not in the כסתות. The women have put them on their heads, but to what end? That question is discussed in chapter 6 below.

---

[23] Cf. Symmachus and Jerome in the preceding paragraph.

5

Souls in Bags

The phrase כְּסְתוֹתֵיכֶנָה אֲשֶׁר אַתֵּנָה מְצֹדְדוֹת שָׁם אֶת־הַנְּפָשׁוֹת (Ezek 13:20) implies that נפשות are trapped *in* (not *with*!) כסתות. James G. Frazer assumed that the נפשות in question were disembodied souls that were literally trapped, but, as we have seen, a majority of scholars disputes this.[1] Moshe Greenberg, for example, writes:

> A like phrase recurs in Prov 6:26, "a married woman can trap [*taṣud*] an honorable person [*nepeš*]" with her wiles; it is a figure for the enticement of gullibles. Theories based on the notion of the magical catching of disembodied souls (T. H. Gaster, *Myth, Legend and Custom in the Old Testament*, pp. 615ff.) disregard the absence of evidence that *nepeš* ever has such a sense in Hebrew.[2]

The notion that the trapping in our passage is not literal but "a figure for the enticement of gullibles" goes back at least as far as David Qimḥi: לצודד נפשות — כי נפשות הצדיקים התמימים הם כאלו הם נתפשות במצודותכן "to trap souls—for it is as if the souls of the simple, righteous people are caught in your traps."[3] It was adopted by William Lowth as well.[4] At first glance, the parallel cited by Greenberg from Prov 6:26 seems to confirm this interpretation. Closer inspection, however, reveals that the parallel is deficient in a crucial respect; it lacks the locative adverb שם. That adverb is difficult to reconcile with the metaphoric reading. The difficulty was tacitly acknowledged already in 1723 by Lowth:

---

[1] See the introduction, nn. 19–20 and 25–27 above.

[2] Greenberg, *Ezekiel 1–20,* 240. So, too, Karl-Friedrich Pohlmann, *Das Buch des Propheten Hesekiel (Ezechiel)* (2 vols.; ATD 22; Göttingen: Vandenhoeck & Ruprecht, 1996–2001), 192.

[3] See Cohen, מקראות גדולות הכתר — ספר יחזקאל, 66a.

[4] See immediately below.

> Ver. 18 . . . *Will ye hunt the Souls of my People* . . .] . . . that is, will ye make a Prey of Men's Souls by deluding them with fair Hopes and Promises?
>
> . . .
>
> Ver. 20. *Wherewith ye hunt the Souls to make them fly.*] To make them run into those Nets and Snares that you have laid for them: See Ver. 18. The Metaphor is continued from the manner of hunting and pursuing living Creatures, by that means to drive them into the Toils prepared for them.[5]

When we compare Lowth's translation of אֲשֶׁר אַתֵּנָה מְצֹדְדוֹת שָׁם אֶת־ הַנְּפָשׁוֹת with that of the Authorized Version of 1611 (*"your pillowes wherewith yee there hunt the soules to make* them *flie"*), we see that there is a crucial difference. Lowth has omitted the word *there* (not to mention *pillowes*), no doubt because it contradicts his interpretation; he takes it for granted that the deluded souls are metaphorically portrayed as being trapped in nets and snares, not in pillows. Ferdinand Hitzig, who emended שם to בם "with them," made the point explicit: "שם . . . hangs together with the incorrect interpretation of כסתות as *προσκεφάλαια*."[6]

It is clear, therefore, that the locative adverb שם "there, in that place" places the trapped נפשות in כסתות. This is not a problem if the latter are empty pillow casings (rather than pillows), and the former are souls (rather than people). We can judge the size of the pillow casings used by the women from the fact that they sewed them on their arms. It seems unlikely that they were large enough to hold נפשות, if the latter were people. Disembodied souls, however, were thought to be immaterial and smaller than people in a number of cultures.[7] Judging from New Kingdom *shabti* figures, even a material *ba* would be small enough to fit easily into a pillow casing.[8]

---

[5] William Lowth, *A Commentary upon the Prophet Ezekiel* (London: W. Mears, 1723), 91–92.

[6] Ferdinand Hitzig, *Der Prophet Ezechiel* (Kurzgefasstes exegetisches Handbuch zum Alten Testament 8; Leipzig: Weidmann, 1847), 91.

[7] See at chapter 13, nn. 9–14 below.

[8] See the "wooden *shabti* figure representing the deceased holding the *ba* in his hand" (Eighteenth Dynasty) in John H. Taylor, *Death and the Afterlife in Ancient Egypt* (London: British Museum Press, 2001), 22 fig. 9. See also the small *ba*-souls clutched to the breast on the *shabti* of Suneru (Nineteenth Dynasty; ibid., 123 fig. 86 and http://www.britishmuseum.org/explore/highlights/highlight_image.aspx?image=ps328134.

The verse says, then, that the women trap disembodied souls in their כסתות. Before they are filled with מספחות and their opening is sewn up, כסתות are bags that can be used to hold things. This fact greatly increases the attractiveness of Frazer's interpretation. Indeed, it can now be said that Frazer's two major prooftexts for disembodied souls are mutually reinforcing. In addition to Ezek 13:20, Frazer cites 1 Sam 25:29: וְהָיְתָה נֶפֶשׁ אֲדֹנִי צְרוּרָה בִּצְרוֹר הַחַיִּים אֵת ה׳ אֱלֹהֶיךָ וְאֵת נֶפֶשׁ אֹיְבֶיךָ יְקַלְּעֶנָּה בְּתוֹךְ כַּף הַקָּלַע "the נפש of my lord will be bound up in the bundle of the living/life in the care of the Lord, your God; but He will sling away the נפש of your enemies (as) in the pocket of a sling." Both speak of souls in bags.[9]

But why use pillow casings instead of ordinary bags? I submit that the answer to that question lies in the concept of the "dream-soul," discussed in the next chapter.

---

jpg&retpage=15187); the *shabti* of Meryre (Eighteenth Dynasty; http://www.metmuseum.org/collection/the-collection-online/search/549215); the *shabti* of Wepwautmes (Nineteenth Dynasty; https://escholarship.org/uc/item/6cx744kk); and an anonymous *shabti* (New Kingdom; http://data.fitzmuseum.cam.ac.uk/id/object/53890). The *ba*-souls depicted in New Kingdom papyri of the *Book of the Dead* tend to be larger (relative to the size of their owners), but there is no reason to assume that they are drawn to scale. In any event, even if the נפשות hunted by Ezekiel's women were imagined as material beings larger than a pillow casing, the latter could still be used to immobilize them. A bird stuffed into a sack cannot fly away even if its head does not fit inside the sack.

[9] The terms used for bags in the two verses, כסת and צרור, occur in close proximity to each other in the Mishnah. The former occurs in כָּל הַכֵּלִים יֵשׁ לָהֶם אֲחוֹרַיִם וָתוֹךְ כְּגוֹן הַכָּרִים וְהַכְּסָתוֹת וְהַשַּׂקִּין וְהַמַּרְצָפִים "all *utensilia* have (two distinct surfaces for the purposes of impurity:) an outside [lit., backside] and an inside (—even those that can be turned inside out), e.g., mattress casings, pillow casings, sacks and packing bags" (*m. Kelim* 25:1). The latter occurs in צְרוֹר מַרְגָּלִית טָמֵא צְרוֹר הַמָּעוֹת ר׳ אֱלִיעֶזֶר מְטַמֵּא וַחֲכָמִ׳ מְטַהֲרִין "a pearl pouch (which is opened infrequently) is (susceptible to becoming) impure; a money pouch (which is opened frequently)—R. Eliezer declares it (susceptible to becoming) impure, while the Sages declare it not (susceptible to becoming) impure" (ibid., 26:2). The Mishnah deals with the צרור separately because it is often only a *temporary*, ad hoc bag; if it is opened frequently (as when it is used to hold money), it does not hold its shape but rather reverts to being a flat piece of leather with no discernible outside and inside. Despite this difference, it is clear from the Mishnah that the צרור and the כסת belong to the same semantic field.

6

Pillow-Traps for Dream-Souls

It is well known that, in many cultures, the souls of sleeping people are thought to leave the body.[1] Such a soul is often referred to as a "dream-soul."[2] For many anthropologists, the dream-soul is merely an aspect of the free soul. In the words of Jan N. Bremmer:

> It is the great merit of Scandinavian anthropologists in particular to have collected large amounts of data to show that most "primitive" peoples have thought that man has two kinds of souls. On the one hand, there is what these scholars call the free soul, a soul which represents the individual personality. This soul ... only manifests itself during swoons, dreams or at death (the experiences of the "I" during the swoons or dreams are ascribed

---

[1] James G. Frazer, *The Golden Bough: A Study in Magic and Religion* (13 vols.; New York: Macmillan, 1935–1937), 3:36–42. For some of the Jewish sources, see Louis Ginzberg, *The Legends of the Jews* (trans. Henrietta Szold; 7 vols.; Philadelphia: Jewish Publication Society, 1909–1938), 5:74. See also the intriguing claim of Hans-Peter Hasenfratz, "Religionswissenschaftliches zur Seelenkonzeption: Am Beispiel Altägyptens," in *Der Begriff der Seele in der Religionswissenschaft* (ed. Johann Figl and Hans-Dieter Klein; Der Begriff der Seele 1; Würzburg: Königshausen & Neumann, 2002), 124: "When he [a person] sleeps at night, his *ba* leaves him and roams in the form of a bird ('bird-soul')." Unfortunately, no evidence is provided for this claim, which I have not encountered elsewhere.

[2] Hochegger, "Die Vorstellungen von 'Seele,'" 327-28; Stith Thompson, *Motif-Index of Folk-Literature: A Classification of Narrative Elements in Folktales, Ballads, Myths, Fables, Mediaeval Romances, Exempla, Fabliaux, Jest-Books, and Local Legends* (6 vols.; Bloomington: Indiana University Press, 1975), 2:496–97.

> to this soul). . . . On the other hand, there are a number of body-souls. . . .[3]

According to JoAnn Scurlock, the Mesopotamian *zaqīqu/zāqīqu*-spirit was, in many respects, a dream-soul:

> This spirit was imagined as a sexless (and probably birdlike) phantom able to flit about or slip through small apertures, and as such, it became associated with dreaming, because it could safely depart the body when one was asleep. The contrast between *zāqīqu* and *eṭemmu* thus roughly corresponds to the distinction, found in the folklore of other cultures, between a "free" or "dream" soul on the one hand and a "body spirit" on the other.[4]

Tertullian, born ca. 160 C.E. to pagan parents in or around Carthage, discusses the dream-soul in his treatise on the soul (*De Anima* 44.2–3). Although he recognizes that "it is easy for the common people to consider sleep to be the withdrawal of the soul" (*facile est vulgo existimare secessionem animae esse somnum*), he denies the possibility of "souls fleeing in the absence of death" (*animae sine morte fugitivae*).[5]

The Quran (39:42), too, knows of souls that leave the body during sleep: اللهُ يَتَوَفَّى الْأَنْفُسَ حِينَ مَوْتِهَا وَالَّتِي لَمْ تَمُتْ فِي مَنَامِهَا "It is Allah that takes the souls at the time of their death, and (as for) those (souls) that have not died, (it is Allah that takes them) in their sleep."

A number of rabbinic sources take statements such as בְּיָדְךָ אַפְקִיד רוּחִי "into Your hand I deposit my רוח" (Ps 31:6) and אֲשֶׁר בְּיָדוֹ נֶפֶשׁ כָּל־חָי וְרוּחַ כָּל־בְּשַׂר־אִישׁ "in His hand is the נפש of every living being and the רוח of all human flesh" (Job 12:10) as referring to the soul of a sleeping person, which is deposited into the hand of the Lord in heaven and returned safe and sound in the morning. For example, according to one opinion in *Gen. Rab.*, הנשמה הזו ממלאה את הגוף ובשעה שאדם ישן היא עולה ושואבת לו חיים מלמעלן "this soul (of ours) fills the body, but during the time that a person sleeps it ascends

[3] Jan N. Bremmer, "The Soul in Early and Classical Greece," in *Der Begriff der Seele in der Religionswissenschaft* (ed. Johann Figl and Hans-Dieter Klein; Der Begriff der Seele 1; Würzburg: Königshausen & Neumann, 2002), 160.

[4] Scurlock, "Death," 1892. See also at chapter 1, n. 32 above.

[5] *Quinti Septimi Florentis Tertulliani De Anima* (ed. J. H. Waszink; Leiden: Brill, 2010), 61 lines 14–15, 24, with discussion on p. 474.

and draws life for it from above."[6] According to *Midrash Tanḥuma*, וכשבא לישן הוא מפקיד רוחו ביד הקב"ה, שנאמר בידך אפקיד רוחי "when he goes to sleep, he deposits his spirit into the hand of the Holy-One-Blessed-Be-He, as it says, 'into Your hand I deposit my spirit' (Ps 31:6)."[7] And according to *Deut. Rab.*, כל אומות העולם מכעיסין אותו, והם ישנים וכל הנפשות עולות אצלו, שנא' אשר בידו נפש כל חי, ובבקר הוא מחזיר לכל אחד ואחד נפשו "all (the members of) the nations of the world anger Him, and (yet when) they fall asleep, all (of their) souls ascend to Him, as it says, 'in His hand is the soul of every living person' (Job 12:10), and in the morning He restores to each and every one (of them) his soul."[8]

One rabbinic source, *Midrash Tehillim*, paints a different picture of the soul's nocturnal whereabouts: וכשאדם ישן יוצאה נשמתו ומשוטטת בעולם, והן הן החלומות שאדם רואה "and when a person sleeps, his soul goes out and wanders about in the world, and those are the dreams that a person sees."[9] According to Josephus (*J.W.* 7.8.7 §349), a similar view was held by Eleazar, the leader of the doomed defenders of Masada:

> ὕπνος δὲ τεκμήριον ὑμῖν ἔστω τῶν λόγων ἐναργέστατον, ἐν ᾧ ψυχαὶ τοῦ σώματος αὐτὰς μὴ περισπῶντος ἡδίστην μὲν ἔχουσιν ἀνάπαυσιν ἐφ' αὑτῶν γενόμεναι, θεῷ δ' ὁμιλοῦσαι κατὰ συγγένειαν πάντῃ μὲν ἐπιφοιτῶσι, πολλὰ δὲ τῶν ἐσομένων προθεσπίζουσι.
>
> Let sleep furnish you with a most convincing proof of what I say—sleep, in which the soul, undistracted by the body, while enjoying in perfect independence the most delightful repose,

---

[6] מדרש בראשית רבא (ed. J. Theodor and C. Albeck; Berlin: M. Poppeloyer, 1927), 133–34; קטעי בראשית רבה מן הגניזה (ed. Michael Sokoloff; Jerusalem: Israel Academy of Sciences and Humanities, 1982), 108 line 29. According to the two other opinions recorded there, the soul needs to remain in the body during sleep.

[7] מדרש תנחומא (ed. Salomon Buber; 6 vols.; Vilna: Rom, 1913), 5:145. (Balaq §23) lines 12–13.

[8] מדרש דברים רבה (ed. S. Lieberman; 2nd ed.; Jerusalem: Shalem, 1992), 101 bottom. Cf. the brief prayer uttered by Ashkenazic Jews upon awakening in the morning: מודה אני לפניך מלך חי וקיים שהחזרת בי נשמתי בחמלה . . . "I offer thanks before You, O living and eternal king, (You) who have compassionately put my soul back into me. . . ."

[9] מדרש תהלים המכונה שוחר טוב (ed. Salomon Buber; Vilna: n.p., 1891), 102.

> holds converse with God by right of kinship, ranges the universe and foretells many things that are to come.[10]

It seems clear that the foretelling of things to come is done through dreams. In short, both of these passages refer to the dream-soul.

The dream-soul was studied in detail by Mary H. Kingsley during her travels in West Africa:

> The dream soul. This is undoubtedly the greatest nuisance a man possesses. It seems an utter idiot, and, as soon as you go to sleep, off it ganders, playing with other souls, making dreams. While it is away you are exposed to three dangers: first, it may get caught by a witch, who sets a trap for it, usually a pot half full of some stuff attractive to the dream soul, with a knife or hook of iron concealed in it which the soul gets caught on, but I have seen soul traps made of string, &c. . . . [11]

> Witchcraft acts in two ways, namely, witching something out of a man, or witching something into him. The former method is used by both Negro and Bantu, but it is decidedly more common among the Negroes, where the witches are continually setting traps to catch the soul that wanders from the body when a man is sleeping; and when they have caught this soul, they tie it up over the canoe fire and its owner sickens as the soul shrivels.
>
> This is merely a regular line of business, and not an affair of individual hate or revenge. The witch does not care whose dream-soul gets into the trap, and will restore it on payment.[12]

In short, the wandering soul is supposed to return in the morning; if it does not, if it is lured away and trapped, the person will remain unconscious and eventually die.[13]

The relevance of Kingsley's findings for the hunting of souls in Ezekiel was recognized by Frazer, who cited part of her account in several of his publications.[14] However, such examples of soul hunting

---

[10] *Josephus in Nine Volumes* (trans. H. St. J. Thackeray et al.; LCL; London: William Heinemann, 1934–1976), vol. 3, *Jewish War,* Books 4–7, 602–3.

[11] Mary Kingsley, "Black Ghosts," *The Cornhill Magazine* n.s. 1 (July–December 1896): 83.

[12] Mary H. Kingsley, *Travels in West Africa: Congo Français, Corsico and Cameroons* (London: Macmillan, 1897), 461.

[13] Hochegger, "Die Vorstellungen von 'Seele,'" 280, 327.

[14] Frazer, "Hunting for Souls," 198; idem, *Folk-lore in the Old Testament,* 2:512.

have made little impression on students of Ezekiel, no doubt because of their geographical and chronological distance from ancient Israel. It has not been noted that the hunting of souls was well known in ancient Egypt as well. In the words of Geraldine Pinch: "Among the most terrifying demons were those who hunted the souls of the dead using throwsticks, spears, bird-traps or nets."[15] Spells for avoiding soul traps are found in the Coffin Texts and the *Book of the Dead*.[16] According to H. W. F. Saggs, there are also parallels from Mesopotamia:

> What the Babylonian witches took away from their victims in their hunting (or prowling) is specifically stated, being in the case of a man his *dūtu* or his *baštu*; or in the case of a woman her *inbu*. These terms are commonly translated by words such as "vigour" or "attractiveness," but it seems probable, on the evidence of context and synonym lists, that the Babylonians thought of these as physical entities or substances constituting part of the personality.[17]

Saggs goes on to compare the *dūtu/bāštu*[18] with the *lamassu-* and *šēdu-*spirits, spirits that were viewed by A. L. Oppenheim as "but another example of the widespread concept of multiple and external souls."[19] Similarly, Tzvi Abusch suggests that the *dūtu/bāštu* was one of "a series of divine beings who represented aspects of self or perhaps even different life- or body-souls."[20] Thus understood, the phrase *ša eṭli damqi dūssu īkim* "she took away the *dūtu* of the handsome man," used in describing the activities of a witch in

---

[15] Geraldine Pinch, *Magic in Ancient Egypt* (Austin: University of Texas Press, 1994), 154.

[16] R. O. Faulkner, *The Ancient Egyptian Coffin Texts* (3 vols.; Modern Egyptology Series; Warminster: Aris & Phillips, 1973–1978), 1:277–79 (spell 343); 2:107–27 (spells 473–81); Claude Carrier, *Le* Livre des Morts *de l'Égypte ancienne* (Moyen égyptien, le langage et la culture des hiéroglyphes—analyse et traduction 2; Paris: Cybele, 2009), 655–66 (chapters 153 A–B).

[17] Saggs, "'External Souls,'" 7.

[18] According to the reading of *CAD* (D:202, s.v. *dūtu*), the terms *dūtu* and *bāštu* interchange in *Maqlû* III 8, 11.

[19] Saggs, "'External Souls,'" 7, citing A. Leo Oppenheim, *Ancient Mesopotamia: Portrait of a Dead Civilization* (Chicago: University of Chicago Press, 1964), 199.

[20] Abusch, "Ghost," 380 with n. 38.

Maqlû III 8,[21] can perhaps be viewed as a parallel to Ezekiel's הַנְּפָשׁוֹת תְּצוֹדֵדְנָה לְעַמִּי.

At the end of the day, however, the most revealing parallels to the practices of Ezekiel's women are still those from nineteenth-century West Africa. Like Kingsley and Frazer, Ezekiel appears to be describing a trap for dream-souls—a devious trap exploiting a weakness in their navigation system. The dream-soul, in attempting to return to its sleeping owner in the dark, looks for a head in proximity to a pillow. Ezekiel's women and their apprentices, therefore, sew pillow casings (כסתות) and make cloth patches (מספחות) for use as pillow filling by cutting up clothing. It is possible that the clothing that they cut up belonged to their victims and bore their scent.[22] It has been noted that Babylonian witches, who prowled the streets with nets, "could gain power over the victims by obtaining substances or objects intimately connected with them, such as hair or pieces of old clothing."[23]

We may assume that Ezekiel's women attempted to enhance the efficacy of their pillow-traps through the use a magic spell[24]—a spell designed to draw the attention of dream-souls flying overhead, luring them down to their fate. Such a spell would be the "evil twin" of various Egyptian spells. For example, chapter 89 of the *Book of the Dead* is entitled (in some copies): "spell for letting a *ba* rejoin its corpse in the realm of the dead."[25] One version of the spell reads:

---

[21] Gerhard Meier, *Die assyrische Beschwörungssammlung Maqlû* (Archiv für Orientforschung 2; Berlin: privately published, 1937), 22.

[22] Cf. Jeffers, *Magic*, 94.

[23] Saggs, "'External Souls,'" 4-5, citing Meier, *Maqlû*, 12 (I 33). Cf. Tzvi Abusch and Daniel Schwemer, *Corpus of Mesopotamian Anti-Witchcraft Rituals* (Ancient Magic and Divination 8.1; Leiden: Brill, 2011–), 1:191 lines 2–9: "The sorceress . . . who pulled [my combed-out hair] from the garbage pit, who gathered [the dirt touched by my feet] in the street, who wiped up [my] sp[ittle] from the ground, who scratched off [(bits of) my house] from the wall, who carried off my garment from the fuller's house, [(who tore off my hem)]. . . ." There is no evidence, however, that the Babylonian witches used these objects to trap souls.

[24] Zevit, *Religions*, 562. See also chapter 2, n. 5 above.

[25] Raymond O. Faulkner, *Ancient Egyptian Book of the Dead* (New York: Barnes & Noble, 2005), 98; cf. Louis V. Žabkar, *A Study of the Ba Concept in Ancient Egyptian Texts* (SAOC 34; Chicago: University of Chicago Press, 1968), 132 n. 39.

> O bringer, O runner, . . . mayest thou grant that this Ba of mine come to me from wherever it may be. If there be any delay in bringing to me my Ba from wherever it may be, thou wilt find the Eye of Horus standing up against thee, as well as that of Osiris. O ye gods, who draw the bark of the lord of millions [= who tow the boat of the sun-god Re/Ra to the underworld each night] . . . , who bring Bas to (their) mummies, whose hands are filled with the ropes, who hold firm (your) spears, drive away the enemy, so that the bark may rejoice and the great god proceed in peace.[26]

This spell was widely known in Egypt from the New Kingdom down to the Ptolemaic period. According to Stephen Quirke:

> The importance of the composition can be seen in its independent use as a separate writing on short papyri to be worn as amulets, in this life or the next. . . . As a key composition securing *ba*-soul to body, the written content and illustration are often inscribed down the front of Late Period to Ptolemaic Period sarcophagus lids. It is also included in a Late Period manual of words to recite over amulets for protection of the body at burial. . . .[27]

The spell reflects a fear that was evidently widespread among the Egyptians: that the *ba*-soul's daily commute would be disrupted, that it would be prevented from rejoining the body. This is a fear similar to the one exploited by Ezekiel's women. The latter used magic to draw the soul *away from* the body, luring it with pillow casings and filling. The Egyptians used magic to draw the soul *towards* the body. They, too, used a concrete object as a lure or landing beacon. Some versions of chapter 89 of the *Book of the Dead* have a postscript containing instructions for use: "to be recited over a golden *ba* [= an amulet in the shape of a human-headed bird] inlaid with precious stones that has been placed on his [= the deceased's] breast."[28] Such amulets are known from Late Period

---

[26] Žabkar, *Ba Concept,* 132; cf. Carrier, *Le Livre,* 317–18.

[27] Stephen Quirke, *Going Out in Daylight – prt m hrw: The Ancient Egyptian Book of the Dead – Translation, Sources, Meanings* (London: Golden House Publications, 2013), 206.

[28] Carrier, *Le Livre,* 318; Faulkner, *Book of the Dead,* 98; Orsolya Illés, "Single Spell Book of the Dead Papyri as Amulets," in *Totenbuch-Forschungen: Gesammelte Beiträge des 2. Internationalen Totenbuch-Symposiums Bonn, 25. bis 29. September 2005* (ed. Burkhard Backes, Irmtraut Munro, and Simone Stöhr; Wiesbaden: Harrassowitz, 2006), 124.

burials.[29] They were designed to ensure that flying souls did not land in the wrong place.

Another Egyptian spell of this type is the "spell for bringing the *ba* to the body."[30] It begins: "O you who drag away *ba*s and cut off shadows, O you gods, lords of the living heads (or, heads of the living), may you bring the *ba* of Osiris-Khentamentiu to him."[31] According to Assmann, this spell appears "on anthropoid stone sarcophagi of the Late Period . . . with almost canonical regularity on the upper surface, the breast of the mummy, where the *ba* was supposed to land when it came to unite with the corpse."[32]

A faint, hellenized echo of such spells can perhaps be discerned in the doctrine of the soul that Josephus (*J.W.* 2.8.11 §154) attributes to the Essenes:

> Καὶ γὰρ ἔρρωται παρ᾽ αὐτοῖς ἥδε ἡ δόξα, φθαρτὰ μὲν εἶναι τὰ σώματα καὶ τὴν ὕλην οὐ μόνιμον αὐτῶν, τὰς δὲ ψυχὰς ἀθανάτους ἀεὶ διαμένειν, καὶ συμπλέκεσθαι μὲν ἐκ τοῦ λεπτοτάτου φοιτώσας αἰθέρος ὥσπερ εἱρκταῖς τοῖς σώμασιν ἴυγγί τινι φυσικῇ κατασπωμένας. . . .
>
> For it is a fixed belief of theirs that the body is corruptible and its constituent matter impermanent, but that the soul is immortal and imperishable; and that these souls, emanating from the finest ether, become entangled, as it were, in the prison-house of the body, to which they are dragged down by a sort of natural spell. . . .[33]

---

[29] Quirke, *Going Out*, 206.

[30] T. George Allen, "Additions to the Egyptian Book of the Dead," *JNES* 11 (1952): 177–86; Hans D. Schneider, "Bringing the *Ba* to the Body: A Glorification Spell for Padinekhtnebef," in *Hommages à Jean Leclant* (ed. Catherine Berger, Gisèle Clerc, and Nicolas Grimal; 4 vols.; Cairo: Institut français d'archéologie orientale, 1994), 4:355–62. I am indebted to Robert K. Ritner for these references and for calling this spell to my attention.

[31] Jan Assmann, *Death and Salvation in Ancient Egypt* (Ithaca, N.Y.: Cornell University Press, 2005), 88.

[32] Ibid.

[33] *Josephus in Nine Volumes*, 2:380–83, with slight changes. For the body as the prison of the soul, see also ibid., 3:602–3 (*J.W.* 7.8.7 §§344–45). Note that Josephus's own view appears to be different from that which he attributes to the Essenes. He asserts (in an admittedly polemical context) that the body is the "fond companion" of the soul, rather than its prison; see Jonathan Klawans, *Josephus and the Theologies of Ancient Judaism* (New York: Oxford University Press, 2012), 119.

Now, the idea that the soul becomes entangled (that is, trapped or imprisoned) in the body is attested already in Plato's *Phaedo* (81e). In other respects, too, "Josephus' description of the Essene view of immortality is highly colored by Greek thought."[34] It is "a kind of self-conscious translation of Essene beliefs into their Greek counterparts."[35] Nevertheless, there is a difference between Plato and Josephus's Essenes. Plato speaks of the soul being attracted to the body by a desire (ἐπιθυμία), while Josephus's Essenes speak of souls being dragged down to their place of imprisonment by a spell (ἴυγξ), albeit a natural one. Assuming that there is no Greek source for Josephus's formulation, it may well be based on an authentic Essene teaching. Perhaps the Essenes used this formulation to attract followers who believed that souls could be trapped by magical means.[36]

We now have a better understanding of the behavior condemned by Ezekiel. Cloth pillow filling was prepared, perhaps by cutting up clothing belonging to intended victims, and a spell was presumably recited over it. It was placed on the heads of tall women, where flying dream-souls could make it out from above and/or pick up its scent. The women then persuaded their gullible listeners (שֹׁמְעֵי כָזָב) that their dream-souls, lured by the pillow filling and the spell recited over it, were now trapped inside the (previously empty) pillow casings.

---

[34] Todd S. Beall, *Josephus' Description of the Essenes Illustrated by the Dead Sea Scrolls* (SNTSMS 58; Cambridge: Cambridge University Press, 1988), 105.

[35] C. D. Elledge, *Life after Death in Early Judaism: The Evidence of Josephus* (WUNT 2/208; Tübingen: Mohr Siebeck, 2006), 58. So, too, Jason von Ehrenkrook, "The Afterlife in Philo and Josephus," in *Heaven, Hell, and the Afterlife: Eternity in Judaism, Christianity, and Islam* (ed. J. Harold Ellens; 3 vols.; Psychology, Religion, and Spirituality; Santa Barbara: Praeger, 2013), 1:110.

[36] For magic in Josephus's time, see Gideon Bohak, *Ancient Jewish Magic: A History* (Cambridge: Cambridge University Press, 2008). Bohak notes (p. 85) that Josephus "repeatedly described the Essenes' interest in occult lore and divination." Indeed, immediately after presenting the views of the Essenes concerning the soul, Josephus (*J.W.* 2.8.12 §159) goes on to speak about their practice of divination: Εἰσὶν δ' ἐν αὐτοῖς οἳ καὶ τὰ μέλλοντα προγινώσκειν ὑπισχνοῦνται. . . . "There are some among them who profess to foretell the future . . . " (*Josephus in Nine Volumes*, 2:384–85). It is worth recalling that Ezekiel's מתנבאות made a similar claim.

7

From Dream-Souls to Bird-Souls

Aquila and Jerome rendered the words הַנְּפָשׁוֹת לְפֹרְחוֹת as if they meant "the flying souls" (τὰς ψυχάς τὰς πετομένας, *animas volantes*).[1] In my view, these renderings, although imprecise, reflect a tradition that contains an important kernel of truth: the verse does speak of flying souls. This rendering has been abandoned by modern translations and commentaries on Ezekiel; almost without exception, they take פֹּרְחוֹת to mean "birds" or the like.[2]

Aquila and Jerome undoubtedly understood הַנְּפָשׁוֹת לְפֹרְחוֹת as a reference to bird-souls. The concept of bird-souls is well known in the ancient Near East and elsewhere,[3] and it may be useful to review some of its manifestations.

---

[1] *Origenis Hexaplorum* (ed. Frederick Field; Oxford: Clarendon, 1875), 800 n. 49; *Biblia sacra iuxta Vulgatam versionem* (5th ed.; ed. Robert Weber and Roger Gryson; Stuttgart: Deutsche Bibelgesellschaft, 2007), 1281; Korpel, "Avian Spirits," 104. As usual, Aquila renders the preceding אֶת with σὺν.

[2] The modern interpretation goes back at least as far as Ewald, *Die Propheten*, 2:396 (*zugvögel*). In my view, the correct approach is that of van der Toorn (*From Her Cradle*, 123), who combines the two interpretations: "they are 'flying souls,' an expression based on the idea that the dead can manifest themselves in the shape of birds."

[3] See Georg Weicker, *Der Seelenvogel in der alten Litteratur und Kunst: Eine mythologisch-archaeologische Untersuchung* (Leipzig: B. G. Teubner, 1902); Gaster, *Myth*, 769; Thompson, *Motif-Index*, 2:498, 501–2; and Spronk, *Beatific Afterlife*, 100 n. 3, 167, and 255.

Pictorial evidence for this concept comes from Egypt, where a human-headed bird is part of the hieroglyph for *b3* (*ba*) "soul"[4] and where "the illustrations that first appear in the *Book of the Dead* depict the *ba* as a bird with a human head and occasionally other human attributes, symbolizing both its human nature and its mobility."[5] This evidence has been used to shed light on Ezekiel's הַנְּפָשׁוֹת לְפֹרְחוֹת by a few biblical scholars.[6] One study of Ezekiel's phrase also pointed to an Egyptian calendar (Papyrus Cairo 86637) which relates that, when Ra killed all of the gods, the latter "took on the shape of fishes, (while) their 'souls' (*ba*'s) took on the shape of birds flying up to heaven. The corpses had become fishes, and the souls, birds."[7] We may add that, in the inscriptions from Medinet Habu, Ramses III twice uses the expression "their soul (*ba*) is flown away" in describing the defeat of his enemies.[8]

There may be parallels in Mesopotamia and at Ugarit as well. According to JoAnn Scurlock, the Mesopotamian *zaqīqu* was a

---

[4] Alan H. Gardiner, *Egyptian Grammar* (3rd ed.; London: Oxford University Press, 1957), 473 sign G53.

[5] James P. Allen, "Ba," *Oxford Encyclopedia of Ancient Egypt*, 1:162. For color depictions of the *ba* in many settings, see Taylor, *Journey*, 17, 19, 25, 56, 73, 90–91, 101, 104, 114–15, 118, 131, 143, 170, 210, 228, 248. Two of these images can be seen at http://www.britishmuseum.org/research/collection_online/collection_object_details/collection_image_gallery.aspx?partid=1&assetid=685479&objectid=113333; and http://www.britishmuseum.org/research/collection_online/collection_object_details/collection_image_gallery.aspx?partid=1&assetid=819318&object id=114834. For additional depictions of the *ba* in copies of the *Book of the Dead*, see http://totenbuch.awk.nrw.de.

[6] Adolphe Lods, *La croyance à la vie future et le culte des morts dans l'antiquité israélite* (2 vols.; Paris: Fischbacher, 1906), 1:71; van der Toorn (see n. 2 above); and Korpel, "Avian Spirits," 100.

[7] Korpel, "Avian Spirits," 100, with slight changes; cf. Christian Leitz, *Tagewählerei: Das Buch* ḥ3t nḥḥ pḥ.wy ḏt *und verwandte Texte* (2 vols.; Ägyptologische Abhandlungen 55; Wiesbaden: Harrassowitz, 1994), 1:39.

[8] William F. Edgerton and John A. Wilson, *Historical Records of Ramses III: The Texts in* Medinet Habu *Volumes I and II* (SAOC 36; Chicago: University of Chicago Press, 1936), 41, 72; *ANET*, 263b; Žabkar, *Ba Concept*, 119; K. A. Kitchen, *Ramesside Inscriptions Translated & Annotated* (7 vols.; Oxford: Blackwell, 1993–2014), 5:27, 46.

dream-soul and "probably birdlike."[9] Some scholars have compared Ezekiel's phrase with a description of the dead found in "Ishtar's Descent to the Underworld" (as well as "Gilgamesh"): "They are clothed like birds, with feathers/wings."[10]

At Ugarit there may be a reference to the bird-soul in *CAT/KTU* 1.161, a text that Paolo Xella interprets as a "ritual in honor of deceased kings of Ugarit."[11] Near the end of the ritual (line 30), we find an intriguing avian reference: *tqdš/tqdm ʿṣr*.[12] The meaning of this, according to Xella, is "you will consecrate (*tqdš*) a bird";[13] according to Josef Tropper, it is "one should offer (*tqdm*) birds."[14] It has always been assumed that the bird(s) in question was/were sacrificed; Klaas Spronk and Tropper compare the Hittite practice of sacrificing birds to the spirits of the dead.[15] However, in discussing a different Ugaritic text, Spronk argues for a different connection between birds and the spirits of the dead:

---

9 Scurlock, "Death," 1892. Cf. the Mesopotamian evidence for the concept of the disembodied soul adduced by Saggs ("'External Souls'").

10 Lods, *La croyance*, 1:71; Korpel, "Avian Spirits," 99. Cf. Stephanie Dalley, "The Descent of Ishtar to the Underworld," in Hallo and Younger, eds., *The Context of Scripture*, 1:381 n. 4: "Underworld creatures are often represented with feathers in Mesopotamian iconography." Other scholars (Saggs, "'External Souls,'" 8; Korpel, "Avian Spirits," 99) have compared S. N. Kramer's translation of a line in what is now called "Dumuzi and Geštinana": "Dumuzi—his soul (ZI) left him like a hawk flying to a bird." However, more recent scholars translate that line very differently; see Jeremy Black, "The Imagery of Birds in Sumerian Poetry," in *Mesopotamian Poetic Language: Sumerian and Akkadian* (ed. Marianna E. Vogelzang and H. L. J. Vanstiphout; Cuneiform Monographs 6; Proceedings of the Groningen Group for the Study of Mesopotamian Literature 2; Groningen: Styx, 1996), 31; and "Dumuzid and Ĝeštin-ana" (t.1.4.1.1) lines 33–46 in The Electronic Text Corpus of Sumerian Literature.

11 Xella, "Death," 2062.

12 For the reading(s), see Pierre Bordreuil and Dennis Pardee, "Le rituel funéraire ougaritique RS. 34.126," *Syria* 59 (1982): 122, 128; and Lewis, *Cults*, 27–28.

13 Xella, "Death," 2062.

14 Tropper, *Nekromantie*, 146, with a note stating that ʿṣr is a collective singular.

15 Spronk, *Beatific Afterlife*, 193; Tropper, *Nekromantie*, 150.

> The common ancient Near Eastern conception of the spirits of the dead taking the physical form of birds is also attested in the literature of Ugarit. The *rpʾum* are described as fluttering (*ndd*; . . .); they are startled like birds (*ndd* D-stem . . .). Apparently they were believed to come like birds to the holy place to enter the company of the gods.[16]

Spronk's argument is based on the assumption that Ugaritic *n-d-d* has the specific meaning "flutter," alongside a more general meaning unconnected to birds, such as "go quickly." The assumption has been refuted by Marjo C. A. Korpel,[17] but even so, Spronk's idea may still have value for understanding *CAT/KTU* 1.161. In commenting on that text, Oswald Loretz mentions the widespread depiction of spirits as birds without explaining its relevance.[18] I suggest that the birds, representing the spirits of the deceased kings, may have been consecrated as guests at the sacrificial meal. In the Bible, terms for "consecrate" from the root ק-ד-ש are used of guests invited to purify themselves for sacrificial feasts (1 Sam 16:5; Zeph 1:7).

Evidence for the bird-soul concept has also been cited from ancient Israel. Theodor H. Gaster begins his discussion of "the winged soul" by quoting יְמֵי־שְׁנוֹתֵינוּ בָהֶם שִׁבְעִים שָׁנָה . . . כִּי־גָז חִישׁ וַנָּעֻפָה "the span of our life is seventy years . . . ; they pass by quickly and we fly away" (Ps 90:10).[19] Daniel Lys cites verses in which the נפש is called, or compared to, a bird, e.g., אֵיךְ תֹּאמְרוּ לְנַפְשִׁי נוּדִי הַרְכֶם צִפּוֹר "how can you say to my נפש, 'Flee to your (plur.) mountain, O bird'" (Ps 11:1); and נַפְשֵׁנוּ כְּצִפּוֹר נִמְלְטָה מִפַּח יוֹקְשִׁים הַפַּח נִשְׁבָּר וַאֲנַחְנוּ נִמְלָטְנוּ "our נפש is like a bird escaped from the fowler's trap; the trap broke, and we escaped" (Ps 124:7).[20] In such verses, we are dealing with poetic language, to be sure, but the poet's decision to use bird imagery may owe something to the bird-soul concept. In the words of Frazer, "Often the soul is conceived as a bird ready to take flight. This conception has probably left traces in most languages, and it lin-

[16] Spronk, *Beatific Afterlife*, 167.
[17] Korpel, "Avian Spirits," 101.
[18] Loretz, "Nekromantie," 300 n. 64, citing Spronk, *Beatific Afterlife*, 193.
[19] Gaster, *Myth*, 769.
[20] Lys, *Nèphèsh*, 179; cf. Saggs, "'External Souls,'" 10.

gers as a metaphor in poetry."[21] One literary critic cites these words in analyzing the bird-soul symbolism of William Butler Yeats.[22]

A compelling parallel to Ezekiel's phrase was pointed out by Adolphe Lods: "Ezekiel portrays souls as birds trapped by the prophetesses. . . . This conception must have been current in his time. They attributed to the souls of the dead the whistling and twittering sound of small birds."[23] The passage in question (Isa 8:19) reads דִּרְשׁוּ אֶל־הָאֹבוֹת וְאֶל־הַיִּדְּעֹנִים הַמְצַפְצְפִים וְהַמַּהְגִּים הֲלוֹא־עַם אֶל־אֱלֹהָיו יִדְרֹשׁ בְּעַד הַחַיִּים אֶל־הַמֵּתִים "inquire of the ghosts and familiar spirits that chirp and coo; for a people may inquire of its divine beings—(inquiring) of the dead on behalf of the living."[24] The claim that this

[21] Frazer, *Golden Bough*, 3:33–34.

[22] James L. Allen, "Yeats's Bird-soul Symbolism," *Twentieth Century Literature* 6 (1960): 117–22.

[23] Lods, *La croyance*, 71, with a reference to Isa 8:19.

[24] The translation of this verse is from NJPS with a few revisions. Instead of the rendering "divine being(s)," used by the NJPS here and in 1 Sam 28:13, it might be more accurate to render "otherworldly being(s)" or "preternatural being(s)," thereby avoiding any implication that the dead were deified and worshiped in Israel; cf. Lewis, *Cults*, 49–51, 115–16; John Day, "The Development of Belief in Life after Death in Ancient Israel," in *After the Exile: Essays in Honor of Rex Mason* (ed. John Barton and David J. Reimer; Macon, Ga.: Mercer University Press, 1996), 233; and Rainer Albertz and Rüdiger Schmitt, *Family and Household Religion in Ancient Israel and the Levant* (Winona Lake, Ind.: Eisenbrauns, 2012), 433 and 470 with n. 32. This assumes, of course, that the beings in question were spirits of the dead. For the view that they were "chthonic gods summoned to assist in the retrieval of a conjured ghost," see Brian B. Schmidt, "Memory as Immortality: Countering the Dreaded 'Death after Death' in Ancient Israelite Society," in *Judaism in Late Antiquity* (ed. Jacob Neusner; 5 vols.; Leiden: E.J. Brill, 1995–2001), 4:90; and idem, "Gods and the Dead," 161. For the view that the dead were, in fact, deified, see Elizabeth Bloch-Smith, "From Womb to Tomb: The Israelite Family in Death as in Life," in *The Family in Life and in Death: The Family in Ancient Israel; Sociological and Archaeological Perspectives* (ed. Patricia Dutcher-Walls; New York: T&T Clark International, 2009), 128–29; and Francesca Stavrakopoulou, *Land of Our Fathers: The Roles of Ancestor Veneration in Biblical Land Claims* (New York: T&T Clark, 2010), 70. For the related controversy concerning the collocation of *ilānu* "the gods" with *eṭemmū* "spirits of the dead" at Nuzi and with *mētū* "the dead" at Emar, see Akio Tsukimoto, *Untersuchungen zur Totenpflege (*kispum*) im alten Mesopotamien* (AOAT 216; Neukirchen-Vluyn:

verse (and, we may add, Isa 29:4) describes the spirits of the dead as making bird sounds was made by Spronk and Brian B. Schmidt as well,[25] but none of these scholars thought it necessary to prove that הַמְצַפְצְפִים וְהַמַּהְגִּים refer to bird sounds. The best prooftext is כְּסוּס עָגוּר כֵּן אֲצַפְצֵף אֶהְגֶּה כַּיּוֹנָה "I chirped like a swift or a swallow, I cooed like a dove" (Isa 38:14). Here, as noted already by Rashi (to Isa 8:19), we find the verbs of Isa 8:19 associated with specific birds. According to Tropper, Isa 8:19 should also be compared to the description of death in Qoh 12:4, with the phrase וְיָקוּם לְקוֹל הַצִּפּוֹר "and one rises at the sound of a bird" understood to mean that birdlike speech begins even before death.[26]

The conception of the soul as a bird is developed further in a Syriac poem by Jacob of Serug (451–521 C.E.), based on the *Acts of Thomas*, about the heavenly palace built by the apostle Thomas for the king of India. One passage relates that the tormented soul of

---

Neukirchener Verlag, 1985), 104–5, cf. 153 (Old Assyrian); Wayne T. Pitard, "Care of the Dead at Emar," in *Emar: The History, Religion, and Culture of a Syrian Town in the Late Bronze Age* (ed. Mark W. Chavalas; Bethesda, Md.: CDL, 1996), 124–28; and Schmidt, "Gods and the Dead," 141–63.

[25] Spronk, *Beatific Afterlife*, 255; and Brian B. Schmidt, *Israel's Beneficent Dead: Ancestor Cult and Necromancy in Ancient Israelite Religion and Tradition* (FAT 11; Tübingen: J. C. B. Mohr, 1994), 153. See also Torge, *Seelenglaube*, 70–71; and cf. Christopher B. Hays, *Death in the Iron Age II and in First Isaiah* (FAT 79; Tübingen: Mohr Siebeck, 2011), 271 n. 310: "One also notes that ghosts are said to 'twitter from below' in the Sumerian-Akkadian incantation series *Utukkū lemnūtu* 5:6." The Akkadian verb used there is *ṣabāru* "to twitter (said of birds)"; see M. J. Geller, *Evil Demons: Canonical* Utukkū lemnūtu *Incantations* (SAA Cuneiform Texts 5; Helsinki: Neo-Assyrian Text Corpus Project, 2007), 118, 208; and *CAD* Ṣ:2–3, s.v. *ṣabāru*. Unfortunately, the relevance of the passage is uncertain, since the subject of "twitter" seems to be "the evil Utukku demons" mentioned four lines above (Tablet 5, line 2). These demons are distinguished from ghosts in the list of evil spirits that occurs frequently in these incantations (Geller, *Evil Demons*, xiii). On the other hand, one passage (Tablet 6, lines 1–2) implies that there is no difference: "The evil Utukku demon is a ghost (*eṭimmu*) of the mountain spring, the evil Utukku demon is a ghost who constantly flits about the mountain spring" (Geller, *Evil Demons*, 127, 214).

[26] Tropper, *Nekromantie*, 290–91. Cf. the citation of the verse in *ʾAbot R. Nat.*, immediately below.

Gad, the king's brother, was sent back from heaven by the angels to rejoin his dead body:

ܗܦܟܬ ܨܦܪܐ ܢܦܫܐ ܠܩܢܐ ܕܢܦܩܬ ܡܢܗ. ܦܓܪܐ ܗܘܐ ܡܝܬܐ ܠܚܝܐ ܘܩܢܐ ܙ̈ܘܥܐ ܘܪ̈ܓܫܐ.[27]

The bird[28]—the soul—came back to the nest from which it had departed. The dead person returned to life, and he acquired movement [lit., movements] and sensation [lit., senses].

Here we see a logical development of the image. If the soul is a bird, then the body must be its nest. According to one manuscript, this development of the image is also found earlier in the story, at the point where the angels take Gad's soul to heaven:

ܚܛܦܘܗ̇ ܠܨܦܪܐ ܡܢ ܩܢܗ̇ ܒܕܡܘܬ ܢ̈ܨܐ.[29]

They snatched the bird from its nest like hawks.

Finally, we may mention Ziony Zevit's comment concerning the bird-souls in the Egyptian calendar cited above: "Such birds may be represented in a decorated Iron II tomb from Tel ʿEton."[30]

Important evidence for the meaning of פֹּרְחוֹת, hitherto ignored, comes from rabbinic literature,[31] where the verb פ-ר-ח "fly" is often

[27] Jacob of Serug, *Homilae Selectae Mar-Jacobi Sarugensis* (ed. Paul Bedjan; 5 vols.; Leipzig: Harrassowitz, 1905–1910; reprinted, Piscataway, N.J.: Gorgias Press, 2006), 3:788; cf. R. Schröter, "Gedicht des Jacob von Sarug über den Palast, den der Apostel Thomas in Indien baute," *ZDMG* 25 (1871): 344 verses 536–37.

[28] For this translation, see the vocalization in the edition by Bedjan, cited in the previous footnote; Michael Sokoloff, *A Syriac Lexicon: A Translation from the Latin, Correction, Expansion, and Update of C. Brockelmann's* Lexicon Syriacum (Winona Lake, Ind.: Eisenbrauns, 2009), 1298b, s.v. צפרא: "of small bird of the spirit"; and especially Henoch Yalon, פרקי לשון (Jerusalem: Bialik, 1971), 145–46. As noted by Yalon, Schröter takes צפרא to mean "morning," but this leaves the metaphor of the body as a nest unexplained. And Schröter himself, in addenda to his article, provides proof that צפרא does not mean "morning"; see at n. 29 below.

[29] For the last five words, see Schröter, "Gedicht," 342 verse 469. For the first two words, see the variant reading in idem, "Nachträge zu dem . . . Gedicht des Jacob von Sarug: 'über den Palast, den der Apostel Thomas in Indien baute,'" *ZDMG* 28 (1874): 604 verse 469.

[30] Zevit, *Religions*, 562; cf. 246.

[31] For the bird-soul in rabbinic literature, including many of the

predicated of the soul (נשמה/נפש) when consciousness is lost for any reason, including death and fainting:

> *Tg. Neb.* (1 Sam 25:29): And as for the soul (נפש) of your enemies—may He cause it to fly away (יְפָרְחִנַּהּ) as one makes fly (מפרחין) a stone with a sling.

> *ʾAbot R. Nat.* (First Recension, Addition 2): "And one rises at the sound of a bird" (Qoh 12:4)—This refers to the soul. Just as a bird flies (פורח) up into the air, so, too, when a person dies his soul flies (יפרח [צ״ל תפרח] נשמתו) up, as it is written, "Who knows if a man's spirit rises upward" (Qoh 3:21).[32]

> *b. Sanh.* 91a bot.: Antoninus said to Rabbi (Judah the Prince): The body and the soul (גוף ונשמה) can both exempt themselves from punishment. How so? The body can claim: It was (obviously) the soul that sinned, for from the day that it left me, I have been lying (innocently) like an inert stone in the grave. And the soul (ונשמה) can claim: It was (obviously) the body that sinned, for from the day that I left it, I have been flying (innocently) in the air like a bird (שמיום שפירשתי ממנו הריני פורחת באויר כצפור).

> *Lev. Rab.*: The mosquito flew away (פרח), and the wicked Titus's soul flew away (פרחה [צ״ל פרחת?] נשמתיה).[33]

> *Pesiq. Rab Kah.*: The Egyptians would enter and see them and their souls would fly up above them (נפשן פורחת מעליהן).[34]

> *Cant. Rab.*: When Israel heard the word אנכי (Exod 20:2) at Sinai, their souls flew away (פרחה נשמתן), . . . as it is written: "My soul went out when he spoke" (נַפְשִׁי יָצְאָה בְדַבְּרוֹ; Song 5:6).[35]

---

sources cited below, see V. Aptowitzer, "Die Seele als Vogel: Ein Beitrag zu den Anschauungen der Agada," *MGWJ* 69 (1925): 150–68.

[32] אבות דרבי נתן (ed. Salomon Schechter; Vienna: Ch. D. Lippe, 1887), 160 lines 37–38.

[33] מדרש ויקרא רבה (ed. Mordecai Margulies; New York: Jewish Theological Seminary of America, 1993), 502 line 6.

[34] פסיקתא דרב כהנא (ed. Bernard Mandelbaum; 2 vols.; New York: Jewish Theological Seminary of America, 1962), 106 lines 2–3.

[35] מדרש רבה על חמשה חומשי תורה וחמש מגילות (2 vols.; Vilna: Rom, 1884), 64 a–b.

It is worth comparing these locutions with their biblical counterparts. In *Cant. Rab.*, the rabbis themselves paraphrased נַפְשִׁי יָצְאָה with פרחה נשמתן—both in reference to fainting.[36] We may also compare פרחה (צ״ל פרחת?) נשמתיה (*Lev. Rab.*) with וַיְהִי בְּצֵאת נַפְשָׁהּ כִּי מֵתָה (Gen 35:18), both in reference to death. There is little evidence of conceptual discontinuity here; the major change is the replacement of י-צ-א with the more vivid verb פ-ר-ח.[37] The rabbinic topos appears to be a relic of an ancient popular conception. In *b. Sanh.*, י-צ-א is replaced by פ-ר-ש, while פ-ר-ח appears in the participle, describing a permanent (or, at least, prolonged) state after death. From that point of view, this פורחת is the closest parallel to the פֹּרְחוֹת of our verse.

What about the -ל in לְפֹרְחוֹת? A number of translations and commentaries translate "like (birds)"[38] or "as if they were (birds)."[39] However, the preposition -כ would be more appropriate to this interpretation (cf. צוֹד צָדוּנִי כַּצִּפּוֹר in Lam 3:52). Zevit renders with "of (birds)," adding: "The translation 'souls of birds' assumes a relative clause lacking the relative pronoun *ʾšr*, a phenomenon well attested in Hebrew poetry."[40] Finally, Carl Friedrich Keil compares וְשִׁלַּחְתִּי אֶת־הַנְּפָשׁוֹת . . . לְפֹרְחֹת with לַחָפְשִׁי יְשַׁלְּחֶנּוּ (Exod 21:26) and renders the preposition with "zu (Fliegenden)."[41] Similarly, but more clearly,

---

[36] In other cultures, too, the free soul "manifests itself during swoons"; see at chapter 6, n. 3 above. The connection is reflected in two Greek words for "swoon" derived from the Greek word for "soul": ἀψυχέω and ἀποψύχω. They are compared with נַפְשִׁי יָצְאָה in Norbert Kilwing, "נֶפֶשׁ und ΨΥΧΗ: Gemeinsames und Unterscheidendes im hebräischen und griechischen Seelenverständnis," in *Studien zu Psalmen und Propheten: Festschrift für Hubert Irsigler* (Herders Biblische Studien 64; Freiburg: Herder, 2010), 385 n. 42. I am indebted to Maurya Horgan for this reference.

[37] This replacement is virtually unknown in the less colorful language of tannaitic literature.

[38] RSV, GWT, NRSV, NJPS; Wevers, *Ezekiel*, 88; Zimmerli, *Ezekiel 1*, 298; Greenberg, *Ezekiel 1–20*, 234.

[39] Ewald, *Die Propheten*, 2:396; Smend, *Der Prophet Ezechiel*, 79; Brownlee, *Ezekiel 1–19*, 193, 194.

[40] Zevit, *Religions*, 561 n. 172. In support of this suggestion, one might compare הַנְּפָשׁוֹת לְפֹרְחוֹת with הַנְּפָשׁוֹת . . . לְעַמִּי and נְפָשׁוֹת לְכֶנָה.

[41] Carl F. Keil, *Biblischer Commentar über den Propheten Ezechiel* (Leipzig: Dörffling & Franke, 1868), 108 = *Biblical Commentary on the Prophecies of Ezekiel*, 1:174.

Korpel takes the preposition as "indicating the result or aim" (with a reference to *HALAT*, 484, s.v. לְ, meaning no. 13) and translates "turning them into (fledglings)."[42]

In my view, Keil and Korpel are right. We are dealing with what might be called the "ingressive -ל." BDB gives its meaning as "*into* (εἰς), of a transition into a new state or condition, or into a new character or office."[43] Ingressive -ל is most commonly used with verbs of being and making (e.g., ה-י-י ל- "become, turn into [intransitive]"; שׂ-י-ם ל- "cause to become, make into [lit., put]"; נ-ת-ן ל- "cause to become, make into [lit., give]"; ה-פ-ך ל- "turn into [transitive]"; ע-שׂ-י ל- "make into"; ב-נ-י ל- "build into"), but there are examples with other verbs. Thus, we find לְעֶבֶד/לַעֲבָדִים with מ-כ-ר "sell" (Deut 28:68, Ps 105:17, Esth 7:4); in English, people are sold either "into slavery" or "as slaves," but in BH they are sold (according to the literal meaning of the idiom) "into slaves." We also find לַעֲבָדִים with כ-ב-שׁ "subdue" (Jer 34:11; Neh 5:5; 2 Chr 28:10) and ל-ק-ח "take" (Gen 43:18; 2 Kgs 4:1); these phrases are particularly relevant, because of their semantic similarity to מְצֹדְדוֹת . . . לְפֹרְחוֹת. They take on additional importance because of the semantic equivalence between וַיִּכְבְּשׁוּם לַעֲבָדִים וְלִשְׁפָחוֹת (Jer 34:11) and וַתִּכְבְּשׁוּ אֹתָם לִהְיוֹת לָכֶם לַעֲבָדִים וְלִשְׁפָחוֹת (Jer 34:16). In this pair, we see that לַעֲבָדִים is equivalent to לִהְיוֹת . . . לַעֲבָדִים; no wonder, then, that virtually all medieval Jewish exegetes begin their paraphrases of לְפֹרְחוֹת with the words להיות פורחות.[44] Thus, Korpel's interpretation of the preposition of לְפֹרְחוֹת appears to be the standard interpretation of Jewish exegetes in the Middle Ages.

I conclude that the meaning of לְפֹרְחוֹת is not "like birds," "as birds," "of birds," or "into birds" but "into bird-souls," that is, "(turning them) into bird-souls." The phrase כִּסְּתוֹתֵיכֶנָה אֲשֶׁר אַתֵּנָה מְצֹדְדוֹת שָׁם אֶת־הַנְּפָשׁוֹת לְפֹרְחוֹת means: "your (empty) pillow casings in which you (pretend to) trap (dream-)souls[45] (and turn them) into bird-souls." The expression פֹּרְחוֹת in our passage should be viewed as a technical term referring to bird-souls. Since bird-souls are most commonly encountered at the time of expiration, the use of this

---

[42] Korpel, "Avian Spirits," 104 n. 23, 107.

[43] BDB, 512a, s.v. לְ, meaning no. 4.

[44] So Rashi, David Qimḥi, Eliezer of Beaugency, Isaiah of Trani, Menaḥem b. Simeon, and Joseph Ḥayyun.

[45] For this tentative rendering, see below.

term may reflect the women's claim that the owners of the trapped souls did not have long to live (v. 19). In any event, the inability of such souls to fly when they are trapped does not negate their status as bird-souls; trapped bird-souls are still bird-souls, just as trapped birds are still birds. In other words, the etymology of פֹּרְחוֹת is no more significant than the etymology of עוֹף; neither implies that the ability to fly will not be taken away. It is worth recalling that the winged Egyptian *ba* is not always portrayed in flight.

What about וְשִׁלַּחְתִּי אֶת־הַנְּפָשׁוֹת אֲשֶׁר אַתֶּם מְצֹדְדוֹת אֶת־נְפָשִׁים לְפֹרְחֹת at the end of v. 20? Two syntactic points must be made. First, the phrase לְפֹרְחֹת is often taken as modifiying וְשִׁלַּחְתִּי אֶת־הַנְּפָשׁוֹת rather than אַתֶּם מְצֹדְדוֹת אֶת־נְפָשִׁים, but this is unlikely because the earlier occurrence of לְפֹרְחֹת in the verse must modify אַתֵּנָה מְצֹדְדוֹת שָׁם אֶת־הַנְּפָשׁוֹת. Second, the clause beginning with אֲשֶׁר is universally assumed to be a relative clause, no doubt because of its similarity to אֲשֶׁר אַתֵּנָה מְצֹדְדוֹת שָׁם אֶת־הַנְּפָשׁוֹת לְפֹרְחוֹת earlier in the verse. This makes נְפָשִׁים, already *morphologically* anomalous because of its masculine plural ending, *syntactically* anomalous as well, because of its failure to be replaced by a resumptive pronoun.[46] However, אֲשֶׁר has other uses in BH, and in one of them it is semantically equivalent to יַעַן אֲשֶׁר "because." I would conjecture that נְפָשִׁים was a technical term for "dream-souls,"[47] just as פֹּרְחוֹת was a technical term for "bird-souls." If so, the meaning may be: "And I shall free (from your clutches) the souls (of those who listen to your lies), for you (are pretending to) trap dream-souls (and turn them) into bird-souls."

At this point, a brief summary of the past six chapters is in order. Ezekiel 13:17–21, I have argued, has been only partially understood until now because of the obscure technical terms that it contains. It describes the manufacture of pillows, using terms whose precise

---

[46] This is not completely unparalleled; cf. אֶת־הַשָּׂדֶה instead of אתוֹ in וַיִּקְבְּרוּ אתוֹ בִּמְעָרַת שְׂדֵה הַמַּכְפֵּלָה אֲשֶׁר קָנָה אַבְרָהָם אֶת־הַשָּׂדֶה לַאֲחֻזַּת־קֶבֶר מֵאֵת עֶפְרֹן הַחִתִּי (Gen 50:13). The use of אֶת with indefinite נְפָשִׁים is a less serious issue because it has many parallels.

[47] Was there a masculine noun נָפָשׁ* "dream-soul" (contrasting with feminine נֶפֶשׁ "soul, self, person, etc."), related to the masculine Arabic *nafas* "breath" (contrasting with feminine *nafs* "soul, self, person, etc.")? Did it derive its meaning from the verb להנפש "to rest [lit., take a breather, catch one's breath]"? In that case, it would denote the state of the soul when its owner is sufficiently at rest to be dreaming.

meaning is known from rabbinic references to pillows. The women and their apprentices sew pillow casings (כסתות), and they cut up clothing—stolen, perhaps, from their intended victims—into the cloth patches (מספחות) that served as pillow filling in ancient Israel. They use these to attract and trap heedless dream-souls (נפשים) rushing back to the pillows of their owners in the morning, after a "night on the town." Trapped inside the empty pillow casings, the dream-souls turn into bird-souls (פרחות), awaiting the imminent demise of their owners, unless the latter agree to ransom them. It should be clear that this passage, when properly understood, provides compelling evidence for a belief in disembodied souls.

Ezekiel clearly condemns the *behavior* of the women, but what about their *beliefs*? Were *any* of them acceptable? Daniel I. Block gives a nuanced answer:

> Some have interpreted these *něpāšôt* as "souls" independent of the body, analogous to Bab. *ilu, ištaru, lamassu,* and *šēdu,* spiritual "demons," whose presence determines one's identity and fate or fortune. . . . Accordingly, the aim of a witch "hunting" for souls would be to gain control over these demons, and thereby exercise power over the human person. This interpretation would not mean that Ezekiel had bought into the Babylonian notion of external, portable, souls, since such notions are quite un-Hebraic. However, his compatriots may well have. Since they had no scruples about adopting pagan religious ideas from their environment and adapting them syncretistically to their own patterns of belief and practice, they probably also adopted many non-Israelite anthropological notions. Ezekiel's adoption of this language represents a rhetorical accommodation to the prevailing notions of his addressees without assent, a pattern observed frequently in the book. Attractive as this interpretation may be, however, most continue to understand *něpāšôt* in its normal Hebraic sense, as a holistic designation for "persons."[48]

This answer suggests that Ezekiel's compatriots accepted the un-Hebraic, Babylonizing beliefs of the women—beliefs that posited the existence of external souls—while Ezekiel himself rejected them.

In my view, this is only partly true. Ezekiel did not reject the

[48] Block, *Book of Ezekiel,* vol. 1, *Chapters 1–24,* 415; so, too, Lys, *Nèphèsh,* 161-62.

beliefs of the women in toto. What he condemned as a lie was their claim of having the power to trap souls[49] and to kill them or keep them alive.[50] However, despite the modern scholarly consensus, there is no indication in the text that he rejected the women's underlying belief in the existence of disembodied נפשות. Indeed, as we shall see in the next chapter, there is no reason to assume that that belief is found only here in the Hebrew Bible.

[49] The clause הַנְּפָשׁוֹת תְּצוֹדֵדְנָה לְעַמִּי in v. 18 is an angry question: "Can you (really) trap souls belonging to my people"? The *dagesh* in הַנְּפָשׁוֹת is perfectly compatible with an interrogative *he*ʾ. The latter takes *dagesh* not infrequently when prefixed to a word whose first letter is pointed with *shewa*; see GKC 296 §100 l.

[50] Cf. v. 19: "proclaiming the death of souls that will/should not die, and the survival of souls that will/should not live—lying to my people, who listen to (your) lies."

8

Disembodied נפשות Elsewhere in the Hebrew Bible

Now that we have established that Ezek 13 speaks of disembodied נפשות, it is time to broaden our search. There is no reason to assume that belief in the disembodied נפש is reflected in only one passage in the Hebrew Bible. We need to take another look at some of the other disembodied נפשות that have been consigned to limbo for the past century—set aside as inconclusive or late.

As mentioned above, James Frazer's second major prooftext is 1 Sam 25:29: וְהָיְתָה נֶפֶשׁ אֲדֹנִי צְרוּרָה בִּצְרוֹר הַחַיִּים אֵת ה׳ אֱלֹהֶיךָ וְאֵת נֶפֶשׁ אֹיְבֶיךָ יְקַלְּעֶנָּה בְּתוֹךְ כַּף הַקָּלַע "the נפש of my lord will be bound up in the bundle of the living/life in the care of the Lord, your God; but He will sling away the נפש of your enemies (as) in the pocket of a sling." Like Ezek 13:20, it speaks of נפשות being in things other than a human body—the bundle of the living/life (צְרוֹר הַחַיִּים) in David's case, and the pocket of a sling (כַּף הַקָּלַע) in the case of his enemies. Like כסת in Ezek 13:20, the word צרור refers to a kind of bag in both BH and MH; indeed, the mishnaic tractate *Kelim* discusses the כסת and the צרור in close proximity to each other.[1] Frazer conceded that the expressions in 1 Sam 25:29 were probably figurative, but he felt that the choice of this unusual metaphor was significant nevertheless. It is true that other interpretations of the verse have been offered,[2] but Frazer's interpretation should perhaps be revisited in the light of our interpretation of כסת.

---

[1] See chapter 5, n. 9 above.

[2] See especially Otto Eissfeldt, *Der Beutel der Lebendigen: Alttestamentliche Erzählungs- und Dichtungsmotive im Lichte neuer Nuzi-Texte*

Three other prose passages seem to locate the נפש outside of the human body, even if only implicitly: בְּצֵאת נַפְשָׁהּ כִּי מֵתָה "when her נפש went out, for/when she died" (Gen 35:18), וַתָּשָׁב נֶפֶשׁ־הַיֶּלֶד עַל־קִרְבּוֹ וַיֶּחִי "the נפש of the child came back inside him [lit., to his inside] and he revived" (1 Kgs 17:22), and נַפְשִׁי יָצְאָה בְדַבְּרוֹ "my נפש went out when he spoke" (Song 5:6). From the first two we see that "the נפש departs at death and returns with life."[3] Although most scholars take נפש in these two verses as meaning "life," this interpretation is problematic. It is difficult to reconcile with the phrase עַל־קִרְבּוֹ "to his inside" (1 Kgs 17:22),[4] since life is not an entity that can be located in space. That is why we never find חיים "life" occurring in any expression similar to רוּחִי בְּקִרְבִּי "my רוח, which is inside me" (Isa 26:9); אֲשֶׁר־בּוֹ נֶפֶשׁ חַיָּה "that has a living נפש in it" (Gen 1:30); or נַפְשִׁי בִּי "my נפש is in me" (2 Sam 1:9). It is telling that, in passages where one might have expected to find אֲשֶׁר־בּוֹ חַיִּים* "that has life in it," we find instead אֲשֶׁר־בּוֹ רוּחַ חַיִּים "that has the רוח of life in it" (Gen 6:17; 7:15).

Additional evidence that נפש does not mean "life" in וַתָּשָׁב נֶפֶשׁ־הַיֶּלֶד עַל־קִרְבּוֹ (1 Kgs 17:22) comes from its poetic counterpart: שׁוּבִי נַפְשִׁי לִמְנוּחָיְכִי "Return, my נפש, to your resting places (for the Lord has been good to you)" (Ps 116:7). Here the psalmist, having been saved from death, turns to his נפש and tells it to return to its resting places, that is, its usual haunts. It is true that most translators have rendered the term מָנוֹחַ here as "rest," but there is good reason to follow *HALAT* in taking it to mean "resting-place."[5] Even those who do not accept *HALAT*'s plausible view that the noun מָנוֹחַ has the meaning "resting-place" *everywhere* in the Bible should at least concede that it has that meaning when it functions in the sentence

(Berichte über die Verhandlungen der Sächsischen Akademie der Wissen–schaften zu Leipzig, Philologisch-Historische Klasse 105.6; Berlin: Akademie-Verlag, 1960).

[3] Charles A. Briggs, "The Use of נפש in the Old Testament," *JBL* 16 (1897): 18; cf. Aubrey R. Johnson, *The Vitality of the Individual in the Thought of Ancient Israel* (Cardiff: University of Wales Press, 1964), 9.

[4] The significance of this phrase is stressed by Kilwing ("נֶפֶשׁ und ΨΥΧΗ," 386 with n. 48) as well.

[5] *HALAT,* s.v. See already Charles A. Briggs and Emilie G. Briggs, *A Critical and Exegetical Commentary on the Book of Psalms* (2 vols.; ICC; Edinburgh: T&T Clark, 1906–1907), 2:397, 399: "Return, my soul, to thy resting place."

as the goal of a verb of motion.[6] In my view, Ps 116:7 and 1 Kgs 17:22 are mutually elucidating. On the one hand, 1 Kgs 17:22 suggests that the "resting-places" of the psalmist's נפש are his innards. The plural number of מְנוּחָיְכִי matches the plural number of קְרָבַי "my innards" in בָּרְכִי נַפְשִׁי אֶת־ה׳ וְכָל־קְרָבַי אֶת־שֵׁם קָדְשׁוֹ "my soul, bless the Lord, and all my innards, (bless) His holy name" (Ps 103:1). (Note that קְרָבַי, standing in parallelism to נַפְשִׁי, must refer to the places in the body where the נפש resides.) On the other hand, Ps 116:7, where every translation available to me renders נפש with "soul," supports my claim that נפש does not mean "life" in 1 Kgs 17:22. In short, there seems to be little difference between the action requested in "Return, my נפש, to your resting places" and that depicted in "The bird—the soul [ܢܦܫܐ]—came back to the nest from which it had departed."[7] If so, Ps 116:7 and 1 Kgs 17:22 must be viewed as evidence for disembodied נפשות.

The interpretation of נפש as "life" makes even less sense in Song 5:6, since the latter refers to fainting—not death. That "my נפש went out when he spoke" refers to fainting[8] is confirmed by an Egyptian parallel, viz., the phrase *b3.ỉ sbw* "my soul departed,"[9] collocated with *ḫm.n.ỉ wỉ* "I lost consciousness,"[10] in a passage from the Egyptian story of Sinuhe:

> I found His Majesty upon the Great Throne set in a recess (paneled) with fine gold. As I was stretched out on my belly, *I lost consciousness* in his presence. This God addressed me in a friendly way, and I was like a man caught by nightfall. *My soul departed*[[11]] and my body shook. My heart was not in my body: I could not tell life from death.[12]

---

[6] Cf. מְנוּחָה in Deut 12:9 and Ps 95:11.

[7] See at chapter 7, nn. 27–28 above.

[8] See chapter 7, n. 36 above, and the text preceding it.

[9] Literally, "my soul went"; see Adolf Erman and Hermann Grapow, *Wörterbuch der aegyptischen Sprache* (7 vols.; Leipzig: J. C. Hinrichs, 1926–1963), 3:429, s.v. *sbj* "gehen."

[10] So rendered by Robert K. Ritner in the translation immediately below. Literally, "I did not know myself"; see Erman and Grapow, *Wörterbuch*, 3:278, s.v. *ḫmj*, *ḫm* "nicht kennen."

[11] So John A. Wilson, "The Story of Sinuhe," in *ANET*, 21 line 255; and Žabkar, *Study of the Ba Concept*, 118.

[12] William Kelley Simpson, Robert K. Ritner, and Vincent A. Tobin,

Now, the fact that X י-צ-א נפש has a different *referent* in Song 5:6 than it does in Gen 35:18 does not imply that it has a different *meaning*.[13] It makes more sense to assume that X י-צ-א נפש has a single meaning with different applications: *temporary* departure of the נפש in Song 5:6 vs. *permanent* departure of the נפש in Gen 35:18. That assumption is more economical, and it fits perfectly with the finding of the Scandinavian anthropologists, cited above, that the free soul "only manifests itself during swoons, dreams or at death."[14] However, it would be difficult to maintain such an assumption if נפש meant "life" in the expression X י-צ-א נפש.

There is another hint that נפש does not mean "life" in this expression. If it did, we would have expected to find X יצאו חיי* "the life of X went out" in the Bible alongside X יצאה נפש. Such a phrase is nowhere to be found, presumably because motion can be attributed only to an entity that can be located in space. We would also have expected to find X כלתה נפש with the same meaning as X כלו חיי and Akk. *iqtû napšat X*,[15] viz., "the life of X ended." We do not find this either. Instead, we find X כלתה נפש with the meaning "X longed for." These differences suggest that נפש and חיים are not synonyms, at least in expressions referring to the termination of life.

The phrase צֵאת נַפְשָׁהּ in Gen 35:18 has both prebiblical and postbiblical parallels. In the Ugaritic account of the murder of Aqhat, we find the expression *yṣat/tṣi . . . npšh* (*CAT/KTU* 1.18 IV), and it is worth noting that the Ugaritic dictionaries seem completely at ease with the meaning "soul" for *npš*.[16] They render *tṣi km rḥ npšh*

Literature of Ancient Egypt: An Anthology of Stories, Instructions, Stelae, Autobiographies, and Poetry (3rd ed.; New Haven: Yale University Press, 2003), 64 with one change. The italics are mine. Cf. Stephen Quirke, *Egyptian Literature 1800 BC: Questions and Readings* (Egyptology 2; London: Golden House, 2004), 67–68.

[13] The distinction between *reference* and *sense/meaning* has been commonplace since the publication of Gottlob Frege's paper "Über Sinn und Bedeutung" (*Zeitschrift für Philosophie und philosophische Kritik* n.F. 100 [1892]: 25–50).

[14] See at chapter 6, n. 3 above.

[15] For this expression, see *CAD* N:298–99, s.v. *napištu*, and Q:178, s.v. *qatû*.

[16] Joseph Aisleitner, *Wörterbuch der ugaritischen Sprache* (Berichte über die Verhandlungen der Sächsischen Akademie der Wissenschaften zu Leipzig, Philologisch-Historische Klasse 106.3; Berlin: Akademie-Verlag,

as "may his soul go out like a breath"[17] and *yṣat km rḥ npš[h]* as "es entwich seine Seele wie ein Wind"[18] quite unselfconsciously. The Mishnah uses expressions such as עם יציאת נפש "at the moment of expiration [lit., soul departure]" (*Šabb.* 23:5), עד שתצא נפשו "until he expires" (*Yebam.* 16:3, *Ohol.* 1:6), and כדי שתצא נפשם "long enough for them to expire" (*Yebam.* 16:4) in legal contexts.[19] Thus, the form of the expression remained virtually unchanged for well over a millennium, and there is no compelling reason to assume that its meaning changed. Note also that the Galilean Aramaic counterpart of X יצאה נפש is X נשמת (צ״ל פרחת?) פרחה "X's soul flew away," and that it, too, is used of both death and fainting.[20] As noted above, this more vivid verb is used of disembodied souls already by Ezekiel.

Perhaps we should also take a second look at the expressions וְאַתָּה צֹדֶה אֶת־נַפְשִׁי לְקַחְתָּהּ "but you are lying in wait for my נפש to take it" (1 Sam 24:11 [12]) and וַיְבַקְשׁוּ אֶת־נַפְשִׁי לְקַחְתָּהּ "they have sought my נפש to take it" (1 Kgs 19:10, 14), together with the many other examples of נפש as the object of ל-ק-ח "take" and/or ב-ק-ש (*piʿel*) "seek."[21] Even if these expressions are metaphorical, the metaphors may well have a nonfigurative origin—one that assumes the existence of a free, separable soul.

In these expressions, נפש is customarily interpreted as a synonym of חיים "life,"[22] but if that interpretation is correct, why do we never find examples of חיים itself as the object of ל-ק-ח or ב-ק-ש?[23] Could it be that the referent of חיים, unlike the referent

1963), 211–12, s.v.; Gregorio del Olmo Lete and Joaquín Sanmartín, *A Dictionary of the Ugaritic Language in the Alphabetic Tradition* (Handbook of Oriental Studies 67; Leiden: Brill, 2003), 637, s.v.

[17] Olmo Lete and Sanmartín, *Dictionary*, 637, line 13 and 985, lines 26–27.

[18] Aisleitner, *Wörterbuch*, 134, lines 8–9. In *HALAT* (673a meaning no. 7), by contrast, the corresponding biblical phrase is treated under the meaning "life."

[19] In one place (*Šeqal.* 6:2), the Mishnah describes the departure of the soul using נשמה instead of נפש, but that description is in a *narrative* context rather than a *legal* one.

[20] See at chapter 7, nn. 31–37 above.

[21] Also as the object of ר-ד-ף "pursue" in Ps 7:6 and 143:3.

[22] See, for example, Hans Walter Wolff, *Anthropology of the Old Testament* (Philadelphia: Fortress, 1974), 19–20.

[23] In one verse, we may well find חיים as the object of ת-פ-ש. According

of נפש, is too abstract to be sought or taken in BH?[24] In answering these questions, we should not be misled by the fact that the taking of a נפש results in loss of life, or by the fact that in English we *do* speak of taking a person's life. Nor should we be misled by the fact that the distinction between נפש and חיים is blurred in biblical poetry, where the two nouns occur in parallelism, e.g., אַל־תֶּאֱסֹף עִם־חַטָּאִים נַפְשִׁי וְעִם־אַנְשֵׁי דָמִים חַיָּי "do not bring my נפש in (to be) with sinners, and with murderers, my חיים" (Ps 26:9); כִּי־שָׂבְעָה בְרָעוֹת נַפְשִׁי וְחַיַּי לִשְׁאוֹל הִגִּיעוּ "for my נפש has become sated with misfortune, and my חיים has reached Sheol" (Ps 88:4); etc. What such examples show is not that נפש can be used with the meaning "life" but that חיים can be used as a poetic epithet for the soul—especially (with the exception of Jonah 2:7) when it corresponds (as a "B-word") to נפש in a parallel colon. This use of חיים is related in some way to the use of חיה "living (creature)" as a term for soul, as can be seen by comparing יִרַדֹּף אוֹיֵב נַפְשִׁי וְיַשֵּׂג וְיִרְמֹס לָאָרֶץ חַיָּי "let the enemy pursue my נפש and overtake it; let him trample my חיים to the ground" (Ps 7:6) with כִּי רָדַף אוֹיֵב נַפְשִׁי דִּכָּא לָאָרֶץ חַיָּתִי "for the enemy pursued my נפש; he crushed my חיה to the ground" (Ps 143:3). The poetic use of חיים may also be compared to the poetic use of כבוד in בְּסֹדָם אַל־תָּבֹא נַפְשִׁי בִּקְהָלָם אַל־תֵּחַד כְּבֹדִי "may my נפש not come into their council; may my כבוד not be joined to their company" (Gen 49:6). Indeed, in one tricolon, we find all three nouns corresponding to each other: יִרַדֹּף אוֹיֵב נַפְשִׁי וְיַשֵּׂג וְיִרְמֹס לָאָרֶץ חַיָּי וּכְבוֹדִי לֶעָפָר יַשְׁכֵּן "let the enemy pursue my נפש and overtake it; let him trample my חיים to the ground; and

---

to R. Saadia Gaon, אִם־לְשָׁלוֹם יָצָאוּ תִּפְשׂוּם חַיִּים וְאִם לְמִלְחָמָה יָצָאוּ חַיִּים תִּפְשׂוּם (1 Kgs 20:18) means something like, "If they come in peace, take them alive; if in war, take life from them"; see Richard C. Steiner, *A Biblical Translation in the Making: The Evolution and Impact of Saadia Gaon's* Tafsīr (Cambridge, Mass.: Harvard University Center for Jewish Studies, 2010), 130, and the literature cited in n. 9 there. It should be obvious, however, that חַיִּים תִּפְשׂוּם—instead of, say, הכום נפש—is used by literary license to create the play on תִּפְשׂוּם חַיִּים.

[24] Cf. Abraham Ibn Ezra's assertion, in his commentary to Qoh 12:7, that that verse (especially the clause וְהָרוּחַ תָּשׁוּב אֶל־הָאֱלֹהִים "and the רוח returns to God") "refutes those who claim that רוח is an accident (מקרה)"—an abstract attribute that has no existence without some underlying substance—"because an accident cannot (be said to) return." This last assertion is not true of a modern language like English, but it may well be true of Biblical Hebrew.

let him make my כבוד dwell in the dust" (Ps 7:6). These poetic uses of חיים and כבוד may well derive from the fact that without the נפש a person has neither life nor honor.

It should be obvious that the correspondence of נפש and חיים in parallel cola is less revealing than the co-occurrence of the two terms in a single clause. We should therefore ponder the significance of נָקְטָה נַפְשִׁי בְּחַיָּי "my נפש is disgusted with my חיים" (Job 10:1). In this example, at least, the two terms are clearly not interchangeable. We should also contemplate the meaning of בָּרְכִי נַפְשִׁי אֶת־ה׳ . . . הַסֹּלֵחַ לְכָל־עֲוֺנֵכִי הָרֹפֵא לְכָל־תַּחֲלֻאָיְכִי: הַגּוֹאֵל מִשַּׁחַת חַיָּיְכִי "my נפש, bless the Lord . . . who forgives all your sins, heals all your diseases, redeems your חיים from the pit . . ." (Ps 103:2–4). Here again we see that the terms נפש and חיים are quite distinct. The clear implication of this passage is that the נפש has חיים (cf. וחיתה/תחי נפש- in Gen 12:13, 19:20, 1 Kgs 20:32, Isa 55:3, Jer 38:17, 20, Ps 119:175) or *a* חיים, just as it has sins and diseases. Indeed, comparison of Ps 103:4 with Job 10:1 makes one wonder if a person's נפש (or, at least, one part of it) was thought to have a חיים of its own, distinct from the חיים of the person and surviving for a certain amount of time in the grave.[25]

As we have already noted,[26] the belief that the soul can exist outside of the body is not identical to the belief that it is separate and distinct from the body, but the latter belief is probably a necessary condition for the former. Thus, we might also want to look again at passages that used to be viewed as evidence for soul-body dualism—passages in which the term נפש is contrasted with an expression referring to the body. In Job 2:5–6, the expression for "body" that stands in opposition to נפש is עצם ובשר "flesh and bone [lit., bone and flesh]" (cf. Gen 2:23). In v. 5, the Adversary says to the Lord: אוּלָם שְׁלַח־נָא יָדְךָ וְגַע אֶל־עַצְמוֹ וְאֶל־בְּשָׂרוֹ אִם־לֹא אֶל־פָּנֶיךָ יְבָרְכֶךָּ "But lay a hand on his flesh and bone, and he will surely curse You to Your face." The Lord accepts the implied proposal, with one caveat: הִנּוֹ בְיָדֶךָ אַךְ אֶת־נַפְשׁוֹ שְׁמֹר "He is hereby in your power; only his נפש you must safeguard."[27] In this example, it is certainly possible to render נפש as "life" instead of "soul"; that is not the case, however, in at

[25] See chapter 10, n. 22 below, and at chapter 11, nn. 19–21 below.

[26] See chapter 1, n. 4 above.

[27] In other words, when you lay a hand on his בשר, be careful not to harm the נפש הבשר that resides in it. For the נפש הבשר, see at n. 40 below and in chapter 9, *passim*.

least some of the examples below. Another passage that appears to belong here is יִכֶל בְּשָׂרוֹ מֵרֹאִי וְשֻׁפּוּ עַצְמוֹתָיו לֹא רֻאּוּ וַתִּקְרַב לַשַּׁחַת נַפְשׁוֹ וְחַיָּתוֹ לַמְמִתִים "his flesh is too wasted to be visible; his bones too rubbed away to be seen; his נפש comes close to the Pit; his חיה, to the executioners" (Job 33:21–22). Here again we have a passage that speaks of a person as having a body (בשר and עצמות) and a נפש // חיה.

The expression employed in Job 2:5 is sometimes abbreviated, with either בשר "flesh" or עצם "bone" used to refer to the body by means of synecdoche (*pars pro toto*). In Proverbs, we find these two synecdochic terms for the body interchanging, with וּלְכָל־בְּשָׂרוֹ מַרְפֵּא "and a cure for his whole בשר [= body]" (4:22) occurring alongside וּמַרְפֵּא לָעָצֶם "and a cure for the עצם [= body]" (16:24).

These abbreviated expressions for "body" can, like the full expression, stand in opposition to נפש. For our purposes, the most important example of this is מִנֶּפֶשׁ וְעַד־בָּשָׂר יְכַלֶּה "from (its) נפש to (its) בשר shall He destroy (it)" (Isa 10:18). Most of the major English versions take מִנֶּפֶשׁ וְעַד־בָּשָׂר to be a merism[28] denoting an entire person,[29] similar to English *body and soul*. If so, the clause refers to

[28] So, too, Jože Krašovec, *Der Merismus in Biblisch-Hebräischen und Nordwestsemitischen* (BibOr 33; Rome: Biblical Institute Press, 1977), 109 no. 112a; Claus Westermann, "נֶפֶשׁ *nepeš* soul," *TLOT* 2:752 meaning 3; and Joseph Blenkinsopp, *Isaiah 1–39: A New Translation with Introduction and Commentary* (AB 19; New York: Doubleday, 2000), 255. Blenkinsopp's translation cleverly adjusts the merism to its context: "The best of his woodlands and orchards (כְּבוֹד יַעְרוֹ וְכַרְמִלּוֹ) will be destroyed root and branch." The seemingly incongruous use of מִנֶּפֶשׁ וְעַד־בָּשָׂר in this context may reflect the semantic bleaching that affects commonly used idioms; cf. the incongruity of בְּעֵינֵי in הִבְאַשְׁתֶּם אֶת־רֵיחֵנוּ בְּעֵינֵי פַרְעֹה (Exod 5:21), rendered "ye have made our odour to stink in the eyes of Pharaoh" in the Darby Bible. Alternatively, it may indicate that כְּבוֹד יַעְרוֹ וְכַרְמִלּוֹ is a metaphor for the Assyrian nobility. In that case, this would be an example of the mixing of vehicle and tenor in prophetic metaphors—a phenomenon that is far from rare.

[29] The other biblical merism for a person, -מִכַּף רֶגֶל- וְעַד קָדְקֹד "from the soul of your/his foot to the crown of your/his head (Deut 28:35, 2 Sam 14:25, Job 2:7; cf. Isa 1:6), covers only the body. There is another difference between these two merisms. In Isa 10:18, the two co-meronyms are complementary, that is, they designate two parts that, by themselves, make up the whole. In Deut 28:35, etc., they designate only the extremities, the two parts located at opposite ends of the whole. These two types are

total extermination, and we should consider the possibility that וְלֹא־תֹאכַל הַנֶּפֶשׁ עִם־הַבָּשָׂר "and you must not consume the נפש with the בשר" (Deut 12:23) belongs here as well.[30] Otto Sander has correctly pointed to מִנֶּפֶשׁ וְעַד־בָּשָׂר as "a small troublemaker" for the generally accepted view of the biblical נפש, and (seemingly unaware of the examples of נפש // בשר cited below) he proposes to solve the problem by taking the phrase to mean "from the gullet to the genitals."[31] Others suggest that "the two words . . . are basically synon. and both denote the vital force that seeks external manifestation."[32] There is no philological basis for either of these ad hoc solutions; they are motivated, rather, by the belief that "this kind of dualism . . . is never found in the OT and would deny the very foundations of OT anthropology."[33] In my view, this type of argument is unacceptable. Philological analysis of a text should have primacy; it should precede anthropological analysis, not follow it.

In poetry, merisms are very often broken up, with the component nouns used as parallel word-pairs.[34] Thus, the merism *heaven and earth* appears in הַאֲזִינוּ הַשָּׁמַיִם וַאֲדַבֵּרָה וְתִשְׁמַע הָאָרֶץ אִמְרֵי־פִי (Deut 32:1). The merism *body and soul* receives the same treatment. In צָמְאָה לְךָ נַפְשִׁי כָּמַהּ לְךָ בְשָׂרִי (Ps 63:2), the noun בשר, serving as an abbreviated expression for "body," is parallel to נפש. The NJPS, which normally avoids any hint of soul-body dualism, renders this as "my soul thirsts for you, my body yearns for you." We find virtually the same rendering in the tenth century, in Saadia Gaon's Arabic translation: וקד עטשת לך נפסי וכמד לך בדני "my soul has thirsted for you,

---

not always distinguished in Hebrew; see A. M. Honeyman, "*Merismus* in Biblical Hebrew," *JBL* 71 (1952): 11-18. In English, by contrast, it is easy to see that *from head to toe* differs from *body and soul*.

[30] Cf. לֹא־תִקַּח הָאֵם עַל־הַבָּנִים "you shall not take the mother together with her young" (Deut 22:6) as interpreted by Jeffrey H. Tigay (*Deuteronomy* דברים: *The Traditional Hebrew Text with the New JPS Translation* [JPS Torah Commentary; Philadelphia: Jewish Publication Society, 1996], 126): "The same phrase, which also appears in descriptions of warfare [Gen 32:11; Hos 10:14], was evidently a common expression denoting total, cruel extermination."

[31] Otto Sander, "Leib-Seele-Dualismus im Alten Testament?" *ZAW* 77 (1965): 329–32.

[32] Jacob et al., "ψυχή κτλ," 623 n. 69.

[33] Ibid., 623.

[34] Krašovec, *Der Merismus*.

and my body has been heartsick for you."[35] Two additional examples of נפש//בשר are found in Job: אֶשָּׂא בְשָׂרִי בְשִׁנָּי וְנַפְשִׁי אָשִׂים בְּכַפִּי "I will take my בשר in my teeth; I will place my נפש in my hand" (13:14); and אַךְ־בְּשָׂרוֹ עָלָיו יִכְאָב וְנַפְשׁוֹ עָלָיו תֶּאֱבָל "rather it is for *himself* that his בשר feels pain; and for *himself* that his נפש feels grief" (14:22). According to E. Dhorme, both examples exhibit "parallelism between בָּשָׂר and נֶפֶשׁ . . . , as between the body and soul."[36] In any event, the meaning "life" is not possible for נפש in Job 14:22, and that fact must be considered in interpreting Job 2:6.

An example of עצם serving as an abbreviated expression for "body" and contrasting with נפש is, according to most of the major English versions, צוּף־דְּבַשׁ אִמְרֵי־נֹעַם מָתוֹק לַנֶּפֶשׁ וּמַרְפֵּא לָעָצֶם (Prov 16:24). The rendering of the NRSV is typical: "Pleasant words are like a honeycomb, sweetness to the soul and health to the body." Here again Saadia Gaon has a very similar rendering: חלו ללנפס ושפאא ללג׳סם "sweet to the soul and a cure for the body."[37] And here again, the meaning "life" is not possible for נפש. Another example that may belong here—even though it has עצם in the plural and נפש in a new verse—is כִּי נִבְהֲלוּ עֲצָמָי: וְנַפְשִׁי נִבְהֲלָה מְאֹד "(heal me, Lord) for my עצמים are agitated; and my נפש is very agitated" (Ps 6:3–4).

We should also reconsider the meaning of נפש in expressions such as לֹא נַכֶּנּוּ נָפֶשׁ "we won't slay him [lit., smite him (on the) נפש]" (Gen 37:21); וְהִכָּהוּ נָפֶשׁ "and he (shall) slay him [lit., smite him (on the) נפש]" (Deut 19:6, 11); and לְהַכֹּתְךָ נָפֶשׁ "to slay you [lit., smite you (on the) נפש]" (Jer 40:14, 15). The word נפש in this expression is frequently taken to mean "life,"[38] but here again we never find a variant of the expression with חיים instead of נפש. Nor can נפש mean "person" in this expression. We are dealing with a special use of the archaic accusative of limitation found with verbs of smiting in

35 תהלים עם תרגום ופירוש הגאון רבינו סעדיה בן יוסף פיומי (ed. Yosef Qafiḥ; New York: American Academy for Jewish Research, 1966), 154, lines 15–16.

36 E. Dhorme, *A Commentary on the Book of Job* (trans. Harold Knight; Nashville: Thomas Nelson, 1984), 187. For the context of the second example (Job 14:22), see at chapter 11, nn. 42, 46–47.

37 משלי עם תרגום ופירוש הגאון רבנו סעדיה בן יוסף בן יוסף פיומי (ed. Yosef Qafiḥ; Jerusalem: Vaʿad le-Hotsaʾat Sifre Rasag, 1976), 122 line 1.

38 See, for example, Josef Scharbert, *Fleish, Geist und Seele im Pentateuch: Ein Beitrag zur Anthropologie der Pentateuchquellen* (Stuttgarter Bibelstudien 19; Stuttgart: Katholisches Bibelwerk, 1967), 64.

poetry and elevated prose, as in הוּא יְשׁוּפְךָ רֹאשׁ וְאַתָּה תְּשׁוּפֶנּוּ עָקֵב "he shall strike you (on the) head and you shall strike him (on the) heel" (Gen 3:15); מְחַץ מָתְנַיִם קָמָיו "smite his foes (on the) loins" (Deut 33:11);[39] יִרְעוּךְ קָדְקֹד "they will smash you (on the) crown" (Jer 2:16); and הִכִּיתָ אֶת־כָּל־אֹיְבַי לֶחִי "you have struck all of my enemies (on the) cheek" (Ps 3:8). In all of these, the accusative of limitation is used to specify the *part* of a person that is harmed by the smiting. For example, the underlying semantic structure of הִכִּיתָ אֶת־כָּל־אֹיְבַי לֶחִי is probably very similar to that of וַיַּכֶּה אֶת־מִיכָיְהוּ עַל־הַלֶּחִי "and he struck Micaiah on the cheek" (1 Kgs 22:24), and that of בַּשֵּׁבֶט יַכּוּ עַל־הַלְּחִי אֵת שֹׁפֵט יִשְׂרָאֵל "they strike the ruler of Israel on the cheek with a staff" (Mic 4:14). Thus, when we find the word נפש in this construction, it is natural to conclude that it, too, refers to a *part* of the person that exists in space—not a life (which, as noted above, is not an entity that exists in space) but the נפש הבשר that resides in the blood (Lev 17:11; cf. Deut 27:25?)[40] when its owner is conscious. This finding complements what we saw above. Although the נפש is *not* a part of the *body*, it *is* a part of the *person*.

Perhaps we should also reexamine Zedekiah's oath to Jeremiah: חַי־ה׳ אֲשֶׁר עָשָׂה־לָנוּ אֶת־הַנֶּפֶשׁ הַזֹּאת אִם־אֲמִיתֶךָ וְאִם־אֶתֶּנְךָ בְּיַד הָאֲנָשִׁים הָאֵלֶּה אֲשֶׁר מְבַקְשִׁים אֶת־נַפְשֶׁךָ "as the Lord—who has made this נפש for us—lives, I will not put you to death or deliver you into the hands of those men who seek your נפש" (Jer 38:16). Here we find an opposition between ה׳ אֲשֶׁר עָשָׂה־לָנוּ אֶת־הַנֶּפֶשׁ הַזֹּאת and הָאֲנָשִׁים הָאֵלֶּה אֲשֶׁר מְבַקְשִׁים אֶת־נַפְשֶׁךָ. Modern scholars have struggled with the former expression,[41] largely because they have insisted on interpreting it using the meaning "life" for נפש. That meaning is clearly

---

[39] The word order of מְחַץ מָתְנַיִם קָמָיו has deceived many, leading them to believe that מתנים is in the construct state. Thus, the Samaritans emended it to מתני, while some modern scholars argued that it exhibited enclitic *mem*; see William L. Moran, "The Hebrew Language in Its Northwest Semitic Background," in *The Bible and the Ancient Near East: Essays in Honor of William Foxwell Albright* (ed. G. Ernest Wright; Garden City, N.Y.: Doubleday, 1961), 68. In fact, we find virtually the same word order in בַּשֵּׁבֶט יַכּוּ עַל־הַלְּחִי אֵת שֹׁפֵט יִשְׂרָאֵל "they strike the ruler of Israel on the cheek with a staff" (Mic 4:14). There, too, the adverbial specifying the smitten body part precedes the direct object.

[40] See in chapter 9, *passim*, and compare לֹא נַכֶּנּוּ נָפֶשׁ (Gen 37:21) with אַל־תִּשְׁפְּכוּ־דָם (v. 22).

[41] See, for example, the discussion of William McKane in *A Critical*

too abstract for the context, since, once again, lives are not entities that exist in space; it makes little sense to speak of them as being made (עָשָׂה־לָנוּ אֶת־הַנֶּפֶשׁ)[42] or pointed at (הַנֶּפֶשׁ הַזֹּאת). Souls, on the other hand, were viewed in antiquity as manikins capable of being depicted by artists.[43]

And if "life" is too abstract a meaning for נפש in חַי־ה׳ אֲשֶׁר עָשָׂה־לָנוּ אֶת־הַנֶּפֶשׁ הַזֹּאת, what about נפש in הֵן כָּל־הַנְּפָשׁוֹת לִי הֵנָּה "all נפשות belong to Me" (Ezek 18:4) and in אֲשֶׁר בְּיָדוֹ נֶפֶשׁ כָּל־חָי וְרוּחַ כָּל־בְּשַׂר־אִישׁ "in His hand is the נפש of every living being and the רוח of all human flesh" (Job 12:10)? If the נפשות *made* by God are souls, it seems natural to assume that the נפשות *owned* by God and the נפשות *held* by God in his hand are also souls.

Last but not least, it might be beneficial to ponder the significance of passages in which a poet turns to his נפש and addresses it directly, with נפשי "my נפש" in the vocative. The Hebrew Bible contains at least a dozen such passages: Jer 4:19; Ps 42:1, 6; 43:5; 62:6; 103:1, 2, 22; 104:1, 35; 116:7; and 146:1. One of them has already been discussed: שׁוּבִי נַפְשִׁי לִמְנוּחָיְכִי כִּי־ה׳ גָּמַל עָלָיְכִי (Ps 116:7). The psalmist usually puts an imperative before the vocative, exhorting his נפש to bless the Lord or the like, but sometimes he asks it a rhetorical question, e.g., מַה־תִּשְׁתּוֹחֲחִי נַפְשִׁי וּמַה־תֶּהֱמִי עָלָי "Why are you downcast, my נפש; why do you murmur against me?" (42:12). The longest exhortation stretches over five verses (103:1–5). It must be stressed that there are no instances in Psalms of לבי "my heart," פי "my mouth," לשוני "my tongue," שפתי "my lips"—or חיי "my life," for that matter—in the vocative.[44] Thus, it would not be correct to view the vocative use of נפשי as a mere poetic conceit, as in "be still,

---

and Exegetical Commentary on Jeremiah (2 vols.; ICC; Edinburgh: T&T Clark, 1996), 2:956–57.

[42] The phrase חַיִּים וָחֶסֶד עָשִׂיתָ עִמָּדִי (Job 10:12) is too obscure to be considered counterevidence.

[43] See at chapter 13, nn. 9–14 below.

[44] Outside of Psalms, we find אֲנִי טֶרֶם אֲכַלֶּה לְדַבֵּר אֶל־לִבִּי (Gen 24:45), whose literal meaning, "I had not yet finished speaking to my heart," makes it appear as if the servant was addressing his heart. However, virtually all of the major English translations render "*in* my heart," and with good reason. The previous verse makes it clear that the servant's (silent) utterance was a prayer addressed not to himself or to his heart but to God. Moreover, aside from our verse and two others (Gen 8:21 and 1 Sam 27:1), the adverbial used to signal internal speech is בלבו "*in* his

my beating heart." It would be more accurate to compare בָּרְכִי נַפְשִׁי אֶת־ה' "my נפש, bless the Lord" (103:1, 2, 22; 104:1, 35) with בָּרְכוּ עַמִּים אֱלֹהֵינוּ "(O) peoples, bless our God" (66:8). Can this be considered evidence that the psalmist perceives a difference between himself (as the speaker) and his נפש (as the addressee)? In answering that question, we might take our cue from James P. Allen who writes that "the Middle Kingdom literary text known as the *Dialogue of a Man with his Ba* . . . reflects the view of the *ba* as a separate mode of existence—in this case, an alter ego with whom its owner could hold a dialogue."[45] In a classic article, Jan Assmann makes this Egyptian text even more relevant to our question by characterizing it, in an allusion to William Butler Yeats, as "a dialogue between self and soul."[46]

---

heart" rather than אל לבו. It is possible, therefore, that אל is used here with the meaning -ב; cf. BDB, 40b meaning no. 8.

[45] James P. Allen, "Ba," 161. Cf. Joan Padgham, *A New Interpretation of the Cone on the Head in New Kingdom Egyptian Tomb Scenes* (BAR International Series 2431; Oxford: Archaeopress, 2012), 42.

[46] Jan Assmann, "A Dialogue between Self and Soul: Papyrus Berlin 3024," in *Self, Soul and Body in Religious Experience* (ed. A. I. Baumgarten, J. Assmann, G. G. Stroumsa; SHR 78; Leiden: Brill, 1998), 384.

9

The רוח

The primary focus of this monograph is the term נפש. However, some of the most important biblical evidence for disembodied souls does not use that term. Instead, it uses the term רוח or (as we shall see in chapter 10) no term at all.

The precise semantic relationship between the terms נפש and רוח is not easy to determine. The two terms are similar enough in meaning to be used in poetic parallelism, e.g., נַפְשִׁי אִוִּיתִיךָ בַּלַּיְלָה אַף־רוּחִי בְקִרְבִּי אֲשַׁחֲרֶךָּ "my נפש yearns [lit., my נפש I yearn] for You at night, my רוח, which is inside me, seeks [lit., my רוח . . . I seek] You at dawn" (Isa 26:9); אֲדַבְּרָה בְּצַר רוּחִי אָשִׂיחָה בְּמַר נַפְשִׁי "I shall speak in the anguish of my רוח, I shall complain in the bitterness of my נפש" (Job 7:11); and אֲשֶׁר בְּיָדוֹ נֶפֶשׁ כָּל־חָי וְרוּחַ כָּל־בְּשַׂר־אִישׁ "in His hand is the נפש of every living being and the רוח of all human flesh" (Job 12:10).

The semantic similarity between נפש and רוח can also be seen in their apparent interchangeability in certain expressions. For example, in references to revival, it is sometimes the רוח that returns: וַתָּשָׁב רוּחוֹ וַיֶּחִי "(he drank,) and his רוח came back, and he revived" (Judg 15:19); וַתָּשָׁב רוּחוֹ אֵלָיו "(he ate,) and his רוח came back to him" (1 Sam 30:12). And sometimes it is the נפש that comes back: וַתָּשָׁב נֶפֶשׁ־הַיֶּלֶד עַל־קִרְבּוֹ וַיֶּחִי "the נפש of the child (who had stopped breathing) came back inside him [lit., to his inside], and he revived" (1 Kgs 17:22); וְיָשִׁיבוּ אֶת־נַפְשָׁם "(they sought food for themselves) to make their נפש come back" (Lam 1:19). We shall return to this evidence in chapter 12.

We should also note the noun קרב "inside, innard," used to describe the physical location of (1) the prophet's רוח (Isa 26:9), (2) the new רוח of the people (Ezek 36:26), (3) the רוח of every human (Zech

12:1), and (4) a revived child's נפש (1 Kgs 17:21–22).[1] This implies that the רוח of humans, like their נפש,[2] is an entity that can be located in space. It is normally to be found inside people during their life.

What, then, is the relationship between the נפש and the רוח? And what is the relationship between each of them and the נפש הבשר mentioned in כִּי נֶפֶשׁ הַבָּשָׂר בַּדָּם הִוא "for the נפש of the flesh is in the blood" (Lev 17:11)?[3]

The first question has been answered in many ways through the ages.[4] For the moment, only one of these answers need detain us. Eighty years ago, René Dussaud suggested that the נפש is a vegetative soul that resides in the tomb, while the רוח is a spiritual soul that leaves the body after death.[5] This suggestion has been largely ignored, even though similar distinctions, derived from the anthropological study of many cultures, are commonplace in Assyriology and Egyptology.[6]

My own answer bears some similarity to Dussaud's suggestion. It begins, however, with the second question. In my view, the נפש הבשר is what modern anthropologists call the "body soul." Indeed, since the term בשר "flesh" is sometimes used to refer to the body

---

[1] For additional examples and the claim that "*rûaḥ* is always said to be 'within' (*b**qereḇ*) someone," see Sven Tengström et al., "רוּחַ *rûaḥ*," *TDOT* 13:375.

[2] See chapter 8 above.

[3] Alongside this statement that "the נפש . . . is *in* the blood," we find assertions that "the נפש . . . *is* the blood" (Lev 17:14b) and "the blood *is* the נפש" (Deut 12:23); cf. אַל־תְּעַר נַפְשִׁי "do not pour out my soul" (Ps 141:8). This may reflect the view that the blood and the נפש form a homogeneous mixture, a sort of blood-נפש solution (so Ramban to Lev 17:14) and/or the view that the נפש has no physical substance. The native dictionaries of Classical Arabic give the meaning "blood" for *nafs* in addition to "soul," "self," "person," etc. In the view of Edward W. Lane (*Arabic-English Lexicon,* 2828 col a), this is "because the animal soul was believed by the Arabs, as it was by many others in ancient times (see Gen ix. 4, and Aristotle, De Anim. i, 2, and Virgil's Aen. ix. 349), to diffuse itself throughout the body by means of the arteries."

[4] For a sample of rabbinic answers, see n. 14 below and chapter 12, n. 18.

[5] René Dussaud, "La notion d'âme chez les israélites et les phéniciens," *Syria* 16 (1935): 269.

[6] See chapter 1 above.

by synecdoche,[7] the meaning of נפש הבשר may, in fact, be "the body soul" rather than "the flesh soul." In any event, the term suggests that there was another (type of) נפש or—as I prefer for reasons that will become clear later—another *component* of the נפש. There are, therefore, grounds to conjecture that the נפש was viewed as consisting of two components: (1) the נפש הבשר, a bodily component located in the blood, and (2) the רוח, a spiritual component bestowed by God. This conjecture answers both of the questions posed above.

The expression נפש הבשר is commonly abbreviated to הנפש. Indeed, the abbreviated and unabbreviated forms of the expression occur together in a single verse: כִּי נֶפֶשׁ הַבָּשָׂר בַּדָּם הִוא . . . כִּי־הַדָּם הוּא בַּנֶּפֶשׁ יְכַפֵּר "for the נפש הבשר is in the blood . . . for it is the blood that, by means of the נפש (in it), effects expiation" (Lev 17:11). Thus, the term נפש can refer to the body soul alone, as well as to the entire bipartite soul (the body soul with the רוח). This semantic analysis provides a plausible solution to a problem that has long puzzled scholars, especially those for whom the primary meaning of נפש is "life, vitality"; viz., how did נפש acquire the meaning "corpse" (Num 6:6; 19:13; etc.)?[8] I suggest that the meaning "corpse" developed by synecdoche from the meaning "body soul," just as the meaning "person" developed (probably much earlier) by synecdoche from the meaning "soul."[9]

In line with this conjecture, we might hypothesize that every creature that has בשר with blood in it (perhaps only blood with a pulsating flow, the דם הנפש of the rabbis)[10] has a נפש בשר, but only a creature that has בשר with both a נפש בשר and a רוח חיים in it (Gen 6:17; 7:15) can be said to have a נפש חיה (Gen 1:30) and, by synecdoche, *be* a נפש חיה (Gen 1:24; etc.). This may be the point of וַיִּפַּח בְּאַפָּיו

---

[7] See the discussion of Isa 10:18; Ps 63:2; Prov 4:22; Job 13:14; and 14:22 in chapter 8 above.

[8] See at chapter 12, nn. 9–10. Cf. the comment of Isaiah of Trani at Introduction, nn. 15–16.

[9] See chapter 12, n. 8.

[10] See, for example, *t. Zebaḥ.* 8:17: אין לך שמכפר אלא דם הנפש בלבד שנ' כי הדם הוא בנפש יכפר אי זהו דם הנפש כל זמן שמקלח "Nothing effects expiation other than נפש-blood, as it is said: 'for it is the blood that, by means of the נפש (in it), effects expiation' (Lev 17:11). Which (part of the blood issuing from a slaughtered animal) is נפש-blood? As long as it spurts (it is still part of the נפש-blood)."

נִשְׁמַת חַיִּים וַיְהִי הָאָדָם לְנֶפֶשׁ חַיָּה (Gen 2:7), assuming that the phrase נשמת חיים is either equivalent to רוח חיים (as many scholars have asserted)[11] or elliptical for נשמת רוח חיים (Gen 7:22).

In groping toward this conjecture during a year-long sabbatical leave, I was unaware that similar portraits of the biblical soul had been sketched in the past. The earliest one is found in the writings of Philo of Alexandria, e.g., *Who Is the Heir* §55:

> ἐπειδὴ γὰρ ψυχὴ διχῶς λέγεται, ἥ τε ὅλη καὶ τὸ ἡγεμονικὸν αὐτῆς μέρος, ὃ κυρίως εἰπεῖν ψυχὴ ψυχῆς ἐστι, . . . ἔδοξε τῷ νομοθέτῃ διττὴν καὶ τὴν οὐσίαν εἶναι ψυχῆς, αἷμα μὲν τῆς ὅλης, τοῦ δ᾽ ἡγεμονικωτάτου πνεῦμα θεῖον.
>
> We use "soul" in two senses, both for the whole soul and also for its dominant part, which properly speaking is the soul's soul. . . . And therefore the lawgiver held that the substance of the soul is twofold, blood being that of the soul as a whole, and the divine breath or spirit that of its most dominant part.[12]

Philo goes on to cite two prooftexts: Gen 2:7 and Lev 17:11. According to George H. van Kooten, Philo's goal is "to reconcile two different, and seemingly contradictory views on the substance of the soul—(1) that of Gen 2,7, according to which, at least in Philo's understanding, the soul consists of *pneuma*; and (2) that of Lev 17,11, which contends that the soul consists of blood."[13] In any event, Philo concludes that the biblical ψυχή = נפש has two parts: "a supe-

---

[11] See already Friedrich Schwally, *Das Leben nach dem Tode: Nach den Vorstellungen des alten Israel und des Judentums einschliesslich des Volksglaubens im Zeitalter Christi; eine biblisch-theologische Untersuchung* (Giessen: J. Ricker, 1892), 5; Johannes Frey, *Tod, Seelenglaube und Seelenkult im alten Israel* (Leipzig: A. Deicher, 1898) 18 n. 1; Robert Henry Charles, *A Critical History of the Doctrine of a Future Life: Or, Hebrew, Jewish, and Christian Eschatology from Pre-prophetic Times till the Close of the New Testament Canon, being Jowett Lectures for 1898-99* (London: Adam & Charles Black, 1899), 41.

[12] *Philo in Ten Volumes* (trans. F. H. Colson and G. H. Whitaker; LCL; London: William Heinemann, 1929–1962), 4:310–11.

[13] George H. van Kooten, "The Anthropological Trichotomy of Spirit, Soul, and Body in Philo of Alexandria and Paul of Tarsus," in *Anthropology in the New Testament and Its Ancient Context: Papers from the EABS-Meeting in Piliscsaba/Budapest* (ed. Michael Labahn and Outi Lehtipuu; Contributions to Biblical Exegesis and Theology 54; Leuven: Peeters, 2010), 102.

rior rational part and a subordinate irrational part."[14] Although the entire ψυχή = נפש consists of blood, one of its parts dominates the other. The dominant part consists of πνεῦμα = רוח, a spirit of divine origin. Perhaps we are to think of this spirit as being dissolved in the blood of the ψυχή = נפש.[15]

Philo's distinction between the πνεῦμα and the ψυχή is reflected also in the writings of Josephus and Paul of Tarsus.[16] For Josephus (*Ant.* 1.1.2 §34), both the πνεῦμα and the ψυχή appear as soul-types or soul-components in a single verse: וַיִּיצֶר ה' אֱלֹהִים אֶת־הָאָדָם עָפָר מִן־הָאֲדָמָה וַיִּפַּח בְּאַפָּיו נִשְׁמַת חַיִּים וַיְהִי הָאָדָם לְנֶפֶשׁ חַיָּה (Gen 2:7):

> Καὶ δὴ καὶ φυσιολογεῖν Μωυσῆς μετὰ τὴν ἑβδόμην ἤρξατο περὶ τῆς τἀνθρώπου κατασκευῆς λέγων οὕτως: ἔπλασεν ὁ θεὸς τὸν ἄνθρωπον χοῦν ἀπὸ τῆς γῆς λαβών, καὶ πνεῦμα ἐνῆκεν αὐτῷ καὶ ψυχήν.
>
> And here, after the seventh day, Moses begins to interpret nature, writing on the formation of man in these terms: "God fashioned man by taking dust from the earth and instilled into him spirit and soul."[17]

---

[14] Jacob et al., "ψυχή κτλ.," 635. For the history of "soul division" (bipartite and tripartite), see most recently Benjamin P. Blosser, *Become Like the Angels: Origen's Doctrine of the Soul* (Washington, D.C.: Catholic University of America Press, 2012), 17–37. For the application of this idea to the Hebrew Bible, see Zevit, *Religions,* 257: "The Zoharic conception of the tripartite soul maintained that the soul consists of *nefeš*, a physical soul, *rūaḥ*, an emotive soul, and *nešāmāh*, a spark of God in the believer's soul. At death, *rūaḥ* ascends to a celestial garden, *nešāmāh* returns to God, but *nefeš* lingers near the gravesite as an active presence." Cf. Abraham Ibn Ezra, יסוד מורא וסוד תורה: מהדורה מדעית מבוארת (ed. Joseph Cohen in collaboration with Uriel Simon; Ramat Gan: Bar-Ilan University Press, 2002), 135–36, lines 50–56. For a suggestion that the *eṭemmu* and the *zaqīqu* were "parts of the soul" in Mesopotamia, see Hays, *Death in the Iron Age II,* 43. For more on soul-types and soul-parts in Mesopotamia, see Abusch, "Ghost and God," 372.

[15] See n. 3 above.

[16] Van Kooten, "Anthropological Trichotomy," 99, 114–19.

[17] *Josephus in Nine Volumes*, 4:16–17. Note that Josephus's paraphrase follows the LXX rather faithfully in the first clause of Gen 2:7, but departs from it in the last two clauses: καὶ ἔπλασεν ὁ θεὸς τὸν ἄνθρωπον χοῦν ἀπὸ τῆς γῆς καὶ ἐνεφύσησεν εἰς τὸ πρόσωπον αὐτοῦ πνοὴν ζωῆς, καὶ ἐγένετο ὁ ἄνθρωπος εἰς ψυχὴν ζῶσαν.

At first glance, Josephus's assertion seems odd. Taken in its plain sense, Gen 2:7 (be it the Hebrew text or its Greek rendering in LXX) makes no mention of instilling ψυχή = נפש into man. In the context of that verse, the phrase נפש חיה seems to refer only to what man *is*—not what he *has*. Perhaps the explanation lies in the hypothesis set forth above: only a creature that *has* a נפש חיה can be said to *be* a נפש חיה. Thus, by breathing נשמת רוח חיים = נשמת חיים into man, God activated and vitalized the נפש בשר in his blood, turning it (or the entire bipartite נפש) into a נפש חיה. If Josephus's assertion is, in fact, based on such an interpretation, there is no need to assume that Josephus himself invented it. His assertion may well reflect an earlier tradition, one that gave rise to the views of Philo and Paul of Tarsus as well.[18]

Thanks to Paul and the early Church Fathers, Philo's distinction took on a distinctly Christian flavor, turning into a "trichotomy of spirit, soul, and body"—a tripartite view of man. In modern times, it became, for the most part, the province of New Testament scholars and Christian theologians.[19] At the very end of the nineteenth century, Robert Henry Charles attempted to breathe a new רוח into tripartite man, a רוח that would transport him back to the time of the Hebrew Bible:

> Though the spirit is not personally conceived, yet, since it remains in the man so long as he lives and forms in him a thing apart by itself, it must be regarded as forming part of man's composite personality. Accordingly, we have here a real trichotomy of spirit (רוח), soul (נפש), and body (בסר [*sic*]). But if we examine these elements more closely we see that the soul is the result of the indwelling of the spirit in the material body, and has no independent existence of its own. It is really a function of the material body when quickened by the spirit. So long as the spirit is present,

---

[18] Cf. Van Kooten, "Anthropological Trichotomy," 99–100: "Since this passage [Gen 2:7] is explicitly quoted by Philo, Paul and Josephus, their interpretation seems to reflect a common Jewish understanding of Gen 2,7 LXX in the first century CE."

[19] See, for example, John Bickford Heard, *The Tripartite Nature of Man* (Edinburgh: T. & T. Clark, 1866); and John B. Woodward, *Man as Spirit, Soul, and Body: A Study of Biblical Psychology* (Pigeon Forge, Tenn.: Grace Fellowship International, 2007).

> so long is the soul "a living soul" (נפש חיה), but when the spirit is withdrawn, the vitality of the soul is destroyed, and it becomes a dead soul (נפש מת), or corpse (Num. vi. 6; Lev. xxi. 11). . . . According to this view the annihilation of the soul ensues inevitably at death, that is, when the spirit is withdrawn. This dissolution of the personality at death is frankly recognised in Eccl. xii. 7, and the impersonal breath of life returns to the Supreme Fount of Life: "the spirit shall return to God, who gave it."[20]

Charles's theory is a sophisticated attempt to reconcile the tripartite view of man with the results of critical scholarship, but it appeared at precisely the wrong time. Swept away in an irresistible tide of monism, it is rarely mentioned today.

My own theory, developed independently, has some elements in common with that of Charles but, as we shall see, is by no means identical with it. In a later chapter, I shall develop the theory further, suggesting that the נפש הבשר and the רוח were viewed as being physically attached and as remaining so from the time of the soul's departure at death until the decomposition of the flesh, around twelve months later.[21]

My view of the רוח is an outgrowth of the traditional view championed by Charles A. Briggs in *JBL* and incorporated into BDB. Briggs writes that the term רוח occurs frequently (twenty-five times) with the meaning "spirit of the living, breathing being, dwelling in the בָּשָׂר of men and animals."[22] As examples, he cites אֱלֹהֵי הָרוּחֹת לְכָל־בָּשָׂר "God of the רוחות of all flesh" (Num 16:22; 27:16); יֹצֵר רוּחַ־אָדָם בְּקִרְבּוֹ "creator of the רוח of man within him" (Zech 12:1); אֲשֶׁר בְּיָדוֹ נֶפֶשׁ כָּל־חָי וְרוּחַ כָּל־בְּשַׂר־אִישׁ "in His hand is the נפש of every living being and the רוח of all human flesh" (Job 12:10), etc.

According to Briggs, the רוח "is the spirit that lives in man and that departs at death."[23] Among the examples he gives, we may mention: וַיִּזְכֹּר כִּי־בָשָׂר הֵמָּה רוּחַ הוֹלֵךְ וְלֹא יָשׁוּב "He remembered that

---

[20] Charles, *Critical History*, 42-43. Cf. idem, *Eschatology: The Doctrine of a Future Life in Israel, Judaism and Christianity* (London: Adam & Charles Black, 1913), 42, where "a dead soul" is corrected to "a soul of a dead man."

[21] See chapter 11 below.

[22] BDB, 925a, s.v. רוּחַ, meaning no. 4; Charles A. Briggs, "The Use of רוח in the Old Testament," *JBL* 19 (1900): 137.

[23] Briggs, "Use of רוח," 137.

they were (merely) flesh (with) a רוח that goes and does not return" (Ps 78:39); תֵּצֵא רוּחוֹ יָשֻׁב לְאַדְמָתוֹ "his רוח goes out (and) he returns to his dust" (Ps 146:4); תֹּסֵף[24] רוּחָם יִגְוָעוּן וְאֶל־עֲפָרָם יְשׁוּבוּן "You bring in[25] their רוח and they expire, returning to their dust" (Ps 104:29); אִם־יָשִׂים אֵלָיו לִבּוֹ רוּחוֹ וְנִשְׁמָתוֹ אֵלָיו יֶאֱסֹף, יִגְוַע כָּל־בָּשָׂר יָחַד וְאָדָם עַל־עָפָר יָשׁוּב "if He would turn His attention to it and bring in to Himself His/its רוח and נשמה, all flesh would expire at once and mankind would return to dust" (Job 34:14–15); וְיָשֹׁב הֶעָפָר עַל־הָאָרֶץ כְּשֶׁהָיָה וְהָרוּחַ תָּשׁוּב אֶל־הָאֱלֹהִים אֲשֶׁר נְתָנָהּ "and the dust [= the flesh] returns to the ground, as it was (before), and the רוח returns to God, who bestowed it" (Qoh 12:7; cf. 3:20–21). In all of these examples, רוח occurs in a context that appears to reflect a dualistic conception of the human being.

In retrospect, it appears that Briggs's article marked the end of an era. Less than a decade after its publication, two challenges to the traditional view of the biblical רוח were published—one chronological and the other semantic. The chronological challenge acknowledged that a dualistic conception of the human being could be found in the Hebrew Bible, but only in its latest strata:

> Only through the contact of the Jews with Persian and Greek thought did the idea of a disembodied soul, having its own individuality, take root in Judaism and find its expression in the later Biblical books, as, for instance, in the following passages: . . . "The spirit shall return unto God who gave it" (Eccl. xii. 7).[26]

However, based on our discussion of נפש, there is good reason to believe that "the idea of a disembodied soul" is found in most strata of the Bible. As for the distinction in Ps 104:29; 146:4; Job 34:14–15; and Qoh 12:7 (cf. Qoh 3:20–21) between the earthly destination of the body and the heavenly destination of the spirit, scholars should think twice before dismissing it as a late import from

---

[24] The *aleph*-less form תֹּסֵף is commonly compared to וַיֹּסֶף (2 Sam 6:1); cf. also וַתֹּפֵהוּ (1 Sam 28:24), תֹּבֵא (Prov 1:10), יוֹכְלוּ (Ezek 42:5), etc.

[25] For this rendering, see below.

[26] Isaac Broydé and Ludwig Blau, "Soul," *Jewish Encyclopedia* (New York and London: Funk and Wagnalls, 1907), 11:472b. Cf. Porteous, "Soul," 428b: "Hebrew thought could distinguish soul from body as material basis of life, but there was no question of two separate, independent entities, except for a possible trace of the 'Greek' idea in Job 4:19: 'those who dwell in houses of clay, whose foundation is in the dust [is dust?].'"

Iranian or Greek thought. It appears time and again in Egyptian mortuary literature of the New Kingdom, in expressions such as "thy *ba* to heaven, thy corpse to the underground" (*Book of the Dead*, chapter 169), "thy *ba* is placed in heaven, thy corpse in the underworld" (Theban Tomb no. 65, Hatshepsut), "*ba* to heaven, corpse to the underworld" (Theban Tomb no. 82, Thutmose III).[27] The importance of the distinction in Egyptian theology is discussed by Jan Assmann:

> Before the coffin containing the mummy was deposited in the sarcophagus chamber, and thus in the netherworld, the *ba* was supposed to ascend to the sky during this rite carried out in the sunlight. Dozens of text passages can be cited in support of this point:
>
> Your *ba* to the sky,
> your corpse to the netherworld!
>
> Such formulas are ubiquitous in the mortuary texts of the New Kingdom and later periods, where they lay stress on the positive aspect of the dissociation. The separation of *ba* and corpse was one of the goals of the transfiguration rituals, and it was part of the transformation of the deceased into a transfigured ancestral spirit.[28]

The other challenge to the traditional view involved a shift in the understanding of the term רוח among scholars—a shift similar to the one for נפש. As a result of the shift, רוח in the above examples came to be understood as meaning "breath" rather than "spirit." The shift is evident in a *JBL* article by William Ross Shoemaker published only four years after that of Briggs: "At death the breath returns to God who gave it (Ps. 104^{29} 146^{4} Job 34^{14} Eccles. 3^{21} 12^{7})."[29] According to Shoemaker, it is the breath of humans that returns to God—not their spirit.

A similar replacement of "spirit" with "breath" can be seen in H. W. Wolff's *Anthropology of the Old Testament*. In the chapter entitled "*rūaḥ* – Man as he is Empowered," many of the verses dis-

---

[27] Žabkar, *Ba Concept*, 127–29.

[28] Assmann, *Death*, 91.

[29] William Ross Shoemaker, "The Use of רוּחַ in the Old Testament, and of πνεῦμα in the New Testament: A Lexicographical Study," *JBL* 23 (1904): 32.

cussed above (Judg 15:19; 1 Sam 30:12; Ps 146:4; Job 34:14; Qoh 12:7), are included in the section entitled "Breath";[30] indeed, the chapter[31] does not even contain a section entitled "Spirit." Among the English versions of the Bible, the NJPS appears to be the most consistent in exorcising the "spirit of the living, breathing being, dwelling in the בָּשָׂר of men and animals" that Briggs saw in the verses cited above. It renders רוח with "breath" in seven of them (Num 16:22; 27:16; Zech 12:1; Ps 78:39; 104:29; 146:4; Job 12:10) and with "lifebreath" in one (Qoh 12:7). In Job 34:14, it employs the rendering "spirit," but that is only because it takes the רוח there as God's. According to the NJPS, then, God has a spirit but humans do not.

It is difficult to offer a decisive refutation of this view, but it is still possible to show that the meaning "breath" makes less sense than the meaning "spirit" in at least *some* of the verses in question. Take, for example, אֱלֹהֵי הָרוּחֹת לְכָל־בָּשָׂר "God of the רוחות of all flesh" (Num 16:22; 27:16). If רוח were a mass (uncountable) noun meaning "breath" (i.e., "breathing or the ability to breathe") in this verse, it would not be able to take a plural ending. In my view, it makes more sense to take the epithet as implying that each living creature possesses its own individuated vitalizing spirit.

The same goes for יֹצֵר רוּחַ־אָדָם בְּקִרְבּוֹ "creator of the רוח of man within him" (Zech 12:1). The NJPS renders this as "(who) created man's breath within him," but which meaning of English *breath* fits here? It is difficult to believe that the BH verb י-צ-ר, rendered "form, fashion" by BDB,[32] is used here of creating "the ability to breathe" within a person, or "the act of breathing," or even "air inhaled and exhaled." The NJPS appears to be bending over backwards to avoid the rendering "spirit" used in the other major English versions, e.g., the NRSV: "(who) formed the human spirit within."

Similarly, "breath" does not make much sense in verses that speak of the רוח returning to God. The clearest example is וְיָשֹׁב הֶעָפָר עַל־הָאָרֶץ כְּשֶׁהָיָה וְהָרוּחַ תָּשׁוּב אֶל־הָאֱלֹהִים אֲשֶׁר נְתָנָהּ "and the dust [= the flesh] returns to the ground, as it was (before), and the רוח returns to God, who bestowed it" (Qoh 12:7). Here again it is difficult to believe that what returns to God is a person's ability to breathe, or a person's act of breathing, or the air inhaled and exhaled by a

30 Wolff, *Anthropology*, 33.
31 Ibid., 32–39.
32 BDB, 427b, s.v.

person. One gets the impression from this verse that what returns to God is independent of the flesh and outlives it.[33]

Two other verses that can be shown to belong here are: אִם־יָשִׂים אֵלָיו לִבּוֹ רוּחוֹ וְנִשְׁמָתוֹ אֵלָיו יֶאֱסֹף, יִגְוַע כָּל־בָּשָׂר יָחַד וְאָדָם עַל־עָפָר יָשׁוּב "if He would turn His attention to it and bring in to Himself His/its רוח and נשמה, all flesh would expire at once and mankind would return to dust" (Job 34:14–15); and תֹּסֵף רוּחָם יִגְוָעוּן וְאֶל־עֲפָרָם יְשׁוּבוּן "You bring in their רוח and they expire, returning to their dust" (Ps 104:29). It will be noted that I have taken א-ס-ף to mean "bring in" in these two verses. This meaning for א-ס-ף in the *qal* and the *piʿel* (and the meaning "be brought in" for א-ס-ף in the *nifʿal*) is quite a bit more common than one would imagine from the standard modern dictionaries.[34] It is most obvious in contexts where the meaning "gather, assemble" makes no sense, e.g., where the direct object of the *qal/piʿel* verb (or the subject of the *nifʿal* verb) is (a) a noun or pronoun referring to a single person or animal (e.g., Num 11:30 [וַיֵּאָסֵף מֹשֶׁה אֶל־הַמַּחֲנֶה]; 12:14, 15; Deut 22:2; Josh 20:4; Judg 19:18; 1 Sam 14:52; 2 Sam 11:27; 17:13; Jer 47:6; and Ps 27:10)[35] or (b) a dual noun referring to body parts of a single individual (e.g., Gen 49:33 and 1 Sam 14:19). Note also לֹא־יָבוֹא עוֹד שִׁמְשֵׁךְ וִירֵחֵךְ לֹא יֵאָסֵף "your sun will no longer go down [lit., go in], and your moon will not set [lit., be brought in]" (Isa 60:20), with the two near-synonyms in parallelism. In chapter 10 below, we shall examine additional examples of א-ס-ף interchanging with ב-ו-א in contexts relating to death: וְגַם כָּל־הַדּוֹר הַהוּא נֶאֶסְפוּ אֶל־אֲבוֹתָיו "and also, all of that generation were brought in to their ancestors" (Judg 2:10) and הִנְנִי אֹסִפְךָ עַל־אֲבֹתֶיךָ "therefore, I am about/going to bring you in[36] to your ancestors" (2 Kgs 22:20)

---

[33] The term נפש also appears in Qohelet, mainly as the seat of the appetite.

[34] BDB, 62b. See also in chapter 10 below. The semantic development from "gather = bring together" to "bring in" is easy to explain based on the agricultural use of the root א-ס-ף. The אָסִיף is an "ingathering," in which fruit is both brought *together in* the field and brought *in from* the field. A very similar semantic change is exhibited by the root כ-נ-ס "gather, bring together," which has the meaning "enter, come in" in the *nifʿal* in Mishnaic Hebrew. For an insightful treatment of this development, see Aaron Koller, לבוא ולהיכנס: היבטים סינכרוניים ודיאכרוניים בסמנטיקה של הפועל "לבוא" בעברית העתיקה, *Lešonenu* 75 (2013): 157-59

[35] Cf. Koller, לבוא ולהיכנס, 158.

[36] I have translated אֹסִפְךָ as a participle. Although it can also be an imperfect, in this context (following הִנְנִי), a participle is more likely.

alongside וְאַתָּה תָּבוֹא אֶל־אֲבֹתֶיךָ בְּשָׁלוֹם "as for you, you shall go in to your ancestors in peace" (Gen 15:15) and תָּבוֹא עַד־דּוֹר אֲבוֹתָיו "it [= the נפש] will go in to the circle[37] of its ancestors" (Ps 49:20). According to this interpretation of א-ס-ף, Job 34:14–15 and Ps 104:29 speak of the רוח as being brought in by God "to Himself," that is, into a divine abode. Assuming that this interpretation is correct, it is most natural to take רוח in these verses as referring to a spirit from God that animates flesh during life and returns to God at death, as in Qoh 12:7 (see above) and probably Num 16:22; 27:16 as well. If so, this is further evidence for disembodied רוחות.

[37] For this rendering, see chapter 10, n. 11 below.

10

The Reunion of the Disembodied Soul with Its Kinsmen

The evidence for disembodied רוחות discussed in the previous chapter sheds light on additional evidence for disembodied souls—evidence that is frequently ignored in discussions of the terms נפש and רוח because it uses neither of these terms. I refer to the pentateuchal idiom וַיֵּאָסֶף אֶל־עַמָּיו.

The precise denotation of this expression has long been the subject of controversy.[1] Some scholars have written that it refers to joining one's ancestors *physically*, in the family tomb, at the time of either the primary burial[2] or the secondary burial.[3] Others have argued, more persuasively, that such physical interpretations are

[1] For discussions with references to earlier literature, see Karl-Johan Illman, *Old Testament Formulas about Death* (Publications of the Research Institute of the Åbo Akademi Foundation 48; Åbo: Åbo Akademi, 1979), 43–45; Saul M. Olyan, "Some Neglected Aspects of Israelite Interment Ideology," *JBL* 124 (2005): 608; and Osborne, "Secondary Mortuary Practice," 45.

[2] Gabriel Barkay, קברים וקבורה ביהודה בתקופת המקרא, in קברים ונוהגי קבורה בארץ־ישראל בעת העתיקה (ed. Itamar Singer; Jerusalem: Yad Izhak Ben-Zvi, 1994), 112-13; and Kilwing, "נֶפֶשׁ und ΨΥΧΗ," 394. For Barkay's earlier view, see the next footnote.

[3] Eric M. Meyers, *Jewish Ossuaries: Reburial and Rebirth. Secondary Burials in Their Ancient Near Eastern Setting* (BibOr 24; Rome: Biblical Institute Press, 1971), 14–15; Gabriel Barkay, "The Iron Age II-III," in *The Archaeology of Ancient Israel* (ed. Amnon Ben-Tor; Tel-Aviv: Open University of Israel, 1992), 359; Matthew J. Suriano, "Death, Disinheritance, and Job's Kinsman-Redeemer," *JBL* 129 (2010): 58; Osborne, "Secondary Mortuary Practice,"

impossible in a good percentage of the contexts.[4] The most obvious counterexamples are found in the reports of the deaths of Aaron (Num 20:24; 27:13; Deut 32:50) and Moses (Num 27:13; 31:2; Deut 32:50), who were not buried with any of their kinsmen.[5] Moreover, in the reports of the deaths of Abraham (Gen 25:8–9), Isaac (35:29), and Jacob (49:33; cf. 50:13), the idiom refers to something that occurs after death but before burial—either right before burial (Isaac) or long before burial (Jacob).[6] In the words of James F. Osborne: "The scholarly consensus appears to be that although the phrase does allude to the spirit joining its ancestors in the afterlife, it cannot be understood as referring to burial itself since the formula precedes the specific mentioning of burial."[7]

Although וַיֵּאָסֶף in this expression is conventionally rendered "he was gathered" (leading some to think of gathering bones),[8] there is good reason to believe that its true meaning is "he was brought in." This was first pointed out by Rashi in his commentary to Gen 49:29:

---

45 with n. 67: "to my mind, the use of the verb ʾsf is highly evocative of the gathering together of bones in addition to the spirit."

[4] Magnus Anton Becherer, *Ueber den Glauben der Juden an Unsterblichkeit der menschlichen Seele vor der babylonischen Gefangenschaft* (Munich: Jakob Giel, 1827), 38–39; Gesenius, *Thesaurus*, 131; Alexander Heidel, *The Gilgamesh Epic and Old Testament Parallels* (Chicago: University of Chicago Press, 1946), 187–88; Bernard Alfrink, "L'expression נֶאֱסַף אֶל־עַמָּיו," *OTS* 5 (1948): 128; G. R. Driver, "Plurima Mortis Imago," 141–42; Nicholas J. Tromp, *Primitive Conceptions of Death and the Nether World in the Old Testament* (BibOr 21; Rome: Pontifical Biblical Institute, 1969), 168–69; Desmond Alexander, "The Old Testament View of Life after Death," *Themelios* 11 (1986): 45; Philip S. Johnston, *Shades of Sheol: Death and Afterlife in the Old Testament* (Downers Grove, Ill.: InterVarsity, 2002), 34; Olyan, "Neglected Aspects," 608 n. 23; etc. See also at n. 7 below.

[5] For an attempt to explain away these counterexamples, see Eric M. Meyers, "The Theological Implications of an Ancient Jewish Burial Custom," *JQR* 62 (1971): 97.

[6] Barkay (קברים, 112–13) attempts to circumvent this objection by arguing that BH ק-ב-ר refers not to primary burial but to secondary burial. This is an ingenious proposal, but it is contradicted by many verses, e.g., Gen 23:4; Deut 21:23; 34:6; 2 Kgs 9:34; 13:21; etc.

[7] Osborne, "Secondary Mortuary Practice," 45.

[8] See n. 3 above and at chapter 11, n. 9 below.

> נֶאֱסַף אֶל־עַמָּיו - על שם שמכניסין הנפשות אל מקום גניזתן, שיש אסיפות בלשון עברי שהן לשון הכנסה, כגון (שופטים יט יח) וְאֵין אִישׁ מְאַסֵּף אוֹתִי הַבָּיְתָה, (דברים כב ב) וַאֲסַפְתּוֹ אֶל־תּוֹךְ בֵּיתֶךָ, (ויקרא כג לט) בְּאָסְפְּכֶם אֶת־תְּבוּאַת הָאָרֶץ, הכנסתם לבית מפני הגשמים, (שמות כג טז) בְּאָסְפְּךָ אֶת־מַעֲשֶׂיךָ מִן־הַשָּׂדֶה. וכל אסיפה האמורה במיתה אף היא לשון הכנסה.[9]
>
> נֶאֱסַף אֶל־עַמָּיו—(The expression derives) from the fact that souls are *brought in* to the place where they are hidden away, for there are occurrences of א-ס-ף in the Hebrew language that denote bringing in, such as "no one is bringing me in to his house" (Judg 19:18); "and you shall bring it in, inside your house" (Deut 22:2); "when you have brought in the yield of the land" (Lev 23:39); "when you bring in the fruits of your labor from the field" (Exod 23:16). *And every occurrence of* א-ס-ף *used in (the context of) death likewise denotes bringing in.*

Rashi's rule applies also to the meaning of א-ס-ף in Job 34:14–15 and Ps 104:29, as we saw in the previous chapter. In light of that evidence, it seems quite likely that Rashi is right in taking וַיֵּאָסֶף אֶל־עַמָּיו to mean "he was brought in to his kinsmen."[10]

Further support for this interpretation comes from an examination of occurrences of the formula that have "ancestors" instead of "kinsmen." In two of them—וְגַם כָּל־הַדּוֹר הַהוּא נֶאֶסְפוּ אֶל־אֲבוֹתָיו (Judg 2:10) and הִנְנִי אֹסִפְךָ עַל־אֲבֹתֶיךָ (2 Kgs 22:20)—we find the verb א-ס-ף. Two others—וְאַתָּה תָּבוֹא אֶל־אֲבֹתֶיךָ בְּשָׁלוֹם "as for you, you shall go in to your ancestors in peace" (Gen 15:15) and תָּבוֹא עַד־דּוֹר אֲבוֹתָיו "it [= the נפש] will go in to the circle[11] of its ancestors" (Ps 49:20)—have the verb ב-ו-א. Since ב-ו-א means "come/go *in*" in Biblical Hebrew, the correspondence between it and א-ס-ף is further evidence for Rashi's rule. The meaning of וְגַם כָּל־הַדּוֹר הַהוּא נֶאֶסְפוּ אֶל־אֲבוֹתָיו must be: "And

---

[9] Elsewhere in his commentaries, Rashi points out many examples of this meaning; see Y. Avineri, היכל רש"י (2nd ed.; 2 vols.; Jerusalem: Mossad Harav Kook, 1985), 2/2:74-75; and Koller, לבוא ולהיכנס, 158.

[10] So, too, Barkay, in one of his discussions (קברים, 112–13), but in that discussion he takes וַיֵּאָסֶף אֶל־עַמָּיו as referring to primary burial; see nn. 2 and 6 above (in contrast to n. 3). For a similar suggestion, including a reference to Rashi, see Hélène Nutkowicz, *L'homme face à la mort au royaume de Juda: Rites, pratiques, et représentations* (Paris: Cerf, 2006), 234.

[11] For the rendering "circle," see Olmo Lete and Sanmartín, *Dictionary of the Ugaritic Language*, 279–80, s.v. *dr*.

also, all of that generation were brought in to their ancestors." And the meaning of הִנְנִי אֹסִפְךָ עַל־אֲבֹתֶיךָ must be: "Therefore, I am about/going to bring you in[12] to your ancestors."

All in all, the evidence for Rashi's interpretation is quite compelling. There is no reason to assume that the verbs in וַיֵּאָסֵף מֹשֶׁה אֶל־הַמַּחֲנֶה "Moses was brought in to the camp" (Num 11:30) and וְאַחַר תֵּאָסֵף "(Let her be shut up for seven days outside the camp) and afterwards let her be brought in" (Num 12:14) have a different meaning than the ones in, say, יֵאָסֵף אַהֲרֹן אֶל־עַמָּיו (Num 20:24) and אַחַר תֵּאָסֵף אֶל־עַמֶּיךָ (Num 31:2). If so, the last two examples should be rendered "Let Aaron be brought in (not: gathered) to his kinsmen" and "afterwards you shall be brought in (not: gathered) to your kinsmen."

Let us return now to 2 Kgs 22:20, this time examining the first *two* clauses: לָכֵן הִנְנִי אֹסִפְךָ עַל־אֲבֹתֶיךָ וְנֶאֱסַפְתָּ אֶל־קִבְרֹתֶיךָ בְּשָׁלוֹם "Therefore, I am about/going to bring you in to your ancestors and you will be brought in to your burial places in peace." It seems clear that the first of these clauses speaks of Josiah being brought in to his ancestors by God, while the second speaks of him being brought in to his burial places[13] by men. Moreover, the two clauses seem to correspond to the last two clauses of (וַיִּגְוַע יִצְחָק וַיָּמָת) וַיֵּאָסֶף אֶל־עַמָּיו זָקֵן וּשְׂבַע יָמִים וַיִּקְבְּרוּ אֹתוֹ עֵשָׂו וְיַעֲקֹב בָּנָיו "(Isaac breathed his last and died), and he was brought in to his kinsmen in ripe old age, and (then) Jacob and Esau his sons buried him" (Gen 35:29). The correspondence between הִנְנִי אֹסִפְךָ עַל־אֲבֹתֶיךָ and וַיֵּאָסֶף אֶל־עַמָּיו suggests that the latter, too, speaks of the deceased being brought in to his kinsmen/ancestors *by God.*[14]

Additional information can be gleaned from אַל־תֶּאֱסֹף עִם־חַטָּאִים נַפְשִׁי וְעִם־אַנְשֵׁי דָמִים חַיָּי "do not bring my נפש in (to be) with sinners,

---

[12] For the translation of אֹסִפְךָ as a participle, see chapter 9, n. 36 above.

[13] The noun is plural, perhaps referring to both primary and secondary burial places.

[14] So, too, Annette Krüger, "Auf dem Weg 'zu den Vätern': Zur Tradition der alttestamentlichen Sterbenotizen," in *Tod und Jenseits im alten Israel und in seiner Umwelt: Theologische, religionsgeschichtliche, archäologische und ikonographische Aspekte* (ed. Angelika Berlejung and Bernd Janowski; Forschungen zum Alten Testament 64; Tübingen: Mohr Siebeck, 2009), 139. Unlike Krüger, Nutkowicz (*L'homme,* 234) makes no mention of הִנְנִי אֹסִפְךָ עַל־אֲבֹתֶיךָ. Accordingly, she suggests that וַיֵּאָסֶף אֶל־עַמָּיו refers to the deceased being ushered in to his kinsmen *by the kinsmen themselves.*

and with murderers, my חיים" (Ps 26:9). It shows clearly that what is brought in by God at death is the נפש (// חיים)[15] of the deceased. This leads us back to the two poetic phrases discussed in the preceding chapter: רוּחוֹ וְנִשְׁמָתוֹ אֵלָיו יֶאֱסֹף "if He would bring in to Himself His/its רוח and נשמה" (Job 34:14); and תֹּסֵף רוּחָם "You bring in their רוח" (Ps 104:29). Based on all of these parallels, we conclude that the expression וַיֵּאָסֶף אֶל־עַמָּיו is somewhat elliptical. Although the grammatical subject of the verb is an implicit masculine singular pronoun whose antecedent is (the name of) the deceased, the expression would seem to refer to the נפש/רוח of the deceased being brought in somewhere by God for an initial reunion with the רוחות/נפשות of the deceased's kinsmen/ancestors.

If this conclusion is correct, and I believe that it is, the formula וַיֵּאָסֶף אֶל־עַמָּיו implies the existence of a soul or spirit that leaves the body at death, before interment, and continues to exist in disembodied form. This implication has been pointed out by a few scholars. Alexander Heidel writes:

> There can be no doubt that the figures of speech under discussion have reference to the immortal element in man. A clear indication of that we seem to have in Ps. 49:19–20: "Though in his lifetime (a man) blesses his soul, and (men) praise thee that thou doest well unto thyself, it shall go to the generation of his fathers; they will not see light forever." The subject of the verbal form *tābô* ("it shall go") is *nafshô* ("his soul"). . . . The expressions under consideration cannot mean anything else than that the soul or spirit of a certain person leaves this world at death and enters the afterworld, in which his fathers or certain of his kindred already find themselves. But there is no justification for concluding on the basis of these formulas that those who have gone before are thought of as assembled in Shĕʾôl in the sense of the subterranean spirit world. . . .[16]

G. R. Driver makes a similar point, based on the same prooftext:

> One of the Psalmists seems to make clear what the ancient Hebrews thought when a man was "gathered to his fathers"; for he says that, when a man dies, "his soul shall go to the generation of his fathers" (Ps 49:19). In other words, firstly he expires; then

---

[15] For the use of חיים here, see chapter 8 above.

[16] Heidel, *Gilgamesh,* 188.

> his soul or spirit, i.e., that part of him which is immortal, leaves this world and "is gathered to his fathers" in the world below, where his ancestors already are; and lastly his body is consigned to a grave, commonly the ancestral grave in the world above.[17]

In this discussion, Driver differs from Heidel in locating the reunion of the soul/spirit with the souls/spirits of the ancestors in the underworld. That is the commonly accepted view.[18] How does this view jibe with the verses that speak of the רוח returning to God and being brought in to God? I shall address this question in chapter 11. The only thing that needs to be said here is that none of this affects my central point, viz., that the expression וַיֵּאָסֶף אֶל־עַמָּיו is evidence for disembodied souls.

Another common pentateuchal expression that may belong here is וְנִכְרְתָה הַנֶּפֶשׁ הַהִוא מֵעַמֶּיהָ "that נפש shall be cut off from its kinsmen." In the thirteenth century, Ramban (Naḥmanides) argued in his commentary to Lev 18:29 that expressions of this type imply that the נפש survives death:

> וְנִכְרְתוּ הַנְּפָשׁוֹת הָעֹשֹׂת מִקֶּרֶב עַמָּם — . . . ותדע ותשכיל כי הכריתות הנזכרות בנפש בטחון גדול בקיום הנפשות אחרי המיתה ובמתן השכר בעולם הנשמות, כי באמרו יתברך וְנִכְרְתָה הַנֶּפֶשׁ הַהִוא מִקֶּרֶב עַמָּהּ (במדבר טו ל), וְנִכְרְתָה הַנֶּפֶשׁ הַהִוא מִלְּפָנַי (ויקרא כב ג), יורה כי הנפש החוטאת היא תכרת בעונה, ושאר הנפשות אשר לא חטאו תהיינה קיימות לפניו בזיו העליון.

> וְנִכְרְתוּ הַנְּפָשׁוֹת הָעֹשֹׂת מִקֶּרֶב עַמָּם—. . . You should know and understand that the forms of excision mentioned with reference to the נפש are a great (source for) trust in the existence of the נפש after death and in the granting of reward in the world of נשמות. For

---

[17] Godfrey Rolles Driver, "Plurima Mortis Imago," in *Studies and Essays in Honor of Abraham A. Neuman, President, Dropsie College for Hebrew and Cognate Learning, Philadelphia* (ed. Meir Ben-Horin, Bernard D. Weinryb, and Solomon Zeitlin; Leiden: Brill, 1962), 142.

[18] See, for example, Alfrink, "L'expression נֶאֱסַף אֶל־עַמָּיו," 128; Tromp, *Primitive Conceptions*, 168; Spronk, *Beatific Afterlife*, 240; Lewis, *Cults*, 164–65; and Nutkowicz, *L'homme*, 234. But see also Cook, "Death," 113: "To be 'gathered to one's people' was to escape the fate of Sheol. Sheol is never referenced in biblical texts that speak of the dead being united with their kin in the Hereafter."

> when He, blessed be He, says "and that נפש shall be cut off from the midst of its kin" (Num 15:30) or "that נפש shall be cut off from before Me" (Lev 22:3), it teaches that the נפש that sins is the one that shall be cut off—through its sin—but the other נפשות, which have not sinned, will exist before Him in the splendor on high.[19]

Ramban's discussion, which is rooted in ancient rabbinic exegesis, has been largely ignored by modern scholars. Indeed, a book devoted to BH formulas used in speaking of death makes no mention of the formula וְנִכְרְתָה הַנֶּפֶשׁ הַהִוא מֵעַמֶּיהָ.[20] That this neglect is unjustified has been shown by Jacob Milgrom:

> The other possible meaning of *kārēt* is that the punishment is indeed executed upon the sinner but only after his death: he is not permitted to rejoin his ancestors in the afterlife. . . . This meaning for *kārēt* is supported by the idiom that is its antonym: *neʾĕsap ʾel* 'be gathered to one's [kin, fathers]'. . . . Particularly in regard to the patriarchs, the language of the Bible presumes three stages concerning their death: they die, they are gathered to their kin, and they are buried. . . . "It (the term 'gathered') designates something which succeeds death and precedes sepulture, the kind of thing which may hardly be considered as other than reunion with the ancestors in Sheol" (Alfrink 1948: 128). This biblical term has its counterpart in the contiguous river civilizations of Egypt—for example, "going to one's Ka"—and of Mesopotamia—for instance, "joining the ghosts of one's ancestors". . .—all of which is evidence for a belief in the afterlife that permeated the ancient world and the concomitant fear that a wrathful deity might deprive man of this boon.[21]

Milgrom's suggestion that the expression וַיֵּאָסֶף אֶל־עַמָּיו is the antonym of the expression וְנִכְרְתָה הַנֶּפֶשׁ הַהִוא מֵעַמֶּיהָ is attractive and potentially very important. It implies that, if the former expression refers to a spirit/soul and its kinsmen in the afterlife (as most scholars believe), so does the latter expression. If the former expression speaks of a spirit/soul joining its kinsmen, the latter expression

---

[19] Ramban (Naḥmanides), *Commentary on the Torah* (trans. Charles B. Chavel; 5 vols.; New York: Shilo, 1971–1976), 3:278 with modifications.

[20] Illman, *Old Testament Formulas.*

[21] Jacob Milgrom, *Leviticus 1–16: A New Translation with Introduction and Commentary* (AB 3; New York: Doubleday, 1991), 459–60.

speaks of a spirit/soul being *prevented* from joining its kinsmen—whether through annihilation[22] or some other means.

The importance of this implication is greatly enhanced by the fact that these two expressions account for the bulk of the biblical occurrences of עמים used in the sense of "kinsmen" (rather than "peoples"). As demonstrated by Alfrink, this is a very archaic usage—a fossil preserved only in a few fixed expressions in the Pentateuch.[23] These expressions—and the ideas that they reflect—must therefore be extremely old. In short, this evidence suggests that ideas about disembodied souls and their punishment in the afterlife were current among the Israelites far earlier than generally assumed.

---

[22] So Maimonides, *Mishneh Torah*, Hilkhot Teshuvah 8:1, 5; and ibid., משנה עם פירוש רבינו משה בן מימון, 4:205b lines 23–25. Cf. *t. Sanh.* 13:4 cited in chapter 11 below. Maimonides describes destruction of the soul as the ultimate punishment. For the Egyptians, too, "dying a second time in the realm of the dead" was the ultimate punishment; see Siegfried Morenz, *Egyptian Religion* (trans. Ann E. Keep; Ithaca, N.Y.: Cornell University Press, 1973), 207: "the second death may apply in particular to the soul, since the body has already died during the first death: 'Not to die a second time on the part of the ba of a man.'"

[23] Alfrink, "L'expression נֶאֱסַף אֶל־עַמָּיו," 121–22, followed by Meyers, *Jewish Ossuaries*, 14. For comparative Semitic evidence bearing on the historical semantics of עמים, see Leonid Kogan, "Proto-Semitic Lexicon," in *The Semitic Languages: An International Handbook* (ed. Stefan Weninger; Handbücher zur Sprach- und Kommunikationswissenschaft 36; Berlin: De Gruyter Mouton, 2012), 235. The evidence suggests that, in Proto-West Semitic, the set of relatives denoted by **ʿamm-* included grandfathers and uncles. Additional details can perhaps be gleaned from an Akkadian prayer dating to the first Babylonian dynasty, discussed in Karel van der Toorn, "Dead That Are Slow to Depart: Evidence for Ancestor Rituals in Mesopotamia," in *In Remembrance of Me: Feasting with the Dead in the Ancient Middle East* (ed. Virginia Rimmer Herrmann and J. David Schloen; Chicago: Oriental Institute of the University of Chicago, 2014), 82–84. The prayer, recited by the paterfamilias (the eldest son), asks the moon-god to release three generations of relatives from the underworld so that they can join a feast. "The paterfamilias begins with the name of his great-grandfather (including the name of *his* father); the names of his grand-uncles and his own grandfather follow; the next names are his uncles' and finally his father's" (ibid., 84). See also C. L. Seow, "Am עם," in *DDD*, 25a: "In a Kassite king-list, Amorite *ḫammu* [= *ʿammu*] is interpreted as *kimtum* 'family, kin.'"

11

Afterthoughts on the Afterlife of the Soul

In the previous chapter, we saw that Abraham, Isaac, Jacob, Aaron, and Moses are said to have been "brought in to their kinsmen" at death. Since the texts make clear that this occurred before interment, they must be speaking of a reunion of souls/spirits. But where did the reunion take place? For most scholars, the answer is simple: Sheol.[1] In my view, the matter needs more thought, because the evidence bearing on this question is fragmentary and seemingly contradictory. There are certainly many verses that speak of the dead in the underworld—in the grave and/or Sheol. But, as we have seen, there are also verses that point in the opposite direction—verses that speak of the רוח returning to God, who bestowed it (Qoh 12:7),[2] and of the רוח being brought in by God to himself (Job 34:14), that is, to a divine abode in heaven. Moreover, the conventional wisdom has a flaw that scholars have ignored. We have already seen that the phrase וַיֵּאָסֶף אֶל־עַמָּיו always *precedes* the phrase וַיִּקְבְּרוּ אתו, whenever they both appear (Gen 25:8–9; 35:29; and 49:33–50:13).[3] It must, there-

[1] See chapter 10, n. 18 above and at chapter 10, n. 21 above.

[2] According to the targum ad loc., this verse refers to the soul returning to God to stand trial (למקם בדינא). However, Josephus (*J.W.* 3.8.5 §§372–74) is probably closer to the conception that underlies the verse when, in attempting to dissuade his men from committing suicide, he refers to the soul as θεοῦ μοῖρα τοῖς σώμασιν ἐνοικίζεται . . . τὴν παρακαταθήκην τοῦ θεοῦ "a portion of the Deity housed in our bodies . . . the deposit entrusted by God" (ibid., §372)—a deposit that is to be returned ὅταν ὁ δοὺς κομίσασθαι θέλῃ "when the depositor is pleased to reclaim it" (ibid., §374); see *Josephus in Nine Volumes*, 2:680–81 with slight changes.

[3] See at chapter 10, n. 7 above.

fore, refer to something that happens to the deceased *before* burial.[4] This is possible only if the bipartite נפש is separable from the body. Driver, for example, assumes that, while the corpse is still awaiting interment, the נפש leaves for the underworld.[5] But this assumption is counterintuitive. If the grave where the body is buried is part of Sheol—as many scholars, following J. Pedersen,[6] believe—or even on the way to Sheol,[7] it is difficult to understand why the נפש would feel the need to part company with the body before arriving at their common destination. The only plausible alternative, in my view, is that Gen 25:8–9; 35:29; and 49:33–50:13 are to be understood, in the light of Job 34:14 and Qoh 12:7, as referring to the initial reunion of the bipartite נפש with its kinsmen *in heaven*.

What are we to make of all this? Are we to conceive of Jacob reunited with his kinsmen in heaven (Gen 49:33–50:13) or in the underworld (Gen 37:35)? Must these seemingly contradictory conceptions be assigned to different periods? Is diachronic explanation the only option here, as many would insist?[8] In this case, I believe

---

[4] See at chapter 10, n. 6 (as well as n. 13) above.

[5] See at chapter 10, n. 17 above.

[6] Johannes Pedersen, *Israel: Its Life and Culture* (2 vols.; London: Oxford University Press, 1926–1940), 1:461–62. The suggestion that every grave is part of Sheol is generally attributed to Pedersen today, but, as shown by Spronk (*Beatific Afterlife*, 67–68), it is found in the work of earlier scholars going back at least as far as the middle of the nineteenth century. For Driver's dissenting view, viz., that the grave is located in "the world above," see at chapter 10, n. 17 above.

[7] So Daniel Faivre, *Vivre et mourir dans l'ancien Israël: Anthropologie biblique de la Vie et de la Mort* (Paris: L'Harmattan, 1998), 148.

[8] For a critique of synchronic analysis of biblical ideas about the afterlife, see Mark S. Smith and Elizabeth M. Bloch-Smith, "Death and the Afterlife in Ugarit and Israel," *JAOS* 108 (1988): 281–83. In my view, we need to give equal time to the weaknesses of diachronic analysis of biblical religion. First and foremost among them is heavy reliance on arguments from silence—arguments that are fallacious unless certain strict conditions are met. Such arguments are at the core of claims that a given biblical idea, prohibition, or the like must have originated during a certain period because there is no mention of it before that. Claims of this type have proven to be very seductive to cautious scholars (despite the formulation with "must have" instead of "may have"), and they have achieved widespread acceptance in the field of biblical studies. But

that it is possible—and perhaps even preferable—to provide a synchronic explanation, even if it is only partial and conjectural. Such an explanation should, in my view, be based on four foundations: biblical literature, other ancient Near Eastern sources, archaeological sources, and rabbinic sources (concerning funerary practice and the ideas associated with it). It is important to ensure that every detail of the explanation be based on several of these foundations.

A good place to begin is funerary practice. Palestinian Jews of the Roman period practiced secondary burial—gathering bones and reburying them. This practice, also known as *ossilegium* (= MH ליקוט עצמות), is discussed here and there in rabbinic literature, e.g., נתאכל הבשר היו מלקטים את העצמות "when the flesh was consumed, they would gather the bones" (*m. Sanh.* 6:6, according to MS Parma).[9] A *baraita* preserved in the Palestinian Talmud (*y. Moʿed Qaṭ.* 1.5.80c; *y. Sanh.* 6.10.23d) has the aforementioned clause (without היו) preceded by: בראשונה היו קוברים אותם במהמורות "at first[10] they would bury them in pits." These pits were decomposition pits, used for primary burial until the corpse was reduced to bones.

Is there any mention of such pits in the Hebrew Bible and/or other ancient Near Eastern sources? As noted already by David Qimḥi in his commentary to Psalms, the term used in the *baraita,* מהמ(ו)רות, appears in בְּמַהֲמֹרוֹת בַּל־יָקוּמוּ "(may He make them fall) into pits from which they cannot get up" (Ps 140:11). Later scholars compared מהמרות עמוקות "deep pits" (Ben Sira 12:6) and Ugaritic *l yrt b npš bn ilm mt, b mhmrt ydd il* (*KTU/CAT* 1.5 I 6–8). The meaning of the latter appears to be something like: "Would that you would go

---

that does not make them any less logically precarious, especially given the nature of our sources. As noted by Osborne ("Secondary Mortuary Practice," 43), "it is important to realize that the Hebrew Bible was not written with the needs of future sociological interpretation in the minds of its authors, and thus preserves only a small portion of what was theologically and socially necessary to ancient Judahite culture."

[9] *Mishna Codex Parma (De Rossi 138),* 200b, lines 1–2. For a recent discussion of this and other passages, see Beth A. Berkowitz, *Execution and Invention: Death Penalty Discourse in Early Rabbinic and Christian Cultures* (New York: Oxford University Press, 2006), 128–35, 263–69 (with literature).

[10] Either in the sense of "originally" (signaling a change of practice) or in the sense of "first" (signaling a two-step procedure, as in Deut 13:10).

down into the throat of divine Môt, into the pit of the beloved of Il."[11] It is not clear whether מהמרת had the specific meaning "decomposition pit" (in addition to "burial pit") already in the biblical period, but there does seem to have been another term with that meaning: שַׁחַת בְּלִי (Isa 38:17).[12] And if the phrase בְּאֵר שַׁחַת means "well/pit of

---

[11] For the meaning of מהמרות/*mhmrt* assumed here, see H. L. Ginsberg, "Ugaritic Myths, Epics, and Legends," in *ANET*, 138b ("pit"); Saul Lieberman, תוספתא כפשוטה: באור ארוך לתוספתא (10 vols.; New York: Jewish Theological Seminary of America, 1955–), 5:1235 ("grave pit"); U. Cassuto, "Baal and Mot in the Ugaritic Texts," *IEJ* 12 (1962): 81 ("deep pit"); Moshe Held, "Pits and Pitfalls in Akkadian and Biblical Hebrew," *JANES* 5 (1973): 188 ("pit" or "grave"); Harold R. (Chaim) Cohen, *Biblical Hapax Legomena in the Light of Akkadian and Ugaritic* (SBLDS 37; Missoula, Mont.: Scholars Press, 1978), 121 ("pit, grave"); and Joseph Patrich, קבורה ראשונה קברים ונוהגי קבורה בארץ־ישראל בעת על־פי מקורות חז״ל — לביאורם של מונחים, in העתיקה (ed. Itamar Singer; Jerusalem: Yad Izhak Ben-Zvi, 1994), 193–94 ("grave pit dug in earth or hewn in rock"). If so, the idea may be that a deep hole in the ground, serving as a grave pit, is Mot's throat (cf. Sheol's throat in Isa 5:14 and Hab 2:5) through which the dead are swallowed. If our noun is related to the Arabic verb *hamara* "pour (rain, tears, etc.)," as many scholars assume, its original meaning may have been "cistern"; however, according to Held (loc. cit.), the Arabic etymology "is highly improbable."

[12] The phrase is rendered "rotting pit" by GWT. This interpretation of the phrase goes back to David Qimḥi. He based it on the earlier recognition (reflected already in Saadia Gaon's Arabic translation, if not earlier) that בְּלִי in this verse is the segolate verbal noun from the root ב-ל-י "wear out, waste away," just as בְּכִי and רְעִי are the segolate verbal nouns from the roots ב-כ-י "weep" and ר-ע-י "graze" respectively. The root ב-ל-י and its cognates are used of the gradual deterioration of human flesh in a number of Semitic languages; for Hebrew, see Gen 18:2; Ps 49:15 (causative *piʿel*, with Sheol as the subject), Job 13:28; Lam 3:4; for Syriac, see n. 37 below; for Judeo-Arabic, see the passage from Saadia Gaon, ספר הנבחר באמונות ובדעות cited in n. 17 below. The reading of 1QIsa[a] is controversial. At least one scholar reads כלי instead of בלי; see Blenkinsopp, *Isaiah 1–39*, 481 note z. But the accepted reading is כלו; see Eduard Yechezkel Kutscher, הלשון והרקע הלשוני של מגילת ישעיהו השלמה ממגילות ים המלח (Jerusalem: Magnes, 1959), 187–88; ספר ישעיהו (ed. Moshe H. Goshen-Gottstein; 3 vols.; Jerusalem: Magnes, 1975–1981), 2:169; *The Great Isaiah Scroll (1QIsa[a]): A New Edition* (ed. Donald W. Parry and Elisha Qimron; STDJ 32; Leiden: Brill, 1999), 65, line 9; *Qumran Cave 1.II: The Isaiah Scrolls* (DJD 32; ed. Eugene

decomposition/decay," as some believe,[13] it is at least possible that it refers to something similar.

In addition to this textual evidence, there is archaeological evidence of secondary burial going back to the Neolithic period in the southern Levant and the rest of the ancient Near East.[14] Tombs from Iron Age Israel have a "bone repository," a depression or pit serving as a communal ossuary.[15] The most recent study concludes that "the archaeological and textual evidence . . . combine to provide a compelling case for the existence of a robust secondary mortuary practice in ancient Judah."[16]

The rabbinic practice of *ossilegium* cannot be separated from rabbinic ideas about the afterlife of the soul. According to the Talmud (*b. Šabb.* 152b–153a), decomposition of the flesh after twelve months triggers not only a reburial of the bones but also a change in the behavior of the soul:

> כל שנים עשר חדש גופו קיים, ונשמתו עולה ויורדת; לאחר שנים עשר חדש הגוף בטל, ונשמתו עולה, ושוב אינה יורדת.
>
> For the entire twelve months (after death), his body remains in existence and his soul ascends and descends; after twelve months, the body ceases to exist, and his soul ascends, never to descend again.[17]

Ulrich and Peter W. Flint; Oxford: Clarendon, 2010), part 1, p. 64, line 9. I am indebted to Elisha Qimron for many of these references.

[13] Tromp, *Primitive Conceptions*, 71, citing J. van der Ploeg's rendering and evidence from Qumran; and Othmar Keel, *The Symbolism of the Biblical World: Ancient Near Eastern Iconography and the Book of Psalms* (trans. Timothy J. Hallett; New York: Seabury, 1978), 66.

[14] Eric M. Meyers, "Secondary Burials in Palestine," *BA* 33 (1970): 2–29.

[15] Meyers, *Jewish Ossuaries*, 5–7, 9, 14; Bloch-Smith, *Judahite Burial Practices*, 36–37, 42 (with 42–43 n. 1); Barkay, קברים, 110–12.

[16] Osborne, "Secondary Mortuary Practice," 46.

[17] See the discussion of Saul Lieberman, "Some Aspects of After Life in Early Rabbinic Literature," in *Harry Austryn Wolfson Jubilee Volume on the Occasion of His Seventy-Fifth Birthday* (ed. Saul Lieberman; 2 vols.; Jerusalem, 1965), 2:509–12 (reprinted in Saul Lieberman, *Texts and Studies* [New York: Ktav, 1974], 249–52). Cf. Saadia Gaon, ספר הנבחר באמונות ובדעות (ed. Yosef Qafiḥ; Jerusalem: Sura; New York: Yeshiva University, 1969), 212b, lines 13–14, 23–24 = Saadia Gaon, *The Book of Beliefs and Opinions* (trans. Samuel Rosenblatt; New Haven: Yale University Press, 1948), 257:

According to the Tosefta (*Sanh.* 13:4 and the parallel in *b. Roš Haš.* 17a), souls sentenced to annihilation spend the twelve months confined to the underworld:

> פושעי ישראל בגופן פושעי אומות העולם בגופן יורדין לגיהנם ונידונין בה שנים עשר חודש ולאחר שנים עשר חודש נפשותן (צ״ל נפשן) כלה וגופן נשרף וגיהנם פולטתן ונעשין אפר והרוח זורה אותן ומפזרתן תחת כפות רגלי הצדיקים. . . .
>
> Jews who sin with their bodies and gentiles who sin with their bodies go down to Gehinnom and are punished there for twelve months. After twelve months, their soul perishes, their body is burned up, Gehinnom disgorges them, they turn into ash, and the wind blows them away and scatters them under the soles of the feet of the righteous. . . .

We seem to be dealing with a twelve-month transitional period during which most souls, after the initial reunion with their kinsmen in heaven, oscillate between the body and heaven.[18] In chapter 9, I speculated that the נפש was viewed as consisting of two components: (1) the נפש הבשר, a bodily component, and (2) the רוח, a spiritual component bestowed by God. If so, the soul's oscillation after death may have been understood as the result of the two components pulling in opposite directions—the נפש הבשר toward the body and the רוח toward heaven. And the termination of the oscillation after a year may have been seen as the result of the withering away of the נפש הבשר together with the body—a process that may be alluded to in וְאַתָּה חָשַׁקְתָּ נַפְשִׁי מִשַּׁחַת בְּלִי "You saved my נפש from the decomposition pit" (Isa 38:17).[19] Matthew J. Suriano finds

---

ת׳ם אקול ואי שי יכון חאלהא בעד כ׳רוג׳הא מן אלג׳סם. . . . ופי אול זמאן אלמפארקה תקים מדה לא תסתקר מקרהא אלי אן יבלי אלג׳סם "Next I shall put the question: 'But what is the status of the soul after its exit from the body?' . . . During the first period after its separation from the body . . . the soul exists for a while without a fixed abode until the body has decomposed."

[18] A slightly different interpretation is required if we factor in the assertion in several midrashic sources that the soul ascends to heaven every night when its owner is asleep and returns to the body in the morning when its owner awakens; see chapter 6, nn. 6–8 above. In that case, the transitional period has the appearance of a one-year extension of the soul's practice during life.

[19] The literal meaning may be: "You grasped my נפש (taking/keeping it) out of/away from the rotting pit." Cf. Ugaritic *ḥ-š-k* "grasp" (with plain,

a reference to this process in Job 19: "The idea that stands behind vv. 26–27 is one of a processual death, where the natural decay of the flesh reflects the gradual diminution of the soul."[20] It is presumably the inception of this fading process, affecting the נפש הבשר but not the רוח, that is meant when the Bible speaks of the נפש dying in Num 23:10; Judg 16:30; and Job 36:14.[21]

The Talmud's depiction of the soul's oscillation has an important Egyptian parallel. The ascension of the deceased's *ba* to heaven (*prt r pt*) during the day and its return to the corpse at night is one of the fundamental themes of Egyptian mortuary literature, appearing already in the Pyramid Texts and the Coffin Texts, not to mention the *Book of the Dead*.[22] The parallel, of course, is not complete. In Egypt, the daily commute of the soul did not end after twelve months, for the obvious reason that the embalmed Egyptian corpses did not decompose after twelve months. And in Egypt, the ascension of the soul to heaven, the domain of the sun-god Re, had to take place during the day in order "to assure the deceased of all the benefits of life under the rays of the sun (*prt m hrw* 'to come forth by day')."[23] The Talmud does not specify the frequency of the soul's ascension, but if it occurred once a day, it may well have done so at night.[24] These differences are easily explained; as such, they do not negate the importance of this parallel in assessing the antiquity of this rabbinic belief.

In short, if the rabbinic practice of *ossilegium* goes back to the Iron Age, as archaeologists believe, then it may be legitimate to assume that the rabbinic beliefs associated with that practice go back to the Iron Age as well. In the words of Meyers:

> In sum, by the time ossuaries were in wide usage amongst the Jews, from the middle of the first century B.C.E. and until the fourth century C.E., secondary burial had a rather elaborate theology to go along with it. The roots of that theology are to be

---

unemphatic *k*) in Olmo Lete and Sanmartín, *Dictionary of the Ugaritic Language*, 375, s.v.

[20] Suriano, "Death," 56 n. 26.

[21] See also at chapter 8, n. 25 above.

[22] Žabkar, *Ba Concept*, 126–28.

[23] Ibid., 126–27.

[24] See n. 18 above.

> found in biblical and tannaitic literature and are often clarified by the later talmudic material.[25]

Similarly, Suriano writes:

> The practice of secondary rites continued in the southern Levant during the late first millennium, despite the fact that the bench tomb plan fell out of use by the end of the Persian period. . . . During the early Roman period, the use of bone boxes (or ossuaries) replaced the earlier repositories and charnel rooms in the practice of collective burial. Thus, the ideological significance of secondary rites and collective burials remained in place throughout the first millennium, despite the fact that its specific practice may have changed over time.[26]

Such ideological continuity may well encompass the rabbinic belief in what we may call "transitional soul oscillation" (in contrast to the *eternal* soul oscillation of the Egyptians). This belief provides a coherent explanation for the contradictory snippets of information that the Hebrew Bible provides about the location of souls in the afterlife. Indeed, the Talmud itself (*b. Šabb.* 152b) appeals to it in responding to the sectarian[27] who asked: אמריתו נשמתן של צדיקים גנוזות תחת כסא הכבוד; אובא טמיא[28] היכי[29] אסקיה לשמואל בנגידא? "you say

---

[25] Meyers, "Theological Implications," 113 = Meyers, *Jewish Ossuaries*, 85. For interpretations of secondary burial, see Nissan Rubin, הקבורה השנייה בארץ־ישראל בתקופת המשנה והתלמוד — הצעה למודל שיטתי לקשר שבין קברים ונוהגי קבורה בארץ־ישראל בעת העתיקה, in המבנה החברתי לדרכי הטיפול במת (ed. Itamar Singer; Jerusalem: Yad Izhak Ben-Zvi, 1994), 248–69; Berkowitz, *Execution*, 132–33, 267–68; and Osborne, "Secondary Mortuary Practice," 35–53.

[26] Suriano, "Death," 58. For a different view, see L. Y. Rahmani, *A Catalogue of Jewish Ossuaries in the Collections of the State of Israel* (Jerusalem: Israel Antiquities Authority, 1994), 53–55.

[27] The Vilna edition has צדוקי "Sadducee," a reading that is presumably the product of censorship but, nevertheless, captures the intent (see n. 30 below); all of the other witnesses in the Lieberman online database have מינא or מינאה "sectarian, heretic."

[28] For the theory that טמיא is a noun derived from Akk. *eṭemmū* "spirits of the dead," see Sokoloff, *Dictionary of Jewish Babylonian Aramaic*, 506a, s.v. טמא. If so, it is in apposition to אובא.

[29] This is the reading of all witnesses in the online Talmudic Text

that the souls of the righteous are hidden away under the Throne of Glory (in heaven); (if so,) how did the necromancer *raise up* Samuel through necromancy?"[30]

My conjecture is also capable of explaining why the denizens of Sheol are normally called רפאים rather than נפשות[31] or רוחות. According to the rabbis, virtually all souls spend part of their time in the underworld for twelve months, as long as the flesh exists. After that, they either make their final trip to heaven or they are annihilated. If there was a belief that the soul has two components, as suggested above, there may well have been an associated belief that, at the end of the twelve-month transitional period, the faded נפש הבשר becomes detached from the רוח and joins a/the קְהַל רְפָאִים "assembly of Rephaim" (Prov 21:16) in the darkness of Sheol (Ps 49:19–20; 88:11–13; Job 17:13), while the רוח returns to God and remains permanently in heaven (Num 16:22; Ps 104:29; Job 34:14; Qoh 12:7). It is widely accepted today that one of the meanings of the Hebrew term רפאים is the same as that of the Phoenician term רפאם, viz., "*manes*, shades."[32] If so, a/the קהל רפאים would appear to be a collective of shades. Parallels between the soul/spirit and the body have been noted in cultures that practice secondary burial elsewhere in the world:

> Upon final burial a profound change occurs to the deceased's spirit. No longer in isolation, the soul joins its ancestors and becomes itself an ancestor when the bones of the deceased are placed in the collective family burial.[33]

Indeed, it has been conjectured that the Mesopotamian *eṭemmu*, too, undergoes a transformation after death—that it "gradually

---

Databank (Saul Lieberman Institute) except for the Vilna edition, which reads היכא "where."

[30] The question is reminiscent of Josephus's description (*J.W.* 2.8.14 §165) of the Sadducees: ψυχῆς τε τὴν διαμονὴν καὶ τὰς καθ' ᾅδου τιμωρίας καὶ τιμὰς ἀναιροῦσιν "as for the persistence of the soul after death, penalties in the underworld, and rewards, they will have none of them" (*Josephus* [Thackeray, LCL] 2:386–87).

[31] But see at chapter 13, nn. 4–7 below.

[32] See *DNWSI* 2:1081–82, s.v. *rp*ʾ$_2$, especially the correspondence ארפאם = M(anibus) "shades" in *KAI* no. 117 (line 1), a Latin-Punic bilingual.

[33] Osborne, "Secondary Mortuary Practice," 39.

loses individuality until it becomes part of the collectivity of the ancestors."[34]

This idea may help to explain a key passage in Job's depiction of death, a passage that has puzzled exegetes since antiquity: וְגֶבֶר יָמוּת וַיֶּחֱלָשׁ וַיִּגְוַע אָדָם וְאַיּוֹ "but a man dies and becomes feeble; a human expires and where is he?" (Job 14:10). The renderings of וַיֶּחֱלָשׁ in the Aramaic versions are frequently, but unjustifiably, dismissed[35] or ignored. The targum renders וגברא ימות ויתמקמק "but a man dies and wastes away"; the Peshiṭta has ܘܓܒܪܐ ܢܡܘܬ ܘܢܚܠܐ with precisely the same meaning.[36] Both use verbs that are used elsewhere to denote the rotting of human flesh.[37] Indeed, the Hebrew cognate of the Syriac verb used by the Peshiṭta appears fewer than a dozen verses earlier in the biblical text: וְהוּא כְּרָקָב יִבְלֶה כְּבֶגֶד אֲכָלוֹ עָשׁ "and he wastes away like a rotten thing, like a garment eaten by moths" (Job 13:28).

David J. A. Clines does not mention these renderings, but he, too, believes that the position of וַיֶּחֱלָשׁ after יָמוּת suggests that it refers to something that occurs *after* death:

> In contrast to the fate of a tree is the fate of humankind: the person that is felled (to use the imagery of v 7) by death has no hope, but is "weak." The verb is חלש which means "be weak" (cf. Joel 4:10

---

[34] Abusch, "Ghost," 372. For Abusch, the transformation results from the decay of memory rather than the decay of flesh; see ibid., 373; and his "Etemmu אטים," in *DDD*, 309b. For the transformation from soul to ghost in other cultures, see Karl R. Wernhart, "Ethnische Seelenkonzepte," in *Der Begriff der Seele in der Religionswissenschaft* (ed. Johann Figl and Hans-Dieter Klein; Würzburg: Königshausen & Neumann, 2002), 56–57.

[35] See Gösta Rignell, *The Peshitta to the Book of Job: Critically Investigated with Introduction, Translation, Commentary and Summary* (ed. Karl-Erik Rignell; Kristianstad: Monitor, 1994), 110: "incorrectly rendered by P."

[36] David M. Stec, *The Text of the Targum of Job: An Introduction and Critical Edition* (AGJU 20; Leiden: Brill, 1994), 94*; *The Old Testament in Syriac according to the Peshiṭta Version* (ed. Peshiṭta Institute; Leiden: Brill, 1972–), part II, fascicle Ia (Job), 18.

[37] For the meaning of Targumic Aramaic יתמקמק, cf. MH נימוק (*Ma'agarim*, s.v. מ-ק-ק *nifʿal*), used of the rotting of flesh after death (עַד שֶׁיִּמּוֹק הַבָּשָׂר "until the flesh rots" in *m. Nid.* 10:4, etc.), fetal resorption, the rotting of fruit, etc. For Syriac ܚܠܐ, used of a corpse with the meaning "rot," see Sokoloff, *Syriac Lexicon*, 156a, s.v. ܚܠ. See also n. 12 above.

> [3:10] for חַלָּשׁ contrasted with גִּבּוֹר "mighty"), not "be prostrate" (cf. RSV, NIV, "is laid low") and it has seemed strange to some that first the person "dies," and thereafter is "weak." Gordis thinks it is the figure of *hysteron proteron*,[[38]] the verbs being reversed in sense, "man dies and grows faint" signifying "man grows faint and dies." Others have suggested a different meaning for חלש, such as "snatch away" or "disappear" . . . , and others again emend the verb to yield the meaning "pass away" or "is driven away." These suggestions can be set on one side when it is realized that חלש refers to human loss of power after death as contrasted with the tree's continuing vitality after it is cut down,[[39]] and that the stress is on this verb, not upon "dies." M. Dahood likewise comments that "the poet is evoking the motif of Sheol as the dwelling of weaklings, those of diminished vigor."[40]

In my opinion, the enfeeblement of the body goes hand in hand with the enfeeblement of the נפש הבשר, and וַיֶּחֱלָשׁ refers to both.[41]

The rest of Job's depiction of death, esp. 14:20–22, is also very instructive:

20. תִּתְקְפֵהוּ לָנֶצַח וַיַּהֲלֹךְ מְשַׁנֶּה פָנָיו וַתְּשַׁלְּחֵהוּ׃
21. יִכְבְּדוּ בָנָיו וְלֹא יֵדָע וְיִצְעֲרוּ וְלֹא־יָבִין לָמוֹ׃
22. אַךְ־בְּשָׂרוֹ עָלָיו יִכְאָב וְנַפְשׁוֹ עָלָיו תֶּאֱבָל׃

20. You overpower him permanently and he departs;
You alter his visage and send him away.
21. His sons are honored but he does not know it;
they are humbled but he does not discern them.
22. Rather it is for *himself* that his flesh feels pain;
and for *himself* that his נפש feels grief.[42]

---

[38] For *hysteron proteron* and *anastrophe*, see Richard C. Steiner, "*Muqdam u-Meʾuḥar* and *Muqaddam wa-Muʾaḫḫar*: On The History of Some Hebrew and Arabic Terms for *Hysteron Proteron* and *Anastrophe*," *JNES* 66 (2007): 33–45.

[39] Cf. Rashi ad loc.: וְגֶבֶר יָמוּת וַיֶּחֱלָשׁ - עץ יש לו תקוה אבל גבר ימות ולא יחליף "but a man dies and becomes feeble—a tree has hope, but a man dies and does not regenerate."

[40] David J. A. Clines, *Job 1–20* (WBC 17; Dallas: Word Books, 1989), 328–29.

[41] See at nn. 19–20 above.

[42] See Dhorme, *Commentary*, 206: "his flesh is grieved only for himself, his soul laments only over himself." For rabbinic exegesis of this passage,

The second half of v. 20 appears to refer to the stage after death when the face becomes unrecognizable. According to the rabbis, who lived, of course, in a hot climate without refrigeration, this occurs after three days.[43] Palestinian Jewish sources of the Byzantine period describe the soul as hovering above the body until that change occurs and it becomes certain that the person is gone for good: כל תלתא יומין נפשא טייסא על גופא סבירה דהיא חזרה לגביה כיון דהיא חמייא דאישתני זיויהון[44] דאפוי היא שבקא ליה ואזלה לה "for the entire three days (after death), the soul flies over the body thinking that she will return to it; when she sees that its facial features have changed, she leaves it and goes on her way" (*y. Moʿed Qaṭ.* 3.5.82b).[45]

For our purposes, the most important part of this passage is v. 22, which ascribes a נפש to a person who is dead and buried.[46] Since it also ascribes flesh to that person, it supports our contention that the soul continues to be associated with the body as long as it has flesh.[47]

---

according to which the deceased feels needle-like pricks from maggots as long as the flesh remains, see *b. Ber. 18b* and *Šabb.* 13b, 152b (together with Isa 66:24). For the contrast between flesh and נפש, see the discussion of מִנֶּפֶשׁ וְעַד־בָּשָׂר יְכַלֶּה (Isa 10:18) in chapter 8 above.

[43] See *m. Yebam.* 16:3; and Margulies, מדרש ויקרא רבה, 398, lines 4–5, 875.

[44] This should probably read דאישתני זיווהון although Biblical Aramaic shows that דאישתנו זיויהון is also possible.

[45] Cf. *y. Yebam.* 16.3.15c; Theodor and Albeck, מדרש בראשית רבא, 1290, lines 4–5; Margulies, מדרש ויקרא רבה, appendix (שרידי ויקרא מגניזת מצרים) 70 bot. *Ba*s that hover over bodies (cf. נפשא טייסא על גופא) or descend to the burial chamber through a vertical shaft (cf. נשמתו עולה ויורדת) are depicted in illustrated manuscripts of the *Book of the Dead* from ancient Egypt; see Taylor, *Journey,* 56, 90–91, 101, 104, 131. One of these images, showing a *ba* hovering over a body, can be seen at http://www.britishmuseum.org/research/collection_online/collection_object_details/collection_image_gallery.aspx?partid=1&assetid=819318&objectid=114834.

[46] See Lods, *La croyance,* 60–61 and Dhorme, *Commentary,* 206–7.

[47] Cf. Laurin, "Concept of Man as a Soul," 132: "After death the nephesh ceases to exist, lingering only so long as the body is a body (Job 14^{22}, Ec 12^{7})." This idea can be traced back to Schwally, *Das Leben,* 7: "But even if the *nephesh* does not leave [the body] immediately at the onset of death, this must happen one day, namely, as soon as the body decays into mold and dust." See also Robert Wenning, "'Medien' in der Bestattungskultur im eisenzeitlichen Juda?" in *Medien im antiken Palästina:*

We may also note that the Talmud (*b. Šabb.* 152b) cites these words of Job in support of the view that . . . כל שאומרים בפני המת יודע עד שיתאכל הבשר "the dead know all that is said in their presence . . . until the flesh is consumed." Rashi clarifies the Talmud's exegesis of the verse: וְנַפְשׁוֹ עָלָיו תֶּאֱבָל — כל זמן שיש לו בשר יש לו לנפש צד חיות להבין "his נפש mourns for him—as long as he has flesh, his נפש has an aspect of vitality (sufficient) for understanding."

These inferences from Job 14:22 are remarkably similar to the inferences drawn by Robert E. Cooley from the excavation of Dothan Tomb 1, a Canaanite family tomb of the Late Bronze Age containing 288 skeletons:

> At the time of burial, scrupulous care was exercised in the placement of the corpse and in the arrangement of tomb equipment. This suggests that the body had to be treated with respect on this particular occasion. Once the body was transformed into a pile of bones it was treated with little respect and regard. It was the normal practice to sweep aside the bones and equipment into a heap, destroying both in the process, to make room for subsequent burials. Apparently it was believed that the deceased was conscious of feeling and actually lived in the tomb as long as the flesh was in existence. Therefore, it needed food, drink and personal supplies that were possessions in life. Once the flesh had disappeared the deceased had arrived in the netherworld and no longer needed the mortuary equipment. . . . The end of the trip had been accomplished as indicated by the complete decay of the flesh.[48]

It should be emphasized that Cooley makes no mention of Job 14:22 when he asserts that "it was believed that the deceased was conscious of feeling." His assertion appears to be based purely on the archaeological evidence.

There are other striking parallels between Cooley's article and this chapter, despite the fact that I was completely unaware of his

---

Materielle Kommunikation und Medialität als Thema der Palästinaarchäologie (ed. Christian Frevel; FAT 2/11; Tübingen: Mohr Siebeck, 2005), 129–30.

[48] Robert E. Cooley, "Gathered to His People: A Study of a Dothan Family Tomb," in *The Living and Active Word of God: Studies in Honor of Samuel J. Schultz* (ed. Morris Inch and Ronald Youngblood; Winona Lake, Ind.: Eisenbrauns, 1983), 53.

article until I had almost finished proofreading this monograph. He, too, speaks of "a transitional phase for the deceased: the time required for the flesh to decompose. . . ."[49] And he, too, asserts that "the transition period terminated with the incorporation of the deceased into the world of the dead."[50] I was also unaware of Robert Wenning's argument for the existence of such a period. According to him, comparison between the standard household inventory and the grave inventory shows that the latter was intended only "for the transitional phase of [the deceased's] 'personal presence,' i.e., until the decomposition of the corpse."[51] Thus, the archaeological evidence provides independent confirmation of the textual evidence.

---

[49] Cooley, "Gathered," 58. Cf. at nn. 17 and 18 above.

[50] Ibid. Cf. the "twelve-month transitional period" discussed after n. 31 above.

[51] Wenning, "Medien," 129–30.

12

Semantic Structure

I have argued in this monograph that the Hebrew term נפש has the meaning "soul" in addition to "person," "self," etc. This combination of meanings is not uncommon in Semitic. For example, Classical Arabic *nafs* has the meanings "soul," "person," "self," "life breath," "blood," "body";[1] Sabaic *nafs*[1], the meanings "soul," "person," "self," and "life";[2] and Ethiopic *nafs*, the meanings "soul, spirit," "breath," "person," "self," and "life."[3] And Proto-Semitic **nap(i)š-* is believed to have had the meanings "soul," "vitality, life," "person, personality," and "self."[4] A similar phenomenon is attested in some Indo-European languages. Hittite *ištanza(n)-*, also written ZI-*(a)n-*, normally means "soul" (in the sense of an immortal essence separate from the body), but in later texts it has the meanings "person" and "self" as well.[5] Greek ψυχή originally referred to "a kind of free-soul" that was "associated with the breath," but by the end of the Archaic Age it had come to refer to one's self and the seat of one's emotions.[6]

---

[1] Lane, *Arabic-English Lexicon*, 2827–28, s.v.; Régis Blachère, "Note sur le substantif *nafs* 'souffle vital,' 'âme' dans le Coran," *Semitica* 1 (1948): 69–77.

[2] Beeston et al., *Sabaic Dictionary*, 93, s.v.

[3] W. Leslau, *Comparative Dictionary of Geʿez* (Wiesbaden: Harrassowitz, 1987), 389, s.v.

[4] Militarev and Kogan, *Semitic Etymological Dictionary*, 1:308.

[5] A. Kammenhuber, "Die hethitischen Vorstellungen von Seele und Leib, Herz und Leibesinnerem, Kopf und Person (I. Teil)," *ZA* 56 (1964): 150–212; Melchert, "Remarks on the Kuttamuwa Inscription," 6: "That the Hittites of Anatolia believed in an immortal soul separate from the body has been known for at least half a century."

[6] Bremmer, "Soul," 160–61.

In all of these cases, we find a word for "soul, spirit" used also of the person of which the soul is a part. This should not be viewed as problematic in any way. It is by no means unusual for a single term to denote both whole and part, a semantic phenomenon sometimes called "automeronymy" or "autoholonymy." For example, BH חדש can refer to an entire month or to part of a month, that is, the day of the new moon;[7] ארץ can refer to the entire earth or to part of the earth, that is, an individual land; and בשר can refer to the entire body or to part of the body, that is, the flesh.[8] Thus, it is perfectly natural that Hebrew נפש can be used in the sense of "person" in addition to the sense of "soul."

There is another, less common meaning of Hebrew נפש—the meaning "corpse"—that scholars have viewed as less natural. Claus Westermann writes that "the group of texts in which *n.* means a deceased or a corpse is difficult to explain because *n.* otherwise refers to vitality."[9] Norbert Kilwing agrees that "it seems somewhat surprising that the same word which the Hebrew language uses for 'life,' 'life force,' or 'living creatures' should at the same time mean 'corpse.'"[10]

Westermann's difficulty may arise from his belief that "the meaning 'life' for *n.* is attested more often, more densely, and more uniformly than the meaning 'soul'; the term would have been heard first and foremost in this sense. . . ."[11] In my view, this belief is wrong and—in a diachronic analysis—irrelevant as well. As noted above, one of the meanings of נפש is "body soul," a meaning that can easily develop into "corpse" by synecdoche.[12] Moreover, the semantic range of נפש may be compared to that of Akkadian *eṭemmu*. The latter refers to "part of [the human being that] is . . . immortal . . . , a

---

[7] See Steiner, "Vowel Syncope," 372–73 with nn. 39–41.

[8] For בשר referring to the whole body, see at chapter 8, nn. 28–36 above. In the case of בשר and חדש, the automeronymy is clearly the product of synecdoche, and I suggest that the meaning "person" developed out of the meaning "soul" by the same process. This suggestion is supported by Hittite, where the meaning "person" for *ištanza(n)-* is later than the meaning "soul" (see at n. 5 above).

[9] Westermann,"נֶפֶשׁ *nepeš* soul," 756 meaning 6.

[10] Kilwing, "נֶפֶשׁ und ΨΥΧΗ," 392.

[11] Westermann, "נֶפֶשׁ *nepeš* soul," 752 meaning 4.

[12] See at chapter 9, n. 9.

ghost which exists apparently during life as well as after death";[13] to "souls of former human beings . . . held to be immortal";[14] to "souls . . . believed to depart from the body at death."[15] Nevertheless, "in some contexts, it is spoken of as if it were identical with the corpse, as when *eṭemmu*s are described as 'sleeping' in their graves or lying about unburied."[16]

Let us turn now from the semantic range of the term נפש to the semantic relationship between the terms נפש and רוח. We have already seen that the two terms sometimes form a parallel pair in poetry, e.g., נַפְשִׁי אִוִּיתִיךָ בַּלַּיְלָה אַף־רוּחִי בְקִרְבִּי אֲשַׁחֲרֶךָּ "my נפש yearns [lit., my נפש I yearn] for You at night; my רוח, which is inside me, seeks [lit., my רוח . . . I seek] You at dawn" (Isa 26:9); אֲדַבְּרָה בְּצַר רוּחִי אָשִׂיחָה בְּמַר נַפְשִׁי "I shall speak in the anguish of my רוח, I shall complain in the bitterness of my נפש" (Job 7:11); and אֲשֶׁר בְּיָדוֹ נֶפֶשׁ כָּל־חָי וְרוּחַ כָּל־בְּשַׂר־אִישׁ "in His hand is the נפש of every living being and the רוח of all human flesh" (Job 12:10).[17] Alongside of this syntagmatic evidence, there is also paradigmatic evidence: the two terms interchange in a single environment, apparently without changing the meaning of the clause. A good example is the collocation of the two terms with the root ש-ו-ב, e.g., רוח in וַתָּשָׁב רוּחוֹ וַיֶּחִי "(he drank) and his רוח came back, and he revived" (Judg 15:19); וַתָּשָׁב רוּחוֹ אֵלָיו "(he ate,) and his רוח came back to him" (1 Sam 30:12); and נפש in וַתָּשָׁב נֶפֶשׁ־הַיֶּלֶד עַל־קִרְבּוֹ וַיֶּחִי "the נפש of the child (who had stopped breathing) came back inside him [lit., to his inside], and he revived" (1 Kgs 17:22); וְיָשִׁיבוּ אֶת־נַפְשָׁם "(they sought food for themselves) to make their נפש come back" (Lam 1:19). Assuming that there is no difference in meaning between וַתָּשָׁב רוּחוֹ וַיֶּחִי and וַתָּשָׁב נֶפֶשׁ־הַיֶּלֶד עַל־קִרְבּוֹ וַיֶּחִי, one could easily conclude from this evidence that נפש and

---

[13] Abusch, "Ghost," 373.

[14] Walter Farber, "Witchcraft, Magic, and Divination in Ancient Mesopotamia," in *CANE* 3:1898.

[15] Scurlock, "Soul Emplacements," 1.

[16] Scurlock, "Death," 1892. Cf. the meanings of Akkadian *napištu* ("life," "person," "body," "self," etc.) discussed by Horst Seebass, "נֶפֶשׁ *nepeš*," *TDOT* 9:501: "Important for the light it throws on OT usage is the meaning 'body, corpse' in 'The plain was too small for . . . their bodies (they ran out of land to bury them).'" See, however, Scurlock's claim ("Death and the Afterlife," 1892) that the "*eṭemmu* was a constituent element of the corpse."

[17] See chapter 9 above.

רוח were synonyms, as did some *midrashim* and some modern scholars.[18] Nevertheless, the relationship appears to be more complex.

In chapter 9, I conjectured that the רוח is one of two components of the נפש, the other being the נפש הבשר (Lev 17:11). If my conjecture is correct, the term רוח is, in many contexts, a meronym of the term נפש. This means that the relation between the things that they denote is one of part to whole.[19] It should be noted that such a conclusion would be perfectly compatible with the evidence just cited—both the syntagmatic evidence and the paradigmatic evidence. Let us first deal with the syntagmatic evidence from poetry. The term "semantic parallelism" covers a variety of relationships.[20] Take, for example, Ps 66:14 אֲשֶׁר־פָּצוּ שְׂפָתָי וְדִבֶּר־פִּי בַּצַּר־לִי "(vows) that my lips pronounced, that my mouth uttered in my distress," and Ps 144:1 הַמְלַמֵּד יָדַי לַקְרָב אֶצְבְּעוֹתַי לַמִּלְחָמָה "who trains my hands for battle, my fingers for warfare." Here, שׂפתים is a meronym of פה since the lips are a part of the mouth, and אצבעות is a meronym of ידים since the fingers are a part of the hands. As for the paradigmatic evidence from the apparent equivalence of וַתָּשָׁב רוּחוֹ וַיֶּחִי and וַתָּשָׁב נֶפֶשׁ־הַיֶּלֶד עַל־קִרְבּוֹ וַיֶּחִי, it should be obvious that when the נפש moves from point A to point B, the components of the נפש—the רוח and the נפש הבשר—do so as well, as long as they remain attached to each other.

---

[18] See David Zilber, נפש, נשמה ורוח, וזיקתן לבשר ורוח — במקרא ולאחריו, *Beth Mikra* 16 (1971): 318, 324. On the other hand, a midrash in *Lev. Rab.* (Margulies, מדרש ויקרא רבה, 740, lines 7–9) asserts that the נשמה communicates with the נפש while a person sleeps. Clearly the author did not consider the terms נפש and נשמה to be synonyms. A *baraita* in the Palestinian Talmud (*y. Kil.* 8.4.31c) goes further, implying that the terms נפש and נשמה are distinct not only from each other but also from רוח; see Nissan Rubin, *Time and Life Cycle in Talmud and Midrash: Socio-anthropological Perspectives* (Boston: Academic Studies Press, 2008), 131. For the claim that these three terms allude to distinct powers or faculties of the soul, see Saadia Gaon, ספר הנבחר באמונות ובדעות, 201, lines 3–12 = *The Book of Beliefs and Opinions* (trans. Samuel Rosenblatt; Yale Judaica Series 1; New Haven: Yale University Press, 1948), 243–44.

[19] More precisely, the prototypical human רוח is a part of the prototypical human נפש.

[20] See Stephen A. Geller, *Parallelism in Early Biblical Poetry* (HSM 20; Missoula, Mont.: Scholars Press, 1979), 31–38.

13

Alleged Evidence against the Existence of Disembodied נפשות

The passages in which a disembodied spirit of the dead is called by a name *other* than נפש were cited fifty years ago by Robert Laurin as evidence against the existence of disembodied נפשות:

> The *nephesh* cannot be separated from the body, any more than it can from the spirit.
>
> This can also be seen in the fact that the word *nephesh* is never used of a disembodied spirit or being after death; the inhabitants of Sheol are never called "souls". They are *rephaim*, "shades, ghosts," partial replicas of this life, "sunken beings" (as the root meaning suggests). But this shadowy existence, in which there is a certain resemblance to the earthly form (Ezk 32^{30}, Is 14^{9-11}, I Sam 28^{14}) and where there is a measure of consciousness without pain or bliss (Is 14^{9-11}, Job 3^{17-19}), is indicative of the unitary concept of man. Any sort of life, even in Sheol, must manifest itself in a bodily form or shape.[1]

There are two arguments here, neither one compelling. The first is an argument from silence, based on the premise that the inhabitants of Sheol are called רפאים—not to mention מתים, אלהים

[1] Laurin, "Concept of Man," 132. Cf. already George Foot Moore, *A Critical and Exegetical Commentary on Judges* (ICC; New York: Charles Scribner's Sons, 1895), 362: "There is nowhere a suggestion that the soul survives the man whose life it was; the inhabitants of the nether-world (*sheol*) are not *souls* but shades (*refaīm*, εἴδωλα)."

(1 Sam 28:13), אבות, אִטִּים (Isa 19:3; < Akkadian *eṭemmu*),[2] etc.—but not נפשות.[3] Laurin deduces from this premise that נפש cannot refer to a disembodied spirit of the dead. There is an element of truth here, but more needs to be said. There are, in fact, verses that speak of a person's נפש being rescued from (i.e., taken out of) Sheol, e.g., הֶעֱלִיתָ מִן־שְׁאוֹל נַפְשִׁי "You have brought my נפש up from Sheol" (Ps 30:4; cf. 1 Sam 2:6 and Job 7:9); and וְהִצַּלְתָּ נַפְשִׁי מִשְּׁאוֹל תַּחְתִּיָּה "and You have rescued my נפש from Sheol below"[4] (Ps 86:13).

How are the images in such verses to be interpreted? Are they relevant to our problem? These questions have been debated since the nineteenth century.[5] To my mind, the simplest interpretation is that these verses exhibit the type of hyperbole that we find in exclamations such as כֻּלָּנוּ מֵתִים "all of us are dead" (Exod 12:33) and כֻּלָּנוּ אָבָדְנוּ "all of us have perished" (Num 17:27). Indeed, such exclamations would seem to set the stage for subsequent reports of being rescued from Sheol. The feeling of gratitude that inspired

---

[2] We are probably dealing with a folk etymology here, based on a pronunciation of *eṭemmu/eṭimmu* as [iṭim] or the like. This form was reanalyzed as a plural, possibly under the influence of the native Hebrew word אִט/-אַט "gentleness." With a foreign word, the reanalysis of the final [im] as the plural ending is not surprising. Something similar happened with the final [im] of Israeli Hebrew [fílim] < English *film*. We may also compare English *cherry*, borrowed from Old North French *cherise* but shortened when the latter was taken to be a plural.

[3] The premise of this argument, viz., the claim that there are no נפשות in Sheol, can be traced back to Karl Grüneisen, *Der Ahnenkultus und die Urreligion Israels* (Halle a.S.: Max Niemeyer, 1900), 43–44. See also Schwab, *Der Begriff*, 40; Jacob et al., "ψυχή κτλ," 621; Kilwing, "נֶפֶשׁ und ΨΥΧΗ," 396; and Klaus Bieberstein, "Jenseits der Todesschwelle: Die Entstehung der Auferweckungshoffnungen in der alttestamentlich-frühjüdischen Literatur," in *Tod und Jenseits im alten Israel und in seiner Umwelt: Theologische, religionsgeschichtliche, archäologische und ikonographische Aspekte* (ed. Angelika Berlejung and Bernd Janowski; Forschungen zum Alten Testament 64; Tübingen: Mohr Siebeck, 2009), 427.

[4] Literally: "Sheol, which is below," taking תחתיה as a non-restrictive modifier of שאול with David Qimḥi ad loc. (cf. Isa 14:9, Prov 15:24, and LXX to Deut 32:22) rather than a restrictive one ("lowest Sheol").

[5] For a sample of the debate a century ago, see Grüneisen, *Der Ahnenkultus*, 43–44; and J. C. Matthes, "De doodenvereering bij Israël," *Theologisch Tijdschrift* 35 (1901), 332–33. For a more recent sample, see Kilwing, "נֶפֶשׁ und ΨΥΧΗ," 396; and Nutkowicz, *L'homme*, 249, 333.

these reports is expressed more soberly in a verse that speaks of a נפש dwelling in the silence of the grave/Sheol: לוּלֵי ה' עֶזְרָתָה לִּי כִּמְעַט שָׁכְנָה דוּמָה נַפְשִׁי "Were the Lord not my help, my נפש would soon inhabit the place of silence" (Ps 94:17; cf. 115:17).

It hardly matters that all of these verses are either hyperbolic or counterfactual. Interpreted in the light of Job 14:22,[6] they suggest that, for the Israelites, there were, indeed, נפשות in Sheol—נפשות that belonged to the recently deceased. These נפשות did not remain intact very long. At the end of twelve months, they broke up into their component parts: the רוחות returned to God, while the faded נפשות בשר joined a/the קהל רפאים, acquiring a new designation in the process.[7] Any dearth of נפשות in Sheol must be understood in this way.

Laurin's second argument against disembodied נפשות is that the inhabitants of Sheol retain their bodily form. The most compelling of his three prooftexts is 1 Sam 28:14, where the witch of Endor describes the divine being coming up from the earth: אִישׁ זָקֵן עֹלֶה וְהוּא עֹטֶה מְעִיל "an old man is coming up, and he is wrapped in a robe." As we have seen, the Talmud (*b. Šabb.* 152b) takes it for granted that this is a description of Samuel's disembodied soul (נשמה),[8] a spirit that preserves every detail of his appearance at death, down to his clothing.

For Laurin, who has a similar view, this is evidence that the Israelites had a monistic concept of human beings. This argument ignores the fact that, in a number of cultures, free souls of the living and/or spirits of the dead are depicted as ethereal miniature

---

[6] See at chapter 11, nn. 46–47 above.

[7] See chapter 11, nn. 31–32 above.

[8] See at chapter 11, n. 30 above. In *Gen. Rab.* (Theodor and Albeck, מדרש בראשית רבא, 1186), the Rabbis go further, using our verse to "flesh out" their description of the resurrection at the end of days. Their discussion there, taken together with the interpretation of our verse in *b. Šabb.* 152b, appears to imply that every righteous individual will be resurrected in the image of his/her disembodied soul. Samuel, for example, will come back to life looking just like the spirit conjured up at Endor. One wonders how the Rabbis would have reacted to the technology available today. Doctors now have the ability to convert MRI or CT scans of an individual into holographic images or (with the aid of a 3D printer) three-dimensional ceramic models. For a remarkably lifelike virtual human body that would make any necromancer jealous, see http://www.ucalgary.ca/news/may2007/CAVEman.

replicas of their owners.[9] Take, for example, the ψυχή of the ancient Greeks, whose dualistic concept of humans is often cited as the antithesis of the Hebrew concept:

> The *psuchē* is like a body; as shown on works of art, on vases, it is represented like a miniature body, a *corpusculum*; it is the double of the living body, a replica that can be taken for the body itself that has the same appearance, clothing, gestures, and voice. But this absolute likeness is also a total insubstantiality. The *psuchē* is a nothing, an empty thing, an ungraspable evanescence, a shade; it is like an airy and winged being, a bird in flight.[10]

Similarly, the ancient Egyptian *ba*, generally believed to have been immaterial,[11] is portrayed as a miniature version of the deceased in illustrated manuscripts of the *Book of the Dead*.[12] Finally, it has been conjectured that the ancient Mesopotamian *eṭemmu* "preserves the body image"[13] in spite of being immortal and intangible.[14] Moreover, it is "believed to depart from the body at death."[15]

---

[9] Frazer, *Golden Bough*, 3:26–30.

[10] Jean Pierre Vernant, "Psuche: Simulacrum of the Body or Image of the Divine?" in idem, *Mortals and Immortals: Collected Essays* (ed. Froma I. Zeitlin; Princeton, N.J.: Princeton University Press, 1991), 189, cited in Abusch, "Ghost," 377 n. 31. Cf. Bremmer, "Soul," 164: "Homer describes the warriors at the entrance to Hades still dressed in their bloody armour. . . . On vases, the souls of the dead are even regularly shown with their wounds, sometimes still bandaged."

[11] James P. Allen, "Ba," 161: "Like the soul, the *ba* seems to have been essentially nonphysical"; Taylor, *Death*, 20: "Although not a physical being, the *ba* was credited with many human characteristics." For the contrary view, see Assmann, *Death*, 89–90.

[12] See Taylor, *Journey*, 17, 25, 73. One of these images can be seen at http://www.britishmuseum.org/research/collection_online/collection_object_details/collection_image_gallery.aspx?partid=1&assetid=685479&objectid=113333.

[13] Abusch, "Ghost," 378.

[14] Ibid., 373. For the immateriality of the *eṭemmu*, see also Tropper, *Nekromantie*, 47. For its immortality under normal conditions, see also Farber, "Witchcraft," 1898. Note, however, that the *eṭemmu* can be destroyed through cremation of the body and other means of total annihilation (Abusch, "Ghost," 374–76). Cf. Scurlock, "Death," 1892: "when the body ceased to exist, so did the potentially harmful *eṭemmu*."

[15] Scurlock, "Soul Emplacements," 1.

In short, the Greek ψυχή, the Egyptian *ba*, and (less certainly) the Mesopotamian *eṭemmu* possessed a bodily form, and yet they fit the dictionary definition of *disembodied*: they had no material existence, and after death they were freed from their owner's body.[16] Thus, the idea that "any sort of life, even in Sheol, must manifest itself in a bodily form or shape" is perfectly compatible with a dualistic concept of human beings.

In sum, Laurin's arguments against the existence of disembodied נפשות in the Bible can no longer be accepted. I know of no other arguments worthy of taking their place. It may well be that the Hebrews, Egyptians, and Greeks could not conceive of their souls in the shape of anything but a body—a body resembling their own—but this is quite different from the claim that they could not conceive of their souls as being disembodied.

At the end of the day, the simplest reading of the evidence supports the conclusion of Sven Tengström in *TDOT*:

> Linguistically and conceptually . . . the ancient Israelites were in a position to differentiate . . . between the inward spiritual core of a person and the various outward manifestations of that person's life. A person's spirit or life, accordingly, could be seen as something transcending corporeality. In its consistent view that *rûaḥ* is God's special gift, the OT refers to this transcendent character. We may conclude that it would be wrong to overemphasize the "synthetic" thought or the "monism" of the OT.[17]

---

[16] See chapter 1, n. 3 above.

[17] Tengström, "רוּחַ *rûaḥ*," 379.

14

Conclusions

It has long been accepted by most scholars that "the Hebrew could not conceive of a disembodied נפש"; however, if that is true, he must have been oblivious to beliefs and practices found all over the ancient Near East. The Katumuwa inscription, on a stele recently excavated at Zincirli (ancient Samal), points up the need for a reassessment. In it, Katumuwa exhibits a belief in the existence of disembodied souls by mentioning the presence of his נבש = נפש in the stele. This belief does not reflect Anatolian influence; it is closely tied to beliefs about the soul/spirit (*eṭemmu*) in Mesopotamia, and it is the basis of the secondary meaning "funerary monument" attested for נפש in a number of Aramaic dialects (including those spoken by Jews and the ancient Arabs of Taima), not to mention Mishnaic Hebrew and Epigraphic South Arabian.

A belief in the existence of disembodied נפשות is reflected in many biblical passages as well. The most important of these is Ezek 13:17–21, a prophecy addressed to women posing as prophetesses. When properly understood, this passage provides compelling evidence; however, it has been only partially understood until now because of the obscure technical terms that it contains. It describes the manufacture of pillows, using terms whose precise meaning is known from rabbinic references to pillows. The women and their apprentices were sewing pillow casings (כסתות) and cutting up clothing—stolen, perhaps, from their intended victims—into the cloth patches (מספחות) that served as pillow filling in ancient Israel. They were using the pillow filling—presumably after reciting a spell over it—to attract heedless dream-souls (נפשים) rushing back to the pillows of their owners in the morning, after a "night on the town." Trapped inside the empty pillow casings, the dream-souls would turn into bird-souls (פרחות), awaiting the imminent demise of their owners, unless the latter agreed to ransom them. Or so the women claimed.

Ezekiel condemns this claim as a lie but, contrary to the modern scholarly consensus, there is no indication that he rejects the women's underlying belief in the existence of disembodied נפשות. Indeed, there is no reason to assume that that belief is found only there in the Hebrew Bible. Other biblical passages seem to imply that a נפש is different from a חיים (Ps 103:2–4; Job 10:1); that, unlike a חיים, it has a spatial location (Jer 38:16; Ps 116:7); that, although it resides inside the body (2 Sam 1:9; 1 Kgs 17:22) in the blood of the flesh (Lev 17:11) when its owner is conscious, it is not part of the body (Isa 10:18; Job 2:5–6); and that it can be punished by preventing it from joining its kinsmen in the afterlife (Gen 17:14; Lev 19:8; Num 9:13; etc.). There are also passages (with parallels from Ugarit and Egypt) that depict the נפש as leaving the body when consciousness is lost for any reason, including death (Gen 35:18; 1 Kgs 17:22) and fainting (Song 5:6), as well as passages (with a parallel from Egypt) that depict it as being addressed by its owner (Ps 42:12; 103:1–5; 116:7; etc.). In short, the נפש, although a part of the *person* (Gen 37:21; Deut 19:6, 11; etc.; cf. Gen 3:15; Ps 3:8; etc.), is not a part of the *body* (see above). As a result, it has considerable freedom of movement.

Conflicting reports about the נפש and the רוח in biblical and postbiblical literature can be explained by a simple three-part conjecture: (1) The נפש consists of two components: (a) the נפש הבשר, a bodily component located in the blood (Lev 17:11), and (b) the רוח, a spiritual component bestowed by God (Num 16:22; Qoh 12:7). The two components are attached, even when the נפש is outside the body (as a dream-soul or bird-soul). The רוח—also called רוח חיים (Gen 6:17; 7:15), נשמת רוח חיים (Gen 7:22), and נשמת חיים (Gen 2:7)—was breathed into man by God at creation (Gen 2:7), as a means of turning the נפש בשר in his blood (or the entire bipartite נפש) into a נפש חיה. The term נפש חיה can be used of any activated, vitalized נפש (Gen 1:30) and, by synecdoche, of any creature that has such a נפש (Gen 1:24; 2:7; etc.). Several elements of this part of my conjecture can be found already in the writings of Philo and Josephus. (2) After death, when the נפש leaves the body, the components remain physically connected for a year, but they pull in opposite directions—the

נפש הבשר toward the body and the רוח toward heaven—so that "his soul ascends and descends" for twelve months (*b. Šabb.* 152b). The ascension of the deceased's *ba* to heaven (*prt r pt*) during the day and its return to the corpse at night is one of the fundamental themes of Egyptian mortuary literature. (3) In the decomposition pit used for primary burial down to Roman times—the שחת בלי of Isa 38:17, and the מהמרת of the Palestinian Talmud (*Moʿed Qaṭ.* 1.5.80c; *Sanh.* 6.10.23d; cf. *KTU/CAT* 1.5 I 7–8 and Ps 140:11)—the נפש הבשר fades as the body wastes away (Ps 49:15; Job 14:10, 20–22; *m. Sanh.* 6:6) until, after twelve months, it becomes detached from the רוח. It then joins a/the קהל רפאים "assembly of Rephaim" (Prov 21:16) in the darkness of Sheol (Ps 49:19–20; 88:11–13; Job 17:13), while the רוח returns to God and remains permanently in heaven (Ps 104:29; Job 34:14; Qoh 12:7; *b. Šabb.* 152b–153a) with its kinsmen.

The portrait of the soul sketched here seems to account for the philological facts better than the standard theory, a theory that has held sway for a century. According to the latter, any hint of soul-body dualism found in the Hebrew Bible must be either reinterpreted or attributed to Greek or Iranian influence. Careful analysis of the evidence has shown that this theory can no longer be maintained. One piece of evidence is worth singling out: the expression ונכרתה הנפש ההוא מעמיה and its antonym ויאסף אל עמיו. The latter expression speaks of a spirit/soul joining its kinsmen in heaven (not in Sheol), while the former expression speaks of a spirit/soul being *prevented* from doing so. These two expressions account for the bulk of the biblical occurrences of עמים used in the sense of "kinsmen" (rather than "peoples"). This is a very archaic usage—a fossil preserved only in a few fixed expressions in the Pentateuch. These expressions—and the ideas that they reflect—must therefore be extremely old. In short, this evidence suggests that ideas about disembodied souls and their punishment in the afterlife were current among the Israelites far earlier than generally assumed.

One of the key elements of our theory—the twelve-month transitional period lasting until the decomposition of the corpse—comes from rabbinic literature, but it is supported by archaeological findings. One archaeologist has independently argued for such a period based on the difference between the standard Israelite household inventory and the Israelite grave inventory. Moreover, it is now widely accepted that the rabbinic practice of secondary burial after the decomposition of the flesh stretches back to the Iron Age and beyond. Some scholars go further, asserting that the ideological significance of secondary burial remained in place throughout the first millennium, even though the practice itself evolved during that period. Since secondary burial is intimately connected in Rabbinic Judaism with a belief in the existence of disembodied souls, there is no longer any reason to avoid the conclusion that that belief is very ancient as well.

In fact, it is possible that the Semitic-speaking peoples of the ancient Near East inherited the belief in question from their common ancestors, the speakers of Proto-Semitic. That language is believed to have had a term **nap(i)š* with the meaning "soul," in addition to the meanings "vitality, life," "person, personality," and "self." In at least some of the daughter languages, the reflex of **nap(i)š* clearly denotes a soul that exits the body at death, a free soul capable of existing without a body. This is true of Samalian נבש, Ugaritic *npš*, Arabic *nafs* and, it should now be clear, Hebrew נפש. It may, therefore, be legitimate to reconstruct that denotation for **nap(i)š*, at least in Proto-West Semitic.

Even earlier evidence comes from paleoarchaeological findings in Iraq. Belief in the existence and afterlife of souls is reflected already in Shanidar Cave, whose earliest burials have been dated to around 50,000 B.P. Although a belief that humans have a soul that survives death is not the same as a belief in disembodied souls, it seems clear that the two beliefs often go together.

In the light of all this evidence, it is no longer possible to insist that the Hebrew was unable to conceive of a disembodied נפש. If anything, the opposite now appears to be true. The evidence suggests that a belief in the existence of disembodied souls was part of the common religious heritage of the peoples of the ancient Near East.

APPENDIX 1

The Katumuwa Inscription from Zincirli

Semitists owe a tremendous debt of gratitude to the University of Chicago archaeologists who led the Neubauer Expedition to Zincirli (ancient Samal) in southeastern Turkey. In 2008, they discovered the funerary stele of an official named Katumuwa, inscribed with an Aramaic inscription that refers to the presence of Katumuwa's נבש (= נפש) in the stele.[1] In so doing, they rescued from oblivion not only Katumuwa's נבש but also a "lost" meaning of Hebrew נפש. In view of the importance of this inscription for the subject of this monograph, I have decided to present it here in full, taking the opportunity to supplement the interpretations given in Dennis Pardee's fine *editio princeps*[2] and the subsequent literature with a few ideas of my own.

Transcription[3]

1. אנכ.כתמו.עבד.פנמו.זי.קנת.לי.נצב.ב
2. חיי.ושמת.ותה.בסיר/ד.עלמי.וחגגת.ס

---

[1] See Schloen and Fink, "New Excavations," 1–13; and Eudora J. Struble and Virginia Rimmer Herrmann, "An Eternal Feast at Samʾal: The New Iron Age Mortuary Stele from Zincirli in Context," *BASOR* 356 (2009): 15–49. For photographs, a film, and a book dealing with the inscription, see https://oi.uchicago.edu/museum-exhibits/special-exhibits/remembrance-me-feasting-dead-ancient-middle-east.

[2] Dennis Pardee, "A New Aramaic Inscription from Zincirli," *BASOR* 356 (2009): 51–71; see also idem, "The Katumuwa Inscription," in *In Remembrance of Me: Feasting with the Dead in the Ancient Middle East* (ed. Virginia Rimmer Herrmann and J. David Schloen; Chicago: Oriental Institute of the University of Chicago, 2014), 45–48.

[3] The transcription below is essentially unchanged from the *editio princeps*.

3. יר/ד.זנ.שור.להדד.קר/דפד/רל.ויבל לנג
4. ד/ר.צוד/רנ.ויבל.לשמש.ויבל.להדד.כרמנ
5. ויבל.לכבבו.ויבל.לנבשי.זי.בנצב.זנ.
6. ועת.מנ.מנ.בני.או.
7. מנבניאש.ויהי.לה.
8. נסיר/ד.זננ.ולו יקח.מנ
9. חיל.כרמ.זננ.שא.
10. יומנ ליומנ.ויה
11. רג.בנבשי
12. וישוי
13. לי.שק

Translation

1. I am Katumuwa, servant of Panamuwa, who acquired for myself a stele while
2. still alive and put it in my eternal reception room. The festal offering of
3. this reception room is a bull for Hadad QRPDL/QRPRL, a ram for the Mov-
4. er of Mountains, a ram for Shamash, a ram for Hadad of the Vineyards,
5. a ram for Kubaba, and a ram for my soul, which is in this stele.
6. And (from?) now, whoever from among my sons or
7. from among the sons of anybody (else) should come into possession of
8. this reception room (?), let him purchase, out of
9. the yield of this (adjoining) vineyard, a sheep
10. every year and let him slaugh-
11. ter it beside my soul
12. and present
13. me with a thigh.

Commentary

Line2

בסיר/ד עלמי "in my eternal reception room": The phrase may be compared to אל בית עולמו "to his eternal abode" (Qoh 12:5). There ,too, the suffixed pronoun attached to the genitive noun ע(ו)לם modifies the entire genitive phrase. Several studies interpret the obscure noun סיר/ד based on Epigraphic South Arabian *ms³wd,* which refers to the reception room of a house or tomb.[4] Nevertheless, problems still remain.[5] Another possibility worth considering is that סיד (סְיָד) is a metathesized form of יסד "foundation," used here as a synecdoche for the reception room or the entire funerary complex.

חגגת "the festal offering of": Cf. Mishnaic Hebrew חגיגת "the festal offering of" (*t. Ḥag.* 1:4), not to mention BH חג "festal offering" (Mal 2:3 and Ps 118:27). Pardee takes it for granted that this is a verb (in the D-stem) meaning "I established a feast,"[6] but he is well aware of the problems connected with his interpretation. One of them is lexical: "The verb that the author uses for the establishment of the annual feast in his honor (ḤGG) is not commonly used with this meaning in the related languages. . . ."[7] This is, of course, an understatement. As Pardee himself notes, "The transla-

[4] Giovanni Mazzini, "On the Problematic Term *syr/d* in the New Old Aramaic Inscription from Zincirli," *UF* 41 (2009): 505–7; Gregorio del Olmo Lete, "KTMW and his 'Funerary Chapel,'" *Aula Orientalis* 29 (2011): 308–10; Sanders, "Appetites," 38–40. Olmo Lete also brings Late Aramaic סיד "plaster" into the picture, but this would be written שיד in Old Aramaic (as in Biblical Hebrew), since the initial sibilant of this word is the reflex of Proto-Semitic *ś.

[5] See, for example, Olmo Lete, "KTMW," 308–9. See also my comment on נסיר/ד in line 8 below.

[6] Pardee, "New Aramaic Inscription," 53, 60; and idem, "Katumuwa Inscription"; cf. G. Wilhelm Nebe, "Eine neue Inschrift aus Zincirli auf der Stele des Kutamuwa und die hebräische Sprachwissenschaft," in *Jüdische Studien als Disziplin—die Disziplinen der Jüdischen Studien: Festschrift der Hochschule für Jüdische Studien Heidelberg 1979–2009* (ed. Johannes Heil and Daniel Krochmalnik; Schriften der Hochschule für Jüdische Studien Heidelberg 13; Heidelberg: Winter, 2010), 321: "(der) ich habe feiern lassen"; Sanders, "Appetites," 50 (cf. p. 40): "I . . . ritually instituted."

[7] Pardee, "Katumuwa Inscription," 46.

tion proposed is essentially etymological; in both Hebrew and Aramaic the verb ḤGG denotes 'keeping a feast,' 'observing a feast,' that feast normally involving a pilgrimage."[8] The second problem is syntactic: What is the relationship between this verb and the immediately following noun? Pardee's solution to this problem is quite strained: "If we are indeed dealing with a D-stem form, its direct object is formally {syr/d}, literally 'I made of this chamber(?) a place of feasting.'"[9] In other words, the real meaning of the verb is not "to establish a feast" but "to turn (a chamber or the like) into a place of feasting." The existence of a verb with that meaning in ancient Semitic seems quite improbable. Even contemporary English, with its well-known tolerance for offbeat coinages, does not appear to have such verb. The most promising candidate, **to festalize* (< *festal*), does not show up in a Google search of the Internet, despite the many occurrences of *to sacralize* (< *sacral*). The third problem is once again syntactic. What is the relationship between the object of the alleged verb and the noun phrases that follow it? In other words, how are we to understand 'I made of this chamber(?) a place of feasting: a bull for Hadad. . . .'? André Lemaire takes חגגת as a *qal*

---

[8] Pardee, "New Aramaic Inscription," 60.

[9] Ibid. So, too, Matthew J. Suriano, "Breaking Bread with the Dead: Katumuwa's Stele, Hosea 9:4, and the Early History of the Soul," *JAOS* 134 (2014): 394: "As both Pardee and Sanders note, the term here is a D-Stem of √*ḥgg* with the object being the *syd*. Rather than having a passive sense of 'holding a feast' (as in Hebrew and Aramaic), the verbal form is factitive, resulting in the creation of a specialized space. The sense of this root has been elucidated by the recent edition of a Northwest Arabian inscription (Dedanitic), where it carries the same meaning: M. del Carmen Hidalgo-Chacón Díez, 'Neubearbeitung der dadanischen Inschrift Abū l-Ḥasan 197,' *AulaOr* 27 (2009): 44 NS 48–49." In the cited edition, however, the verb *ḥggw* is not taken to be factitive. It is separated from the noun that follows it and translated "haben das (religiöse) Fest gefeiert" (Hidalgo-Chacón Díez, 44), a translation that is almost identical to the translation given for Hebrew *ḥgg*: "wallfahren, ein (religiöses) Fest feiern" (Hidalgo-Chacón Díez, 48). And Suriano's use of the term "passive" to describe the meaning "holding a feast" is incomprehensible. Sanders ("Appetites," 40) cites the Qatabanian phrase *bḥg* "by order of" as a parallel, but this parallel is distant from the point of view of syntax and semantics, as well as genetics and geography. When dealing with verbs (as opposed to nouns), it is best to adopt a stricter standard.

verb and translates "I celebrated this chapel: a bull for Hadad. . . ,"[10] but that interpretation, too, fails to clarify the relationship between the object of the alleged verb and the noun phrases that follow it. Even in English, it is obvious that a preposition is missing, e.g., "*with* a bull for Hadad. . . ." Moreover, Lemaire's interpretation, like Pardee's, posits a syntactic usage for the verb that is unparalleled elsewhere in Northwest Semitic. The Hebrew evidence is crucial because ח-ג-ג is poorly attested in other Northwest Semitic languages. In Hebrew (Biblical and Mishnaic), the verb ח-ג-ג behaves very much like the verb ח-ל-ם "dream." These verbs frequently take no accusative at all, but when they take an accusative noun, it is always a *cognate* accusative: חג "a festival, as a festival" in the case of the former, חלום "a dream" in the case of the latter. Thus, the interpretations of Pardee and Lemaire are unparalleled in that they take סיר/ד זג to be the direct object of ח-ג-ג. All of these problems disappear once we recognize חגגת as a noun in the construct state.

Line 3

הדד קר/דפד/רל "Hadad QRPDL/QRPRL": Ilya Yakubovich takes this to mean something like "Hadad the Companion" with *qrpdl* reflecting a reconstructed noun **harpatalli-* "companion," derived from the Luwian root *harp* "to associate oneself, to join."[11] Seth L. Sanders accepts this proposal but modifies the gloss to "Hadad the Ally."[12] According to Yakubovich and Craig Melchert (in an e-mail to Sanders), none of the linguistic difficulties inherent in this suggestion is sufficient to rule it out.[13] Nevertheless, it is clear

[10] Lemaire, "Rites," 133–34.

[11] Ilya Yakubovich, "The West Semitic God El in Anatolian Hieroglyphic Transmission," in *Pax Hethitica: Studies on the Hittites and Their Neighbours in Honour of Itamar Singer* (Studien zu den Boğazköy-Texten Herausgegeben von der Kommission für den Alten Orient der Akademie der Wissenschaften und der Literatur, Mainz, 51; ed. Yoram Cohen, Amir Gilan, and Jared L. Miller; Wiesbaden: Harrassowitz, 2010), 396.

[12] Sanders, "Appetites," 44–45.

[13] Another question for Hittitologists is whether "the Ally"—as opposed to "my Ally" or "my Savior"—is plausible as a divine epithet. A deity called "Hadad the Ally" could easily wind up being the ally of my enemy!

that there are a number of uncertainties in the reconstruction that underlies the suggestion. That being the case, it cannot hurt to add another conjectural interpretation—one that takes the phrase to be Samalian: שור להדד קר-פר-(א)ל "a bull for Hadad of Bull-Il's city." This interpretation takes the prepositional phrase להדד קר-פר-(א)ל as being parallel to the phrase [לאלה]י קר זא "for the gods of this city" in the Samalian Hadad inscription (*KAI* no. 214 line 19).[14] Elsewhere in Samalian, the noun קר "city" appears three times in the plural, written קירת "cities." It appears also in Moabite and BH, and it is the morphologically masculine counterpart of קרת "city" attested in Ugaritic, Phoenician, Hebrew, Aramaic, etc.[15] The interpretation assumes that פרל is derived from *פר-אל and is comparable to Ugaritic *ṯr-il* "Bull-Il." The noun פר and/or its feminine counterpart is used of bovines in Hebrew, Ugaritic, and several Late Aramaic dialects, and it has cognates in Arabic and Akkadian. The use of this epithet here is, of course, appropriate to the offering of a bull. For three words written as one, cf. מנבניאש in line 7. For final אל with deleted *alef*, see the discussion of glottal-stop elision in Egyptian Aramaic by Takamitsu Muraoka and Bezalel Porten: "An example illustrating this process is בבל 'Babylon' A6.15:1 as against its historical spelling בבאל ib. 5";[16] cf. Egyptian Aramaic (papyrus Amherst 63) *bytr*^{g} = בית-אל "Bethel."[17] In Samalian, as elsewhere, etymological *alef* is normally expressed in writing (e.g., Samalian רכבאל), but there are exceptions (e.g., יתמר "it was ordered" < *יתאמר

[14] Cf. Nebe, "Eine neue Inschrift," 322: "The QR-component could contain the element *qr* 'city' (*KAI* 214,19)."

[15] See chapter 3, n. 48 above.

[16] Takamitsu Muraoka and Bezalel Porten, *A Grammar of Egyptian Aramaic* (2nd ed.; HO, The Near and Middle East 32; Leiden: Brill, 2003), 23. It is possible that the spelling בבאל is based on a folk etymology and does not reflect the actual pronunciation of the word; even so, the fact that it co-occurs with the other spelling in the same document is revealing.

[17] Note the absence of Demotic *e* = Aramaic ʾ; this is the regular spelling of the divine name in the Aramaic text in Demotic script (VII/13, VIII/9, 13, IX/9, XV/1, 14, XVI/14, 15). There seem to be examples in Biblical Hebrew as well, e.g., עֲרָפֶל < *ערף־אל and כַּרְמֶל < *כרם־אל (alongside ארזי אל and הררי אל). The noun ערפל has cognates in Ugaritic and Aramaic, suggesting that the divine name אל used as a genitive noun was affected by glottal-stop elision already in Proto-Northwest Semitic.

or יאתמר*).[18] The assumed toponym קר-פר-(א)ל would be similar in structure to BH קִרְיַת בַּעַל (Josh 15:60; 18:14). It might refer to Il's abode called *Mbk Nhrm* in Ugaritic texts.[19]

Line 4

צוד/רנ "mountains": Of the various possibilities discussed by Pardee, the most likely, in my view, is that צור is the early spelling of Aramaic טור "mountain," cognate to Hebrew צור "rock [= large, fixed mass of stony material], crag,"[20] Ugaritic *ġr* "mountain," and Sabaic *ẓwr*, *ẓr* "rock, bedrock."[21] In this interpretation, the initial Samalian *ṣade* represents the reflex of *ṯ̣ before it merged with the reflex of *ṭ.[22] The spelling with medial *waw* calls to mind the consonantal *waw* in the Western Aramaic determined form of this noun (Galilean Aramaic טַוְורָה, Samaritan Aramaic טברה).[23] It also calls to mind the name of the mountain range of southern Anatolia, which formed the northern boundary of the kingdom of Samal: Ταῦρος. One might speculate that this towering mountain range got its name from the Aramaic word for "mountain." It is possible that it

---

[18] Tropper, *Die Inschriften*, 220.

[19] For the identification of *Mbk Nhrm* with Baalbek, see Richard C. Steiner, "On the Rise and Fall of Canaanite Religion at Baalbek: A Tale of Five Toponyms," *JBL* 128 (2009): 507–25.

[20] The latter meaning, as a count noun, is naturally clearest in the plural (e.g., Num 23:9; 1 Sam 24:3), but there are good examples in the singular as well (e.g., Exod 33:21–22; Ps 27:5).

[21] Beeston et al., *Sabaic Dictionary*, 173, s.v.

[22] It is difficult to say whether the Semitic words for "chert, flint, stone that can be sharpened by flaking"—Akkadian *ṣurru*, Hebrew צֹר, Arabic *ẓirru*, etc.—are related to the words for "mountain, rock." The same goes for Mehri *ṣā̃wər* "a stone, a rock" and Ḥarsūsi *ṣéwwer* "a stone, a pebble," which seem to point instead to *ṣ; see T. M. Johnstone, *Mehri Lexicon and English-Mehri Word-List* (London: School of Oriental and African Studies, University of London, 1987), 368 s.v.; idem, *Ḥarsūsi Lexicon* (London: Oxford University Press, 1977), 117, s.v.

[23] See Michael Sokoloff, *A Dictionary of Jewish Palestinian Aramaic of the Byzantine Period* (Ramat Gan: Bar-Ilan University Press, 1990), 222a, s.v. טור; and Abraham Tal, מילון הארמית של השומרונים (Leiden: Brill, 2000), 307, s.v. טור.

was originally called "the mountain(s)" in Aramaic and that this appellation eventually turned into the name of the mountains just north of the kingdom (just as the word for "north," שמאל, turned into the name of the kingdom itself). The most likely time for the shift from common noun to proper noun would be the Achaemenid period, after the merger of *ṯ with *ṭ. The excavators of Zincirli found what they believe to be "a fortress built under the aegis of the Achaemenid Persian empire to control the nearby pass over the Amanus Mountains, which the army of Darius III used in 333 B.C.E. to cross over to the Mediterranean coast and attack the army of Alexander the Great from the rear in the Battle of Issos."[24] If so, the Greek name is further evidence that the Aramaic word for "mountain" originally had a medial diphthong [aw]. It is true that Zeev Ben-Ḥayyim[25] takes the consonantal *waw* to be the product of a back-formation, but, even if this is correct, it is not necessary to assume that we are dealing with a late development. It has been shown that many forms considered to be innovations of Galilean Aramaic or Western Aramaic are actually much older.[26] Thus, it is possible that the alleged back-formation is early enough to account for the *waw* of צורן; if not, the *waw* is a *mater lectionis*.[27]

Lines 3-4

נגד/ר צוד/רן "Mover of Mountains": This interpretation assumes that we are dealing with an epithet containing the participle of Aramaic נ-ג-ד "draw, pull." In its earliest attestations (Cowley 26 = *TADAE* A 6.2, lines 4 and 8), this root refers to the pulling of a heavy object

[24] J. David Schloen, "The City of Katumuwa: The Iron Age Kingdom of Samʾal and the Excavation of Zincirli," in *In Remembrance of Me: Feasting with the Dead in the Ancient Middle East* (ed. Virginia Rimmer Herrmann and J. David Schloen; Chicago: Oriental Institute of the University of Chicago, 2014), 38.

[25] Cited in the aforementioned dictionaries (see n. 23 above).

[26] See Richard C. Steiner, "Papyrus Amherst 63: A New Source for the Language, Literature, Religion, and History of the Arameans," in *Studia Aramaica: New Sources and New Approaches* (ed. M. J. Geller, J. C. Greenfield, and M. P. Weitzman; JSSSup 4; Oxford: Oxford University Press, 1995), 202–3.

[27] So Pardee, "New Aramaic Inscription," 61.

to move it from one place to another. In this interpretation of the phrase, we may compare הַמַּעְתִּיק הָרִים "He who moves mountains," appearing as a divine epithet in Job 9:5.[28] Such a divine epithet would be particularly appropriate to the topography of the kingdom of Samal, which was situated in a long, narrow rift valley surrounded by steep mountains.[29] Did the Samalians believe that their valley was formed when one of the gods split the Amanus mountain range and dragged half of it eastward? For the creation of a valley in this manner, see Zech 14:4.

Line 4

הדד כרמנ "Hadad of the Vineyards": This is Pardee's rendering, but in the *editio princeps* he leaves open the possibility that כרמנ is not Semitic: "If not another manifestation of Hadad defined by a non-Semitic word, then the interpretation as 'Hadad of the vineyards' appears likely."[30] André Lemaire favors that possibility, suggesting that כרמנ be identified with a Luwian toponym, such as *Harmana* or *Kammanu*.[31] Emilia Masson, by contrast, asserts that הדד כרמנ "is purely and simply a translation of the Luwian appellative *tuwarsis Tarhunzas* 'Tarhunzas of the vineyard'"—a parallel mentioned by Pardee—and she notes that Tarhunza is rendered by בעל (= הדד) in two bilingual inscriptions.[32] In my view, "Hadad of the Vineyards" makes perfect sense in connection with the vineyard mentioned in line 9; see the section entitled "Funerary Foundations" below.

---

[28] Contrast Pardee, "New Aramaic Inscription," 61: "Perhaps *l ngd ṣwdn*, 'the officer (in charge) of provisions' or 'of the hunts' . . ."; and Emilia Masson, "La stèle mortuaire de Kuttamuwa (Zincirli): comment l'appréhender," *Semitica et Classica* 3 (2010): 53: "The first sequence [נגד/ר] can be interpreted without any risk . . . as a transcription of the divine name Nikarawas/Nikaruhas, attested until now in the final imprecations of two hieroglyphic inscriptions."

[29] Schloen and Fink, "New Excavations," 1.

[30] Pardee, "New Aramaic Inscription," 62.

[31] Lemaire, "Le dialecte araméen," 148–49.

[32] Masson, "La stèle mortuaire," 53.

Line 5

כבבו "Kubaba": In other Aramaic inscriptions, the goddess's name is written כבב or כבבה.[33] The spelling here, with final *waw*, has been taken as reflecting **Kubabuwa*[34] or the Neo-Assyrian form *Kubābu*.[35]

נבשי "my soul": This form, with *bet* instead of original *pe*ʾ, occurs in a number of Northwest Semitic inscriptions, and it has been discussed by many scholars.[36] I shall mention only a few of them. Pardee adopts the view that נבש "is a Samalian/OA isogloss over against the Canaanite dialects."[37] In other words, it is restricted to inscriptions (Zincirli, Fekherye, Sefīre) that most scholars view as Aramaic. Pardee dismisses the occurrence of this form in epigraphic Hebrew (Arad) as a "scribal peculiarity rather than a dialectal feature," and he leaves the occurrence in Phoenician (Zincirli) unmentioned. Takamitsu Muraoka, by contrast, writes that "the phenomenon is not confined to Aramaic, for it is also attested in Phoenician (Zenjirli) and Hebrew of some [*sic*] Arad inscription."[38] Josef Tropper, while viewing the Phoenician form as an Aramaic loanword, believes that Ugaritic *nbšt* is a genuine cognate of נבש,[39] presumably on the assumption that it means something like "living being(s)."[40] All of these scholars have taken the spelling of נבש at face value, assuming that it reflects a *phonetic* variant in the spoken language. Many explanations of the form have been proposed based on this assumption,[41] all of them problematic. One should, therefore, consider the possibility that נבש was phonetically indistinguishable from נפש, both being pronounced [napš]. In that case,

---

[33] Younger, "Two Epigraphic Notes," 166–79; André Lemaire and Benjamin Sass, "The Mortuary Stele with Samʾalian Inscription from Ördekburnu near Zincirli," *BASOR* 369 (2013): 122.

[34] Nebe, "Eine neue Inschrift," 323.

[35] Younger, "Two Epigraphic Notes," 166–79.

[36] See Takamitsu Muraoka, "The Tell-Fekherye Bilingual Inscription and Early Aramaic," *Abr-Nahrain* 22 (1983–1984): 88–89, 112–13, and the literature cited there.

[37] Pardee, "New Aramaic Inscription," 67.

[38] Muraoka, "Tell-Fekherye," 88–89.

[39] Tropper, *Die Inschriften*, 43–44.

[40] See Olmo Lete and Sanmartín, *Dictionary*, 618, s.v. *nbšt*, and the literature cited there.

[41] See the survey in Muraoka, "Tell-Fekherye," 88–89 and 112–13.

נבש would be an inverse spelling,[42] reflecting the neutralization of the /b/ ≠ /p/ opposition before voiceless /š/ in a single form.[43] In other words, we may be dealing with a feature that is purely orthographic, lacking any reflex in the phonology of the spoken lan-

---

[42] For inverse spelling, see Henry M. Hoenigswald, *Language Change and Linguistic Reconstruction* (Chicago: University of Chicago Press, 1960), 9–10; and Joshua Blau, *On Pseudo-Corrections in Some Semitic Languages* (Publications of the Israel Academy of Sciences and Humanities, Section of Humanities; Jerusalem: Israel Academy of Sciences and Humanities, 1970), 52. One of Blau's examples is relevant to ours: "Syriac *zevtâ* 'pitch,' occurring alongside original *zeftâ*."

[43] Ugaritic examples of this neutralization are discussed by Edward L. Greenstein, "A Phoenician Inscription in Ugaritic Script?" *JANES* 8 (1976): 51–52; and W. Randall Garr, "On Voicing and Devoicing in Ugaritic," *JNES* 45 (1986): 46, 51. According to Greenstein, "the root *lbš* 'dress, wear' remains *lbš* in all verbal and some nominal forms, in which *b* is followed by a vowel, but becomes *lpš* (= **lupšu* or **lipšu*) in a nominal formation in which **b* directly precedes voiceless *š*" (Greenstein, "Phoenician Inscription," 51–52). In this case, the neutralization of the /b/ ≠ /p/ opposition before voiceless /š/ does not result in inverse spelling. The same goes for the other two Ugaritic examples cited by Greenstein (ibid.) and Garr ("Voicing," 46, 51), in which the /b/ ≠ /p/ opposition is neutralized before voiceless /k/. In Hebrew, the neutralization of this opposition occurs most commonly before /q/. As noted by Pardee, Arad letter 24 has והבקידם = והפקידם in lines 14–15, alongside בנבשכם in line 18; see Yohanan Aharoni, כתובות ערד (Jerusalem: Bialik, 1975), 48. Beginning in the fourteenth century, the name רבקה appears with an *f* (*Riffka, Ryfka, Ryfke,* etc.) in the European transcriptions collected by Alexander Beider, *A Dictionary of Ashkenazic Given Names: Their Origins, Structure, Pronunciation, and Migrations* (Teaneck, N.J.: Avoteynu, 1996), 557–58. The pronunciation reflected by this rendering, in use to this day, goes back to antiquity, if we may judge from the spelling of the name in the Peshiṭta with a Syriac *peʾ*. Occasionally, neutralization in the *hifʿil*/*ʾafʿel* leads to the creation of doublets in the *qal*, e.g., MH ב-ק-ר ~ פ-ק-ר (also in Targumic Aramaic) and ב-ק-ע ~ פ-ק-ע; see J. N. Epstein, מבוא לנוסח המשנה: נוסח המשנה וגלגוליו למימי האמוראים הראשונים ועד דפוסי ר׳ יו״ט ליפמן הלר (בעל תוי״ט) (3rd ed.; Jerusalem: Magnes, 2000), 1220–21; Abraham Tal, לשון התרגום לנביאים ראשונים ומעמדה בכלל ניבי הארמית (Tel-Aviv: Tel-Aviv University, 1975), 106; Menahem Moreshet, לקסיקון הפועַל שנתחדש בלשון התנאים (Ramat Gan: Bar-Ilan University Press, 1980), 287 n. 30*, 289; and the literature cited there.

guage.[44] A very different possibility—probably incompatible with the preceding one—has been suggested by Militarev and Kogan based on the occurrence of the form *näbs* (alongside *näfs*) "soul" in several of the Semitic languages of Ethiopia (Argobba, Mäsqan, Goggot, and Soddo), a form that they regard as a cognate of Northwest Semitic נבש.[45] In their view, Proto-Semitic probably had (alongside **napš-* and the verbal root **n-p-š* "breathe") "a variant nominal root **nabš-* . . . (see also metathetic **nšb* ≬ **nsb* 'to blow'. . .)."[46] This possibility, too, is well worth considering. Although *näbs* is attested only in *modern* Ethiopian Semitic, it cannot be dismissed as a late development from a modern form **näps*. There was no such modern form because **p* shifted to **f* in an ancestor of the Ethiopian Semitic languages, yielding **nafs*.

ויבל לנבשי זי בנצב זנ "and a ram for my soul, which is in this stele": To capture the tenselessness of the relative clause, one could also render this phrase as "and a ram for my soul in this stele." It is clear that Katumuwa is portrayed in this inscription as speaking at the inaugural feast of the reception room dedicated to his funerary cult. It is also clear that the "ram for my soul in this stele" was to be part of the inaugural feast. But when did that feast take place? Was it before Katumuwa's death or after it? As Pardee notes in the *editio princeps*, the phrase "for my 'soul' that (will be) in this stele" is "hardly a formula that KTMW would employ while participating in a feast during his lifetime."[47] This is a persuasive argument for the view that the inaugural feast was held *after* Katumuwa's demise. However, in his second article, Pardee appears to do an about-face, asserting that "when the author had the stele erected and established the feast, animal sacrifices were made in honor of the named divinities and of the author's soul."[48] This implies that the inaugural feast was held (not merely established) while Katumuwa was alive.[49] As for his earlier argument, Pardee writes: "In

---

[44] My witty friend, John Huehnergard, notes that this suggestion implies that all of the scholarly debate about the form נבש is "apsurd."

[45] Militarev and Kogan, *Semitic Etymological Dictionary*, 308; cf. Leslau, *Comparative Dictionary*, 389b, s.v. *nafsa*.

[46] Militarev and Kogan, *Semitic Etymological Dictionary*, 308.

[47] Pardee, "New Aramaic Inscription," 60.

[48] Pardee, "Katumuwa Inscription," 47.

[49] So, too, Herrmann, "Katumuwa Stele," 54.

stating that his 'soul' was included among the honorees at the inaugural feast, the author appears to be setting up an identification of his living form in attendance at that feast with the representation of that living form on the stele, also in attendance at that feast, and with the continuation of that being in the stele after his death."[50] Pardee's earlier view does not necessitate such speculation and is, therefore, to be preferred.

Line 8

נסיר/ד "reception room (?)": The last three letters of the word spell the word סיר/ד found twice in lines 2–3, but what is the initial *nun* doing here? Has a vowelless preformative *m*- become partially assimilated to the following dental sibilant? The difference in form (נסיר/ד < מסיר/ד [?] vs. סיר/ד) may be matched by a difference in meaning. In this context, the noun should refer to the entire funerary complex, including the vineyard. The assumption appears to be that whoever possesses the נסיר/ד also possesses the vineyard.

זנג "this": This variant of the masculine singular demonstrative pronoun, with suffixed *nun*, is used in line 9 as well, but in line 3 we find זג, the defectively spelled form that alternates with זנה in other Aramaic texts from Samal.[51] As recognized by Pardee, the closest parallel to זנג elsewhere in Aramaic is דנן.[52] For a long time, the latter form was known primarily from the Literary Aramaic of Babylonian Jewry—the official targumim (*Onqelos* and *Jonathan to the Prophets*), legal documents, magical texts, etc.[53] This distribution led Edward M. Cook to believe that it exhibited "the nunation sometimes added to unstressed final vowels in the Late Aramaic period."[54] Not long afterward, it became clear that the form דנן predated the Late Aramaic period, when it began to appear in documents from the Judean

[50] Pardee, "Katumuwa Inscription," 48.

[51] Paul-Eugène Dion, *La langue de Ya'udi: Description et classement de l'ancien parler de Zencirli dans le cadre de langues sémitiques du nord-ouest* (Waterloo, ON: Editions SR, 1974), 59, 63, 156,

[52] Pardee, "New Aramaic Inscription," 64.

[53] Tal, לשון התרגום, 8–9; Sokoloff, *Dictionary of Jewish Babylonian Aramaic*, 344a, s.v. דנא.

[54] Edward M. Cook, "The Orthography of Final Unstressed Long Vowels in Old and Imperial Aramaic," in *Sopher Mahir: Northwest Semitic Studies Presented to Stanislav Segert* = *Maarav* 5–6 (1990): 64–65.

Desert.[55] It is now attested in seven documents from the Judean Desert, dated to the end of the Herodian period and the Bar-Kokhba period.[56] In the most recent treatment of דנן, Margaretha Folmer is aware of some of these Middle Aramaic attestations but not of זנן in our inscription: "We do not have evidence for this pronoun in the older phases of Aramaic. . . . The only evidence for this form is found in documents from the period of Middle Aramaic onwards."[57] Folmer suspects that דנן "probably came into existence prior to the apocopation of the unaccented long final /ā/ of דנה, the first evidence of which is found in the period of Middle Aramaic."[58] Does the new attestation of זנן confirm her suspicion? Is it the ancestor of later דנן? There is still an enormous time gap (eight centuries) between Samalian זנן and Jewish דנן. The extent to which the gap is closed by bringing other examples of suffixed *nun*[59] into the picture depends, of course, on which of those other examples are relevant. According to some scholars, the suffixed *nun* of אדין (~ אזי) "then"—attested already in the fifth century B.C.E.—belongs here.[60] I have my doubts about that. In the other pre-Christian examples, *nun* is suffixed to

[55] Ada Yardeni, שטר מכר ממדבר יהודה: נחל צאלים 9, *Tarbiz* 63 (1994): 308 with n. 2.

[56] Ada Yardeni, אוסף תעודות ארמיות, עבריות ונבטיות ממדבר יהודה וחומר קרוב (Jerusalem: Hebrew University of Jerusalem, 2000), 2:39, s.v. דנן.

[57] Margaretha Folmer, "Rare Demonstrative Pronouns in Targum Onqelos: דנן and דיכי," in *In the Shadow of Bezalel: Aramaic, Biblical and Ancient Near Eastern Studies in Honor of Bezalel Porten* (ed. Alejandro F. Botta; CHANE 60; Leiden: Brill, 2013), 120–21. One error in Folmer's presentation needs to be noted. On p. 96 nn. 39 and 41, she cites Samaritan Aramaic הדנן and כדנן from Abraham Tal, מילון הארמית של השומרונים, 190, s.v. הדנן and כדנן. However, she fails to note the indications there that these are not genuine Samaritan forms. The entry for כדנן states explicitly that it is "from Onqelos." And (as confirmed by the author himself in an e-mail communication) the entry for הדנן indicates that all of the attestations come from insertions made by a later hand in MS N of the Samaritan targum; see Abraham Tal, *The Samaritan Targum of the Pentateuch: A Critical Edition* (3 vols.; Tel-Aviv: Tel-Aviv University, 1980–1983), 3:99 (English section).

[58] Folmer, "Rare Demonstrative Pronouns," 121.

[59] See Klaus Beyer, *Die aramäischen Texte vom Toten Meer* (2 vols.; Göttingen: Vandenhoeck & Ruprecht, 1984–1994), 1:149; Yardeni, שטר מכר, 308 n. 2; and the literature cited there.

[60] Beyer, *Die aramäischen Texte*, 1:149; Elisha Qimron, ארמית מקראית (2nd ed.; Jerusalem: Bialik, 2002), 32.

a final vowel preceded by a nasal: הִמּוֹ > הִמּוֹן (Dan 2:34, 35; 3:22) and תַּמָּה > תַּמָּן (late second century B.C.E.).[61] I suspect that in all of these early cases, the final vowel assimilated to the preceding nasal consonant, becoming a nasal vowel.[62] If so, the suffixed *nun* represents nothing more than nasalization; it does not indicate the presence of final consonantal [n]. Many additional cases of nasalized final vowels were created in Jewish Aramaic and Hebrew when final *nun* and *mem* were (variably?) elided after having nasalized the vowels that preceded them.[63] This elision is sometimes reflected in Greek transcriptions of Palestinian toponyms. Thus, we find Μωδεει and

---

[61] Murabbaʿāt 72:10 (contrasting with three occurrences of זנה in lines 5–6); Beyer, *Die aramäischen Texte*, 1:149; Yardeni, אוסף תעודות, 1:256. It used to be thought that תמן was attested already in the fifth century B.C.E. at Elephantine; see, for example, E. Y. Kutscher, "The Language of the 'Genesis Apocryphon': A Preliminary Study," *Scripta Hierosolymitana* 4 (1958): 4 n. 16 (reprinted in מחקרים בעברית ובארמית [ed. Zeev Ben-Ḥayyim, Aron Dotan, and Gad Sarfatti; Jerusalem: Magnes, 1977], 6 n. 16). However, this attestation is now viewed as a misreading; see Yardeni, שטר מכר, 308 n. 2.

[62] That is to say that the velum, having been lowered to produce the medial nasal consonant, remained lowered during the articulation of the final vowel.

[63] Z. Ben-Ḥayyim, "Traditions in the Hebrew Language, With Special Reference to the Dead Sea Scrolls," *Scripta Hierosolymitana* 4 (1958): 210–11 = idem, מסורת השומרונים וזיקתה למסורת הלשון של מגילות ים המלח וללשון חז"ל, *Lešonenu* 22 (1958): 232–33; Elisha Qimron, *The Hebrew of the Dead Sea Scrolls* (HSS 29; Atlanta: Scholars Press, 1986), 27–28; Richard C. Steiner, "Hebrew: Ancient Hebrew," in *International Encyclopedia of Linguistics* (4 vols.; New York: Oxford University Press, 1992) 2:112; Yoel Elitzur, *Ancient Place Names in the Holy Land: Preservation and History* (Jerusalem: Magnes, 2004), 314–16. Already in 1952, E. Y. Kutscher had collected a large body of evidence for what he viewed as "word-final *m* > *n*" in מחקרים בארמית הגלילית (המשך), *Tarbiz* 23 (1952): 38–43 (Eng. trans. in idem, *Studies in Galilean Aramaic* [trans. Michael Sokoloff; Ramat-Gan: Bar-Ilan University Press, 1976], 58–67, 101–3). However, his evidence (e.g., אדן < אדם in Mishnaic Hebrew) is reminiscent of the orthographic replacement of final *m* with *n* ("dentalization of *m*") in Old French, attested already in the "Sequence of Saint Eulalie" (ca. 880); see Roger Berger and Annette Brasseur, *Les séquences de sainte Eulalie* (Publications romanes et françaises 233; Geneva: Droz, 2004), 138 n. 77. In both cases, the orthographic change appears to be associated with the assimilatory nasalization of vowels and

Μωδαι for מוד(י)עין alongside Μωδεειν and Μωδαιν.[64] The Greek letter *nu* at the end of the latter two forms may reflect (variable preservation of) the final nasal consonant, or it may reflect nasalization of the final vowel without any final nasal consonant. It appears that this nasalization later spread by analogy to other words with final vowels—vowels that were neither preceded nor followed by a nasal consonant—and was written with *nun*.[65] If so, a form such as להלן < להלא "onward" in Galilean Aramaic and Mishnaic Hebrew may well have been pronounced [lhallã] rather than [lhallān] or [lhallā̃n]. In any event, for now we cannot prove a direct link between Samalian זנג and Jewish דנן, and, thus, we cannot exclude the possibility of independent development. Nevertheless, there is a good chance that we are dealing with an Aramaic form that was suppressed in Official Aramaic and went underground, only to emerge centuries later in Jewish literary and legal documents.[66]

ולו יקח "let him purchase": The root ל-ק-ח seems to have the sense here that it has in postbiblical Hebrew and occasionally already in BH, viz., "buy."[67] This is also a meaning of the cognate Akkadian verb *leqû*,[68] and it has been suggested that the Hebrew

---

the subsequent (variable?) deletion of *m* and *n*. In short, I believe that Ben-Ḥayyim's reinterpretation of Kutscher's evidence is correct.

[64] משנת ארץ ישראל: מסכתות מועד קטן וחגיגה עם מבוא ופירוש היסטורי חברתי (ed. Shmuel Safrai and Ze'ev Safrai; Ramat-Gan: Bar-Ilan University Press, 2012), 335.

[65] See again Beyer, *Die aramäischen Texte*, 1:149; Yardeni, שטר מכר, 308 n. 2; and the literature cited there. So, too, in the Urdu alphabet (derived from the Arabic alphabet), nasalized vowels are represented by a *nūn*, which, in final position, loses its superior point (*nūn-e ġunna* "*nūn* of nasalization"). Phoneticians mark nasal vowels with a tilde, e.g., [ã].

[66] For similar examples, see Steiner, "Papyrus Amherst 63," 202–3. In my view, the form דנן should play an important role in any attempt to date the oldest layer of the official *targumim*. This layer may be older than commonly thought. For evidence that an Aramaic translation of the Torah was prepared at the behest of the Achaemenid authorities, see Richard C. Steiner, "The *Mbqr* at Qumran, the *Episkopos* in the Athenian Empire, and the Meaning of *lbqrʾ* in Ezra 7:14: On the Relation of Ezra's Mission to the Persian Legal Project," *JBL* 120 (2001): 636–38.

[67] E. Y. Kutscher, מלים ותולדותיהן (Jerusalem: Kiryath Sefer, 1965), 55. Contrast Pardee, "New Aramaic Inscription," 54: "let him take."

[68] See *CAD* L:139–40, s.v.

verb acquired the meaning as a result of Akkadian influence.[69] It is possible that something similar occurred in Samalian. In any event, this use of ל-ק-ח is not well attested in Aramaic, perhaps because of the root ז-ב-ן "buy," which appears already in Official Aramaic. The converse of ל-ק-ח "buy," viz., נ-ת-ן בכסף "sell,"[70] is attested much earlier, e.g., Gen 23:9; Deut 2:28; 14:25; 1 Kgs 21:6; 21:15. It is parallel to Akkadian *ana kaspi(m) nadānu* "sell,"[71] attested already in Old Akkadian.[72] A variant of this expression is attested at Zincirli in Kulamuwa's Phoenician inscription (*KAI* no. 24 line 8), assuming that ועלמת יתן בש means "a maid he sold for a sheep."

Lines 6–8

מנ מנ בני . . . ולו יקח "whoever from among my sons . . . —let him purchase": A *casus pendens* construction like the ones in the Bible which have "the left-dislocated element . . . connected to the clause with a conjunction."[73] The closest biblical parallel is אֲשֶׁר יִמָּצֵא אִתּוֹ מֵעֲבָדֶיךָ וָמֵת "whoever from among your servants it is found with—he shall die" (Gen 44:9). For additional examples with a conjunction and an indefinite subject ("whoever," "anyone who," etc.), see Exod 9:21; 21:13; and many of the examples collected by S. R. Driver.[74] It is possible that the left-dislocated element is itself derived from a *casus pendens* construction: מנ מנ בני או מנבניאש ויהי לה נסיר/ד זנג "whoever

[69] Kutscher, מלים ותולדותיהן, 55.

[70] For converse terms in semantics, including *buy* and *sell*, see John Lyons, *Semantics* (2 vols.; Cambridge: Cambridge University Press, 1977), 1:279–80.

[71] E. Y. Kutscher, editorial note in Joseph Naveh, כתובות ארמיות קדומות, *Lešonenu* 29 (1965): 186.

[72] CAD N1:49–50, s.v. *nadānu*.

[73] Adina Moshavi, *Word Order in the Biblical Hebrew Finite Clause: A Syntactic and Pragmatic Analysis of Preposing* (Linguistic Studies in Ancient West Semitic 4; Winona Lake, Ind.: Eisenbrauns, 2010), 83. See also the standard grammars and Richard C. Steiner, "Does the Biblical Hebrew Conjunction -ו Have Many Meanings, One Meaning, or No Meaning At All?" *JBL* 119 (2000): 265–66.

[74] S. R. Driver, *A Treatise on the Use of the Tenses in Hebrew and Some Other Syntactical Questions* (3rd ed.; London: Oxford University Press, 1892), 151 §123; reprinted with an introductory essay by W. Randall Garr (Grand Rapids: Eerdmans, 1998).

from among my sons or from among the sons of anybody (else)—he shall come into possession of this reception room (?)." If it is, this is a good example of recursion (also known as "recursiveness" and "recursivity") in Northwest Semitic syntax.

Lines 8–9

מנ חיל כרמ זנג "out of the yield of this vineyard": Pardee's comparison to תְּאֵנָה וָגֶפֶן נָתְנוּ חֵילָם "fig tree and vine have given their חיל" (Joel 2:22)[75] is apt, but he does not supply a rendering for חיל in that verse. The rendering of RSV and NRSV—"full yield"—is probably close to the mark; cf. also the well-attested meaning "wealth" in BH.[76] However, we may be dealing with a technical meaning, similar to that of פרות in Mishnaic Hebrew, viz., "usufruct, profit, interest."[77] English *yield* also has such a technical meaning, as in the phrase "payable out of the yield of an estate."[78] In my view, the prepositional phrase מנ חיל כרמ זנג is an adverbial modifying יקח;[79] others take it as the direct object of יקח[80] or as part of a compound direct object.[81]

Line 9

שא "a sheep": For שא "sheep" at Samal, cf. *KAI* no. 215 line 9 ושאה ושורה "and ewes and cows"; שאה must have had a morphologically masculine counterpart שא,[82] just as שורה had a morphologically masculine counterpart שור, attested in our inscription. Pardee dismisses this simple interpretation of the noun in favor of a more

[75] Pardee, "New Aramaic Inscription," 65.

[76] BDB, 299a, s.v., meaning no. 3.

[77] Marcus Jastrow, *A Dictionary of the Targumim, the Talmud Babli and Yerushalmi, and the Midrashic Literature* (London: Luzac, 1903), 1225, s.v. פרי.

[78] Contrast Pardee, "New Aramaic Inscription," 54: "from the best (produce) of this vine(yard)." There is no need for parentheses in the last word; *krm* means "vineyard" and *gpn* means "vine."

[79] So, too, Sanders, "Appetites," 50.

[80] Pardee, "New Aramaic Inscription," 54, 65; and idem, "Katumuwa Inscription," 45, 48.

[81] Nebe, "Eine neue Inschrift," 318, 325.

[82] So, too, Lemaire, "Rites," 135; and Lemaire and Sass, "Mortuary Stele," 122; contrast Pardee, "New Aramaic Inscription," 54.

speculative one: "(as) a (presentation?)-offering."[83] He is compelled to do so by his assumption that the phrase מנ חיל כרמ זנג, rather than שא, is the direct object of יקח.

Line 10

יומנ ליומנ "every year": The literal meaning is "days to days," that is, "(from) year to year." Pardee aptly compares מימים ימימה, which occurs five times in the Bible, adding: "There [1 Sam 1:3] the meaning 'yearly' for the phrase 'from days to days' appears clear from the structure of the story."[84] It should be added that there are quite a few examples of ימים meaning "full year" in other biblical passages, as pointed out by both the rabbis[85] and modern scholars.[86] This interpretation seems to imply that the ending *-n* is the Common Aramaic plural ending, even though that ending was not in use in Samalian. Lemaire attempts to avoid that implication by suggesting two alternate interpretations for the ending *-n*,[87] but this is unnecessary. For a simpler solution, see the section entitled "The Languages and Dialects of Samal" below.

Lines 9–10

שא יומנ ליומנ "a sheep every year": André Lemaire and Benjamin Sass compare the phrase שאי̇נ לימ "two sheep for the day" appearing twice in their new decipherment of the Samalian funerary inscription from Ördekburnu near Zincirli.[88]

---

[83] Pardee, "New Aramaic Inscription," 54, 65; and idem, "Katumuwa Inscription," 45 (minus the question mark). Cf. Sanders, "Appetites," 50: "an . . . offering."

[84] Pardee, "New Aramaic Inscription," 65.

[85] See, for example, Horovitz and Rabin, מכילתא דרבי ישמעאל, 69 lines 10–13 (Exod 13:10 and Lev 25:29); *b. Ketub.* 57b (Gen 24:55 and Lev 25:29); Rashi to Num 9:22; Rashbam to Gen 40:4; Abraham Ibn Ezra to Gen 27:44.

[86] See BDB, 399b, s.v. יום, meaning no. 6c.

[87] Lemaire, "Le dialecte," 149–50.

[88] Lemaire and Sass, "Mortuary Stele," 122–23.

Lines 10–11

ויהרג "and let him slaughter it": For ה-ר-ג used of slaughtering animals for feasts, cf. Isa 22:13. The expected accusative pronoun expressing "it" is absent, because when two coordinate verbs have identical underlying direct objects, the second of those objects may undergo deletion instead of—or after—pronominalization.[89]

Line 11

בנבשי "beside my soul": One of the meanings of the preposition -ב at Samal is "beside, next to."[90] The slaughtering is to take place in close proximity to the stele, which contains Katumuwa's soul.

Line 12

וישוי "and let him present": The root ש-ו-י was previously known at Samal in the noun שי "gift"[91] < **šayy-* < **šawy-*.[92] The verb and the noun occur together in an Aramaic text in Greek script: *αμμουδ αμασαι σειιαια ιααβνα λα(ι) ζαβδαια σαυιει να αμμοδ ζαβδαια* = עמוד עמסי שייא יהבנא // לזבדיא שוינא עמוד זבדיא "we donated the pillar of the gift bearers;[93] for the offerings, we bestowed the pillar of offerings."[94] The

[89] Cf. Muraoka and Porten, *Grammar*, 273. Contrast Pardee, "New Aramaic Inscription," 54: "he is also to perform the slaughter (prescribed above)"; and 66: "No direct object is expressed after HRG in the new inscription, but it appears highly likely that the reference is to the festal sacrifice of a bull and several rams established by the first part of the text." Pardee's rendering seems to assume that the omission of the object following the transitive root ה-ר-ג is an example of "absolute use," comparable to English *he's eating*.

[90] See *KAI* no. 215 line 18 and no. 216 line 8, according to *DNWSI*, 138, s.v. b_2 meaning no. 1c.

[91] *KAI* no. 214 line 18.

[92] See Richard C. Steiner, "Poetic Forms in the Masoretic Vocalization and Three Difficult Phrases in Jacob's Blessing: יֶתֶר שְׂאֵת (Gen 49:3), יְצוּעִי עָלָה (Gen 49:4), and יָבֹא שִׁילֹה (Gen 49:10)," *JBL* 129 (2010): 223. Note, however, that the reading שי in *KAI* no. 214 line 18 has recently been challenged by Lemaire ("Rites," 132, 135).

[93] For the phrase עמסי שייא, cf. BH נֹשְׂאֵי מִנְחָה.

[94] Steiner, "Poetic Forms," 223. For the Greek text, see Manfred

verb is also known from the Bible: הוֹד וְהָדָר תְּשַׁוֶּה עָלָיו "you bestowed splendor and majesty upon him" (Ps 21:6). As for the related noun, it is attested in the Bible and in the Lachish ewer.[95] Lemaire and Sass entertain the possibilty that וישוי means "and let him roast."[96]

Funerary Foundations

This inscription appears to be intended for a specific occasion, the festal inauguration of Katumuwa's funerary cult.[97] In the first part, it prescribes the offerings for that occasion; in the second part, it sets forth the manner in which his needs will be met after the inauguration, viz., by means of an endowed funerary foundation. Katumuwa's endowment includes a vineyard (line 9),[98] and Katumuwa invites Hadad of the Vineyards to the inaugural banquet (line 4), presumably as a means of ensuring that the vineyard will yield enough income to cover the cost of the yearly offering. It may also include the house—or at least the room—in which Katumuwa erected his stele (lines 1–2).

Funerary foundations are known from Egypt already in the Early Dynastic period[99] and from Anatolia, Syria, and elsewhere

---

Krebernik, "Ein aramäischer Text in griechischer Schrift?" in *"Sprich doch mit deinen Knechten aramäisch, wir verstehen es!" . . . Festschrift für Otto Jastrow zum 60. Geburtstag* (ed. Werner Arnold and Hartmut Bobzin; Wiesbaden: Harrassowitz, 2002), 427. For pillar-shaped cult stands, see LaMoine F. DeVries, "Cult Stands: A Bewildering Variety of Shapes and Sizes," *BAR* 13.4 (July/August 1987): 29.

[95] See Frank Moore Cross, "The Evolution of the Proto-Canaanite Alphabet," *BASOR* 134 (1954): 21; idem, "The Origin and Early Evolution of the Alphabet," *Eretz-Israel* 8 (1967): 16*; and Richard C. Steiner, "*Mattan* and *Shay* in the Lachish Ewer Inscription," to appear in *Eretz-Israel* (Joseph Naveh Memorial Volume).

[96] Lemaire and Sass, "Mortuary Stele," 129 n. 176.

[97] See above.

[98] Cf. Struble and Herrmann, "Eternal Feast," 30. As noted by Pardee ("New Aramaic Inscription," 65), the deictic in כרמ זנג "this vineyard" hints that the vineyard was nearby; moreover, "the area immediately to the east of the chamber where the stele was found appears to have been open at roughly the time the stele was erected, and the presence of a small vineyard there is possible."

[99] Toby A. H. Wilkinson, *Early Dynastic Egypt* (London: Routledge,

in the Hellenistic and Roman periods.[100] They were endowed with "mortuary estates"—fields, gardens, vineyards, houses, etc.—to provide perpetual care for the dead.[101] Some parts of Katumuwa's inscription, viz., lines 8–10 and lines 3–5, are paralleled in the funerary inscription of a certain Posidonius from Halikarnassos dated to between ca. 350 and 250 B.C.E.:[102]

> Every year in the month of Eleutherios, these [= the officiants] should take four gold staters from the (interest of the) mortgage (on the endowed fields), in the possession of the priests, and carry out the sacrifices.[103]
>
> On the first day, they should offer: to the Good Fortune of the father and mother of Posidonius, a ram; to the Good Spirit (Δαίμονι ἀγαθῶι) of Posidonius and (his wife) Gorgis, a ram. On the second day: to Zeus Patroios, a ram; to Apollo, guardian of Telemessos, a ram; to the Moirai, a ram; to the Mother of the Gods, a goat.[104]

The term Δαίμων "can designate the immortal 'guiding spirit' of an individual," and that appears to be the meaning here.[105] Like the נבש of Katumuwa, the Δαίμων of Posidonius is to receive a ram as a funerary offering; however, Posidonius's endowment appears to be larger than Katumuwa's, since it suffices to pay for a ram *every* year, not just the first year. The correspondence between Δαίμων and נבש in these inscriptions corroborates the common assumption (based

1999), 98–103. See also Robert K. Ritner, "The Cult of the Dead," in *Ancient Egypt* (ed. David P. Silverman; New York: Oxford University Press, 1997), 141.

100 Bernhard Laum, *Stiftungen in der griechischen und römischen Antike: Ein Beitrag zur antiken Kulturgeschichte* (2 vols.; Leipzig: B. G. Teubner, 1914); Robert Parker, "A Funerary Foundation from Hellenistic Lycia," *Chiron* 40 (2010): 103–21.

101 Laum, *Stiftungen*, 1:133–35. For the establishment of vineyards to support the Egyptian king's funerary cult, see Wilkinson, *Early Dynastic Egypt*, 101.

102 Laum, *Stiftungen*, 1:71, 2:111–12 (no. 117). For the date, see Jan-Mathieu Carbon, "Δάρρων and δαίμον: A New Inscription from Mylasa," *Epigraphica Anatolica* 38 (2005): 5 n. 27.

103 Laum, *Stiftungen*, 2:111 (no. 117).

104 Ibid., 2:112.

105 Carbon, "Δάρρων and δαίμον," 6.

on the correspondence between Akkadian *eṭemmu* and נבש)[106] that Katumuwa's נבש is his (immortal) spirit or soul.

The Languages and Dialects of Samal

The sociolinguistic situation at Samal is rather complex. The inscriptions from this site date from the period beginning in the second half of the ninth century and ending in the second half of the eighth century. During that relatively short period, we see a transition from Phoenician to Samalian (usually considered to be a dialect of Aramaic) followed by a transition from Samalian to standard Old Aramaic. In the words of H. L. Ginsberg:

> It would ... seem that at some time in the third quarter of the 8th century B.C.E. the local vernacular, Samalian, was (as a "provincial" dialect) superseded, for purposes of royal epigraphs, by Common Aramaic. Possibly Kilamuwa's ... Samalian votive inscription similarly postdated his Phoenician stele, and likewise bears witness to a language policy: Kilamuwa would then have begun by employing the old cultural language of the region, Phoenician, and then have substituted the native Samalian speech as the official language in the second half of the 9th century B.C.E.[107]

In Pardee's view, the Katumuwa inscription makes the situation even more complex:

> In summary, the new inscription requires that the former relatively neat picture of inscriptions in Samalian, Old Aramaic, and Phoenician be modified. It may now be posited that two principal Northwest Semitic languages were in use in Samʾal, Phoenician (*KAI* 24, ninth century) and Aramaic, with the latter now attested in three distinct dialects, the two that were previously known, Samalian (admitting that Samalian is to be identified as an archaic dialect of Aramaic rather than a distinct Northwest Semitic language) and a local form of Old Aramaic, and a third, attested in the new inscription.[108]

---

[106] See at chapter 1, nn. 29–30.

[107] H. L. Ginsberg, "The Northwest Semitic Languages," in *Patriarchs* (ed. Benjamin Mazar; World History of the Jewish People 2; New Brunswick, N.J.: Rutgers University Press, 1966), 118–19.

[108] Pardee, "New Aramaic Inscription," 68.

The suggestion that "three distinct dialects" of Aramaic were in use at Samal, at virtually the same time, is rather provocative, to say the least—especially if the term *dialect* is being used in its proper sense ("a distinctive variety of the *spoken* language"). One can hardly fault Lemaire for asking, "Is it really necessary to see in this inscription the revelation of a new dialect?"[109] What is the basis for this claim?

Pardee is well aware that the language of the inscription "shows some features that are remarkably characteristic of Samalian, in particular the retention of {ʾnk} as the 1 c.s. pronoun and the particle {wt-}."[110] In addition, it exhibits one of the two most distinctive characteristics of the Samalian dialect:

> No form of the definite article is attested in this inscription, as in Samalian, unlike in ZA,[[111]] where one finds {-ʾ} on both singular and plural nouns.[112]
>
> The principal isogloss by which this dialect differs from ZA is the absence of a post-positive definite article.[113]

Examples of this feature in the Katumuwa inscription are סיר/ד זנ "this reception room" (lines 2–3), נצב זנ "this stele" (line 5), נסיר/ד זנג "this reception room (?)" (line 8), and כרמ זנג "this vineyard" (line 9). In each of these cases, the noun is modified by a demonstrative adjective; in standard Old Aramaic, such nouns *do* take the definite article.[114]

In Pardee's view, this evidence does not suffice:

> The inscription would immediately be classified as Samalian were it not for the m.pl.abs. forms ending in {-n} ({ywmn} twice in line 10, probably {krmn} in line 4, and possibly {ṣwd/rn} in that same line). That masculine plural nouns in the absolute and construct states appear in Samalian with a *mater lectionis* represent-

---

[109] Lemaire, "Le dialecte," 146.

[110] Pardee, "New Aramaic Inscription," 68.

[111] That is, the standard Old Aramaic used at Zincirli, the variety of Aramaic that superseded Samalian in the later royal inscriptions.

[112] Pardee, "New Aramaic Inscription," 67.

[113] Ibid., 68.

[114] One could argue that the definite article is, in reality, redundant for such nouns, but that has little relevance for classification.

ing a vowel marking case (nom. = {-w}, obl. = {-y}) and without a following consonant in the absolute state is broadly accepted today. Indeed, in some respects, this is the defining isogloss of Samalian. . . .[115]

The language of the Katumuwa inscription is a previously unattested dialect of Aramaic, not quite so archaic as the language of the Hadad and Panamuwa inscriptions, but more so than the standardized language of the larger body of Aramaic inscriptions from the Aramaean kingdoms of the ninth to seventh centuries BC.[116]

In my view, it would be rash to posit a new dialect based on a single feature, even if we had access to the spoken language. It seems particularly unwise to make such an assumption when the result is an anomaly, viz., the use of three *distinct* dialects of Aramaic in a single city at the same time.

Fortunately, there is a far simpler and more natural explanation. A few years after Katumuwa prepared his stele, during the reign of Bar-Rakib son of Panamuwa II, standard Old Aramaic replaced Samalian in the royal inscriptions of Samal. For Jonas C. Greenfield, the replacement illustrates the "interplay of language and politics," since standard Old Aramaic was the lingua franca of the Assyrian Empire, and Bar-Rakib was at pains to stress in his inscriptions that he was a loyal vassal of Tiglath-pileser, the ruler of that empire.[117] Ian Young strengthens Greenfield's thesis by pointing to "other examples of subservience to foreign culture and ideas in this reign."[118]

Greenfield presented the replacement as an abrupt change, resulting from a political decision. The evidence of the subsequently discovered Katumuwa inscription raises the possibility that Bar-Rakib's political decision was the culmination of a gradual sociolinguistic change beginning in the time of his father. In other words, it is possible that standard Old Aramaic was viewed as more

---

115 Pardee, "New Aramaic Inscription," 66.

116 Pardee, "Katumuwa Inscription," 45.

117 Jonas C. Greenfield, "The Dialects of Early Aramaic," *JNES* 37 (1978): 95.

118 Ian Young, "The Languages of Ancient Samʾal," *Maarav* 9 (2002): 104–5.

prestigious than Samalian already in the time of Panamuwa II and Katumuwa—at least by educated scribes. To my mind, the simplest explanation for the use of the plural suffix *-n* in Katumuwa's inscription is that (1) Katumuwa or his scribe viewed Samalian as a provincial variety of Aramaic,[119] one with lower status than the standard variety of Old Aramaic used throughout the Assyrian Empire; and (2) Katumuwa or his scribe viewed the plural suffix *-n* as a sociolinguistic marker of standard Aramaic and used it to add prestige to the inscription.[120] In other words, Katumuwa or his scribe agreed with Pardee's assertion that the absence of the plural suffix *-n* "is the defining isogloss of Samalian"![121]

A somewhat similar solution has been proposed by Paul Noorlander: "Impressionistically, one could even adduce the Aramaic of Bar-Rākib as the final destination of the gradual Aramaization of Śamʾāl, in which the Kattimuwa stele exhibits a transitional stage."[122] It is clear from Noorlander's discussion that what he has in mind is

---

[119] This view of Samalian is held by many modern scholars as well. See, for example, Ginsberg, "Northwest Semitic," 118–19 (cited in part at n. 107 above); and Tropper, *Die Inschriften*, 307–11.

[120] Cf. Schloen and Fink, "New Excavations," 10: "KTMW's mortuary inscription is written . . . in the local West Semitic Samalian dialect (or an Aramaized version of it)." Since the influence of standard varieties on varieties with lower prestige is very well known, one example from Late Aramaic should suffice. The Babylonian Geonim spoke a variety of Eastern Aramaic similar to the vernacular recorded in the Talmud, but their writings reflect the influence of a "high Babylonian" literary language—an archaic variety preserved in traditional legal documents. The extent of this influence varies with the genre and its degree of formality. Thus, the influence is more pronounced in the opening lines of the responsa of the Geonim than it is in the rest of their writings. For the evidence and the plausible claim that this reflects style shifting rather than dialectal variation, see Matthew Morgenstern, הארמית הבבלית היהודית בתשובות הגאונים — עיונים בתורת ההגה, בתצורת הפועל, בכינויים ובסגנון (Ph.D. diss., Hebrew University, 2002), i (English abstract), 13–15.

[121] Centuries later, the absence of the masculine plural suffix *-n* would become a/the defining feature of *Eastern* Aramaic.

[122] Paul Noorlander, "Samʾalian in Its Northwest Semitic Setting: A Historical-Comparative Approach," *Orientalia* 81 (2012): 229. (I am indebted to John Huehnergard for this reference.) Nebe ("Eine neue Inschrift," 330) speaks of "the transitional stage to the Aramaic of Zincirli in its last phase."

a gradual change in the *spoken* language (from Samalian—not Aramaic, in his view—to Aramaic): "That would require the postulation of intense contact with an Aramaic-speaking community, such that even inflectional borrowing took place."[123]

It is probably best to proceed with caution at this point. It is not impossible that the plural suffix *-n* appeared as an affectation in the speech of Samalian courtiers. In that case, we might claim to have discovered a new *sociolect* of *Samalian* (rather than a new *dialect* of *Aramaic*). In my view, such a claim would go beyond the available evidence because we cannot take for granted that Katumuwa used the plural suffix *-n* in speech as well as in writing. But even if the claim is true, we cannot speak of "three distinct dialects." We are dealing, rather, with style shifting along a continuous spectrum from the vernacular to the standard language.

The use of Phoenician at Samal is also quite instructive. The Phoenician inscription (*KAI* no. 24) dates to the reign of Kulamuwa (late ninth century B.C.E.), as does one of the Samalian inscriptions (*KAI* no. 25). This seems to be evidence for Phoenician–Aramaic bilingualism, at least among the educated elite. Such bilingualism is precisely the sociolinguistic context needed to explain the way that the twenty-two-letter Phoenician alphabet was adapted for use with the twenty-nine-consonant Old Aramaic phonemic inventory.

It is widely accepted that Proto-Semitic *ṣ́, *ś, *ṯ, *ḏ, *ṯ̣, *ḫ, and *ġ were preserved as separate phonemes (albeit not always with their original pronunciation) in standard Old Aramaic,[124] where they were written with *qof, šin, šin, zayin, ṣade, ḥet,* and *ʿayin,* respectively. The result was polyphony: *qof* was used to represent the reflexes of *ṣ́ and *q; *šin* was used to represent the reflexes of *ś, *ṯ, and *š; *zayin* was used to represent the reflexes of *ḏ and *z; *ṣade* was used to represent the reflexes of *ṯ̣ and *ṣ; and so on. Later (after a series of mergers), we find *qof, šin, šin, zayin,* and *ṣade* replaced by *ʿayin, samekh, taw, dalet* and *ṭet,* respectively—but only for the reflexes of *ṣ́, *ś, *ṯ, *ḏ, *ṯ̣, respectively. There can be little doubt that the orthographic replacement reveals that the earlier spellings represent the Semitic phonemes in question at a time when they were still unmerged,

---

123 Noorlander, "Samʾalian," 229.

124 For *ḫ and *ġ in Aramaic, see Richard C. Steiner, "On the Dating of Hebrew Sound Changes (*Ḫ > Ḥ and *Ġ > ʿ) and Greek Translations (2 Esdras and Judith)," *JBL* 124 (2005): 229–67.

but why were they written that way at first? For example, why was *t* not used to represent the sound [θ] by Aramaic scribes already in the Neo-Assyrian period, as it was by Akkadian scribes back then?[125] The question becomes more compelling once one notes the strange asymmetry of the standard Old Aramaic orthographic system, in which *šin* (rather than *samekh*) is grouped with *zayin* and *ṣade*.[126] Of course, the same asymmetrical treatment of *ṯ is found in Canaanite in general and Phoenician in particular. The asymmetry must have been transferred from Phoenician to Aramaic together with the alphabet itself.[127] Bilinguals simply used the Phoenician spelling of lexical items like *šql* "shekel" and *y-š-b* "sit," even though Old Aramaic did not have a /š/ in them. This evidence suggests that the main principle used in adapting the Phoenician alphabet to Old Aramaic was etymological rather than phonetic.[128]

The asymmetry transferred to Aramaic from Phoenician through the etymological adaptation of the alphabet clearly bothered the Aramaic scribes of Tell Fekherye. Not knowing Phoenician, they found the use of *šin* to represent *ṯ inexplicable. They eliminated the problem by using *samekh* to represent *ṯ.[129] This spelling reform can be viewed as the product of a simple phonetic analogy: *ṯ : *samekh* = *ḏ : *zayin* = *ṯ̣ : *ṣade*. Alternatively, it can be viewed as an example of the etymological adaptation of an alphabet by bilingual

[125] Richard C. Steiner, "Addenda to *The Case for Fricative-Laterals in Proto-Semitic*," in *Semitic Studies in Honor of Wolf Leslau on the Occasion of his Eighty-fifth Birthday, November 14th, 1991* (ed. Alan S. Kaye; 2 vols.; Wiesbaden: Harrassowitz, 1991), 2:1506. The contrast between the two groups of scribes is most striking in the bilingual inscription from Tell Fekherye, where we find [θ] in a single personal name (*Adad-itʾi* = הדיסעי) written in two different ways; see Ali Abou-Assaf, Pierre Bordreuil, and Alan R. Millard, *La statue de Tell Fekherye et son inscription bilingue assyro-arameénne* (Études assyriologiques; Paris: Recherche sur les civilisations, 1982), 18, 43–44, 80.

[126] More precisely, there is a mismatch between the orthography and the phonology, for /š/ does not belong to any phonological triad.

[127] Richard C. Steiner, *Early Northwest Semitic Serpent Spells in the Pyramid Texts* (HSS 61; Winona Lake, Ind.: Eisenbrauns, 2011), 48 with n. 127.

[128] See Joshua Blau, *Phonology and Morphology of Biblical Hebrew: An Introduction* (Winona Lake, Ind.: Eisenbrauns, 2010), 74–75.

[129] Abou-Assaf, Bordreuil, and Millard, *La statue*, 43–44, 80.

scribes being susceptible to later correction by scribes based on the phonetic principle.[130]

There is one radical departure from Canaanite orthography in Old Aramaic: the use of *qof* rather than *ṣade* to represent the reflex of *ṣ́. With this phoneme, the bilingual scribes who adapted the Phoenician alphabet to Aramaic abandoned the etymological principle in favor of phonetic considerations. Perhaps the reflex of *ṣ́ had become so different phonetically from the reflexes of *ṣ and *ṯ̣ (and so similar to the reflex of **q*) that it seemed odd to represent it with *ṣade*.

This account assumes, of course, that we know something about the realization of the reflex of *ṣ́ in Old Aramaic. However, this assumption has been challenged by John Huehnergard:

> The pronunciation represented by <Q> might well have become normative very early, or it might even represent something close to the assumed Proto-Semitic pronunciation (or at least one allophone thereof). All that can be said is that the reflex of *ṣ́ had not merged with *ṣ in the texts in which it is written with <Q>; in other words, no change can be said with certainty to have occurred, unlike the situation in Ugaritic and in Canaanite, where such a merger did take place.[131]

This statement appears to assume that, when it comes to ancient texts, only a phonemic merger can prove that a phonetic change has occurred. If so, it follows that there is no proof that *ṣ́ changed

---

[130] A somewhat similar example can be cited from Arabic. It was apparently bilingual Nabateans who adapted the twenty-two-letter Aramaic alphabet for use with Arabic. Their use of *ṭet, ḥet* and *ʿayin* to write the Arabic reflexes of *ṯ̣, *ḫ and *ġ, respectively, was probably based, at least in part, on the *etymological* principle of adaptation (Blau, *Phonology and Morphology*, 75). Jews, however, later used *kaf* and *gimel* to write the Arabic reflexes of *ḫ and *ġ, respectively, based on the *phonetic* principle of adaptation. The same principle underlies the use of *dalet* (instead of *ṭet*) for the Arabic reflex of *ṯ̣ in at least some of our oldest Judeo-Arabic documents; see Joshua Blau, *A Handbook of Early Middle Arabic* (Jerusalem: Hebrew University of Jerusalem, 2002), 22.

[131] John Huehnergard, "What Is Aramaic?" *Aram* 7 (1995): 278. I have corrected a typographical error in the passage with the permission of the author.

its pronunciation in Old Aramaic, since it is clear that *ṣ́ was still unmerged in that language. In my view, such an assumption, while normally valid, may be overly stringent in this case. Let us review the evidence pertaining to this question.

There is no reason to doubt that *ṣ́ was articulated in the front of the mouth in Proto-Semitic. In most of the Semitic languages it eventually merged with *ṣ; in Amorite, it was written with the same cuneiform signs as *ṣ and *ṯ̣;[132] in Arabic, it merged with *ṯ̣ or *l.[133] Even Aramaic itself appears to have ṣ as the reflex of *ṣ́ in a non-trivial number of words,[134] possibly a relic of some Pre-Proto-Aramaic stage. Further evidence comes from the doublets and correspondences that indicate that *ṣ́ was the emphatic counterpart of *ś.[135] The evidence of transcriptions (from languages in which *ṣ́ remained unmerged until historical times) points in the same direction. The ancient North Arabian deity *Ruḍā* (*Rḍw, Rḍy*) is called *Ru-ul-ṭa-a-a-u* by Esarhaddon[136] and apparently 'Οροτάλτ by Herodotus (3.8).[137] The

---

[132] Michael P. Streck, "Amorite," in *The Semitic Languages: An International Handbook* (ed. Stefan Weninger; Handbücher zur Sprach- und Kommunikationswissenschaft 36; Berlin: De Gruyter Mouton, 2012), 454.

[133] See, for example, Richard C. Steiner, *The Case for Fricative-Laterals in Proto-Semitic* (American Oriental Series 59; New Haven: American Oriental Society, 1977), 16–20, 36–37, 71; Kees Versteegh, "Loanwords from Arabic and the Merger of *ḍ/ḏ̣*," *Israel Oriental Studies* 19 (1999): 273–86; Jonathan A. C. Brown, "New Data on the Delateralization of *ḍād* and Its Merger with *Ẓāʾ* in Classical Arabic: Contributions from Old South Arabic and the Earliest Islamic Texts on *Ḍ* / *Ẓ* Minimal Pairs," *JSS* 52 (2007): 335–68; and the literature cited there.

[134] Steiner, *Fricative-Laterals*, 149–54; Leonid Kogan, "Proto-Semitic Phonetics and Phonology," in *The Semitic Languages: An International Handbook* (ed. Stefan Weninger et al.; Berlin: De Gruyter Mouton, 2012), 100.

[135] Steiner, *Fricative-Laterals*, 111–22.

[136] Ibid., 92–94.

[137] Javier Teixidor, *The Pagan God: Popular Religion in the Greco-Roman Near East* (Princeton: Princeton University Press, 1977), 69; Steiner, "Addenda," 1503–4; Kogan, "Phonetics and Phonology," 72. This identification makes much more phonetic sense than the ones cited in David Asheri, Alan Lloyd, and Aldo Corcella, *A Commentary on Herodotus Books I-IV* (ed. Oswyn Murray and Alfonso Moreno; Oxford: Oxford University Press, 2007), 407.

Ethiopian toponym that is written *Mḍ* in epigraphic Geez is rendered Ματλια in Greek.[138] These transcriptions raise the possibility that *ṣ́ was realized as an affricate, [tɬʼ],[139] a realization suggested by other considerations as well.[140]

There is also no reason to doubt that *ṣ́ was articulated in the back of the mouth in Old Aramaic and probably already in Proto-Aramaic. Aramean scribes initially used *qof* to write this sound; subsequently, after a further development, they used *ʿayin*. Assyrian scribes rendered it at times with a velar/uvular fricative and at times with a velar/uvular stop, e.g., *Ra-ḫi-a-nu*/*Ra-qi-a-nu* and *-ra-ḫi-i*/*-ra-qí-i* = רקי-.[141] This variation, taken together with other considerations, seems to point to either a velar affricate [kxʼ] or a uvular affricate [qχʼ].[142] Leonid Kogan speaks of a "growing consensus" in favor of this reconstruction.[143]

Similar variation is found in Papyrus Amherst 63,[144] where the reflex of *ṣ́ is rendered sometimes with a velar/uvular fricative and sometimes with a velar/uvular stop. Examples of the former are:

---

[138] See Kogan, "Phonetics and Phonology," 80, and the literature cited there.

[139] Greek -τάλτ may be an attempt to render [tɬʼa:].

[140] André Martinet, "Remarques sur le consonantisme sémitique," *Bulletin de la Société Linguistique de Paris* 49 (1953): 67–78 = idem, *Évolution des langues et reconstruction* (Paris: Presses Universitaires de France, 1975), 248–61; Steiner, *Fricative-Laterals*, 155–56; Kogan, "Phonetics and Phonology," 62–65.

[141] Beyer, *Die aramäischen Texte*, 1:101.

[142] Steiner, *Fricative-Laterals*, 40; Rainer M. Voigt, "Die Laterale im Semitischen, *WO* 10 (1979): 101–2; Steiner, "Addenda," 1500–1501; Qimron, ארמית מקראית, 13; T. Notarius, "*ʔq(n)* 'wood' in the Aramaic Ostraca from Idumea: A Note on the Reflex of Proto-Semitic /*ṣ́/ in Imperial Aramaic," *Aramaic Studies* 4 (2006): 104–5; Steiner, *Early Northwest Semitic Serpent Spells*, 72; see also the next footnote. Note that [q] is used here as it is used by the International Phonetic Association, as a plain (= nonemphatic) voiceless uvular stop.

[143] Kogan, "Phonetics and Phonology," 99 (with literature).

[144] Amherst 63 is a long Aramaic text recorded in the Demotic Egyptian script instead of the normal Aramaic script; see Richard C. Steiner, "The Aramaic Text in Demotic Script," in *The Context of Scripture* (ed. William W. Hallo and K. Lawson Younger Jr.; 3 vols.; Leiden: Brill, 1997–2002), 1:309–27, and the literature cited there.

e.m.r.^{m} *b.ḫ.nh.n.*^{m} = *ʾmr bġnhn* "a lamb in their flocks" (VI/4)[145]

ʿ̅r̅ .rẖ.^{m} *wbrl̅m̅n̅* = *ʿl ʾrġʾ wbrmn* "on earth and on high [lit., in heights]" (XV/3)

Examples of the latter are:

r̅.^{m} *ḥ.k*^{m} *y.t.why*^{m} = *rḥq ydwhy* "he washes/washed his hands" (III/10–11)[146]

.rk^{m} *h.w*^{m} *n.ḥ.š.n*^{m} *šm.y.*^{m} *ṫprs.rn*^{m} = *ʾrk(ʾ) hw(h) nḥšn šmy(ʾ) dprzln* "the earth was (like) pieces of bronze; the heavens, (as though) of pieces of iron" (XVII/11)[147]

⸢š⸣[my]⸢n⸣^{g} *w̿.rk.*^{m} = *⸢š⸣[my]⸢n⸣ w(ʾ)rq* "⸢h⸣[eav]⸢en⸣ and earth" (XXII/6–7)[148]

Despite the superficial similarity between this variation and that in the Assyrian sources, it seems unlikely that they have the same explanation.[149] Nevertheless, at least some of these renderings are

---

[145] Richard C. Steiner and Charles F. Nims, "You Can't Offer Your Sacrifice and Eat It Too: A Polemical Poem from the Aramaic Text in Demotic Script," *JNES* 43 (1984): 93, 98.

[146] Richard C. Steiner and Adina Moshavi, "A Selective Glossary of Northwest Semitic Texts in Egyptian Script," in *DNWSI* 2:1257, s.v. *yd*; 2:1264, s.v. *rḥq*.

[147] Richard C. Steiner and Charles F. Nims, "Ashurbanipal and Shamash-shum-ukin: A Tale of Two Brothers from the Aramaic Text in Demotic Script," *RB* 92 (1985): 70; S. P. Vleeming and J. W. Wesselius, *Studies in Papyrus Amherst 63: Essays on the Aramaic Texts in Aramaic-Demotic Papyrus Amherst 63* (2 vols.; Amsterdam: Juda Palache Instituut, 1985–1990), 1:25.

[148] Vleeming and Wesselius, *Studies*, 1:25.

[149] It is reasonable to assume that the priest who dictated the Aramaic text in Demotic script did so from a written text in which the word for "earth" appeared sometimes as ארק and sometimes as ארע. Such spelling fluctuation is attested elsewhere in even shorter texts; see Muraoka and Porten, *Grammar*, 9: "ארק and ארע occur in the same document dated to 464 BCE (B2.2:6,16) just as in BA Jer 10.11." The priest pronounced ארק with a velar stop and ארע with a velar fricative. The former pronunciation may be a spelling pronunciation, as suggested by Vleeming and Wesselius, *Studies*, 1:25–27. The latter pronunciation shows that the Aramaic reflex of *ṣ́ initially merged with the reflex of *ġ, before the latter merged with the reflex of *ʿ.

clear evidence that the Aramaic reflex of *ṣ́ was articulated in the back of the mouth.

Further evidence that the Old Aramaic reflex of *ṣ́ was articulated in the back of the mouth is found in the Late Aramaic dialects. In a few forms, we find Aramaic *g* as the reflex of *ṣ́ (e.g., ג-ח-ך "laugh"); this reflex appears to be the product of a dissimilation that took place during the period when *ṣ́ was written with *qof*.[150]

What about the reflexes of *ṣ́ in Samalian and the dialect of Deir ʿAllā? They, too, are written with *qof*, but there is virtually no evidence concerning their pronunciation beyond that fact. Huehnergard considers it unlikely that this *qof* had the same realization in Samalian and the dialect of Deir ʿAllā that it did in standard Old Aramaic.[151] Indeed, he doubts that these dialects are close relatives of standard Old Aramaic, all descended from Proto-Aramaic (or "Proto-Syrian," as he calls it):

> It must be stressed . . . , however, that the features that lead to the positing of "Proto-Syrian" . . . are extremely weak, and that it is just as likely, if not indeed more likely, that there is no genetic connection between Sam'alian, Deir ʿAllā, and Proto-Aramaic beyond the Proto-Northwest Semitic level. . . .[152]

Huehnergard's skepticism is salutary, and he presents many arguments for his view that I find persuasive. Moreover, he is not alone in his view.[153] At the end of the day, however, I find it difficult to accept his conclusion because of the highly distinctive character of the *ṣ́ isogloss.

In my view, the existence of Proto-Aramaic does not depend on the assumption that *qof* had the same realization in Samalian and the dialect of Deir ʿAllā that it did in standard Old Aramaic. It is sufficient to assume that *ṣ́ = [tłˀ] shifted to [kłˀ] > [kxˀ] in Proto-Aramaic even if, after that, the three dialects went their separate ways. The existence of Proto-Aramaic would not be endangered if it turned out, say, that standard Old Aramaic carried the Proto-Aramaic migration of *ṣ́ = [tłˀ] to [kxˀ] one step further, from velar [kxˀ]

---

[150] Steiner, *Fricative-Laterals*, 113–15.

[151] Huehnergard, "What Is Aramaic?" 278.

[152] Ibid., 282.

[153] The notion that Samalian is a dialect of Aramaic is contested by Noorlander ("Samʾalian," 202–3) as well.

to uvular [qχˀ]. Nor would it make any difference if Samalian and/or the dialect of Deir ʿAllā de-affricated [kxˀ] to [kˀ], thereby merging the reflex of *ṣ́ with the reflex of *q rather than that of *ġ (> *ʿ). None of this would be incompatible with the view that standard Old Aramaic, Samalian, and the dialect of Deir ʿAllā have a common ancestor distinct from the common ancestor of the Canaanite dialects. The migration of *ṣ́ = [tɬˀ] to the back of the mouth would remain the crucial innovation that distinguishes Proto-Aramaic from Proto-Canaanite. Even though this migration was only a phonetic (subphonemic) shift in Proto-Aramaic, it was a rather idiosyncratic innovation, unlikely to have occurred independently in standard Old Aramaic, Samalian, and the dialect of Deir ʿAllā. As such, it deserves, in my view, to be considered the hallmark of a common ancestor that we may call Proto-Aramaic.

At first glance, this conclusion would seem to be at odds with the views of the archaeologists who have been excavating at Zincirli:

> The emergence of the Semitic-speaking dynasty of Iron Age Samʾal is attributed by many scholars to the migration of Aramaeans from the Euphrates River region some 200 km to the southeast. . . . It is true that Aramaic-speaking warlords seized power in various places during this period, sometimes at the expense of Luwian rulers; but there is no direct evidence that this was the case in Samʾal. In fact, the only reason to think that the new rulers of Samʾal were invading Aramaeans, rather than long-indigenous Semitic-speakers who had been resident in the area for a millennium or more, is the linguistic classification of the Samalian dialect (used in a number of locally written alphabetic inscriptions) as a branch of Aramaic. But there is some question as to whether Samalian is actually Aramaic (see Huehnergard 1995). It does not possess a number of morphological innovations shared by other Aramaic dialects. . . . Thus, Samalian could instead be an otherwise unattested branch of Northwest Semitic that developed in this topographically isolated region. . . , being derived from the Amorite dialect brought there during the Middle Bronze Age. In that case, Gabbar[154] may well have been not a roving Aramaean warlord, but a local resident of Amorite heritage who threw off

[154] Gabbar was the founder of the Iron Age kingdom of Samal.

> the Luwian yoke and restored his Semitic-speaking compatriots to a position of power. . . .
>
> There is certainly no archaeological hallmark of the Aramaeans as an invasive ethnic group that can be pointed to at Zincirli. . . .
>
> If this hypothesis of an indigenous political revolution can be confirmed by further research at Zincirli, it would change the historical picture considerably, because the kingdom of Samʾal in northwestern Syria would thus never have been Aramaean. . . .[155]

However, closer examination reveals that the archaeological evidence from Zincirli is quite compatible with the traditional view of Samalian as a dialect of Aramaic. The alleged contradiction is eliminated by Ran Zadok's plausible suggestion that Aramaic developed from one/some of the dialects of Amorite.[156] Based on this suggestion and the archaeological evidence, I would conjecture that the Iron Age Arameans of Samal and their Aramaic dialect are the descendants of the Bronze Age Amorites of Samal and their Amorite dialect.

[155] Schloen and Fink, "New Excavations," 9. Cf. Schloen, "City of Katumuwa," 35.

[156] Ran Zadok, "On the Amorite Material from Mesopotamia," in *The Tablet and the Scroll: Near Eastern Studies in Honor of William W. Hallo* (ed. Mark E. Cohen, Daniel C. Snell, and David B. Weisberg; Bethesda, Md.: CDL, 1993), 315–17.

APPENDIX 2

The Meaning of לְצוֹדֵד

Until recently, it was universally agreed that לְצוֹדֵד (Ezek 13:18) meant "to hunt/trap" and מְצֹדְדוֹת (Ezek 13:20) meant "are hunting/trapping." Nancy R. Bowen has now challenged this two-thousand-year-old consensus by rendering לְצוֹדֵד נְפָשׁוֹת as "in order to make souls dizzy." In a long footnote, she argues for this rendering based on the Akkadian cognate *ṣuddu* "to cause to turn, to make dizzy" taken in conjunction with three arguments: (1) "In the *qōlēl* form of this weak verb one would expect a sense of iterative action, intensive action, or the like (GKC, §72m), which is not reflected in translations"; (2) "This form of the root does not occur anywhere else in Hebrew (including Mishnaic Hebrew and the Dead Sea Scrolls) or Aramaic"; (3) "The form *suddu*[1] occurs frequently precisely in texts that describe the distress to a victim caused by some malevolent being."[2]

The first argument has little force. It is hardly surprising that Bowen found that this sense "is not reflected in translations"; for most verbs, there is no way of capturing this nuance in English.[3] But why limit one's search to translations when there are so many fine commentaries? Indeed, the author's own short list of "the

[1] Here and in three other places in the footnote, the *s* should be corrected to *ṣ*.

[2] Bowen, "Daughters," 429 n. 51. Unless otherwise indicated, all of the quotations below are from this footnote.

[3] It is only on rare occasions that English proves adequate to the task, e.g., מִתְקַטְּלִין "were being slaughtered/massacred" (Dan 2:13) and לְקַטָּלָה "to slaughter/massacre" (Dan 2:14) vs. לְהִתְקְטָלָה "to be killed" (Dan 2:13).

principal commentaries" on Ezekiel[4] includes a commentary by Moshe Greenberg that offers the following explanation: "*ṣoded* is an intensive of *ṣud* 'hunt down' . . . probably with reference to many objects (*nᵉpašot* 'persons')."[5] This explanation rings true. In v. 18, the *polel* infinitive לְצוֹדֵד occurs together with the *piᶜel* participle מְתַפְּרוֹת. The use of the *piᶜel* of ת-פ-ר in the verse presumably has the same explanation as the *polel* of צ-ו-ד; each of them takes a direct object that denotes a large set (of pillow casings and dream-souls, respectively). The phrases כָּל־אַצִּילֵי יָדַי and כָּל־קוֹמָה in the verse support this explanation. The twofold use of "all" is an exaggeration, to be sure, but it is meant to indicate that the sewing and trapping were done on a large scale.

The second argument is also difficult to grasp. The laws of statistics make it likely that there will be verb forms in the Hebrew Bible that do not occur anywhere else in Hebrew or Aramaic; indeed, the *piᶜel* of ת-פ-ר mentioned in the previous paragraph is another such example. It is telling that Bowen does not hesitate to translate מְתַפְּרוֹת as "sew," despite the fact that the *piᶜel* of ת-פ-ר is unattested in Qumran Hebrew and Tannaitic Hebrew (not to mention Aramaic). In the case of לְצוֹדֵד, the *polel* infinitive of צ-ו-ד, the lack of attestation in postbiblical Hebrew and Aramaic is even less noteworthy. The *polel* is an archaic verb stem in Hebrew and Aramaic, hardly to be expected in postbiblical sources. Originally, it seems, most hollow verbs did not take the *piᶜel/paᶜel* stem; the closest equivalent, especially in poetry, was *polel*. Later, when hollow verbs became fully triliteral, the *piᶜel/paᶜel* stem began to replace the *polel* stem. And, indeed, the *paᶜel* of the Syriac cognate of צ-ו-ד is well attested with the meanings "hunt" and "set a trap."[6] It is even used of hunting a נפש in the Peshiṭta to 1 Sam 24:11(12).

Clearly, the fact that "this form of the root does not occur anywhere else in Hebrew . . . or Aramaic" is not a problem. But even if it were a problem, how could it be solved by importing an Akkadian meaning that itself does not occur with this root anywhere else in Hebrew or Aramaic? Indeed, far from eliminating the alleged distributional anomaly, Bowen's suggestion adds a new one. It cre-

---

[4] Bowen, "Daughters," 417 n. 2.

[5] Moshe Greenberg, *Ezekiel 1–20: A New Translation with Introduction and Commentary* (AB 22; Garden City, N.Y.: Doubleday, 1983), 240.

[6] Sokoloff, *Syriac Lexicon*, 1277b, s.v.

ates a situation in which we have a causative *polel* meaning "make dizzy" with no corresponding *qal* meaning "become dizzy"![7]

The third argument might be relevant if לְצוֹדֵד could be viewed as a *borrowing* (as opposed to a *cognate*) of Akkadian *ṣuddu,* but there are several obstacles to such a view. First and foremost among them is "the striking paucity of verbs among the Akkadian loanwords in Aramaic."[8] Furthermore, as noted above, analysis of the sociolinguistic context makes it clear that any words of Akkadian origin borrowed by the Judean exiles would *not* have been borrowed directly from Akkadian. They would have been words used so commonly in Babylonian Aramaic that the exiles might have begun to use them in their own Aramaic speech and in Hebrew.[9] But, as Bowen is at pains to point out, the *polel* of צ-ו-ד is unknown in Aramaic. Thus, a borrowing from Akkadian is highly unlikely.

Nor can we assume that the meaning of Akkadian *ṣuddu* "to cause to turn, to make dizzy" is inherited from Proto-Semitic and that BH לְצוֹדֵד is a cognate that inherited the same meaning. All of the evidence indicates that this is a secondary meaning, the product of semantic development: "hunt" > "prowl" > "turn about, whirl, spin" > "be subject to vertigo." All of these meanings, with the exception of "hunt," are attested for Akkadian *ṣâdu* according to *CAD.*

At the end of the day, it is difficult to see what is gained by importing this meaning from Akkadian. The normal meanings of the root צ-ו-ד fit the context in Ezek 13:18, 20, while even a quick glance shows that the Akkadian meaning "make dizzy" does not. Bowen herself provides tacit acknowledgment of this problem by translating אֲשֶׁר אַתֵּנָה מְצֹדְדוֹת שָׁם אֶת־הַנְּפָשׁוֹת לְפֹרְחוֹת as "(with) which you make souls dizzy (make to go this way and that) like fledgling birds." The parenthetical insertion—"make to go this way and that"—was felt by Bowen to be necessary presumably because fledgling birds do not normally become dizzy. Another context where "make dizzy" makes no sense is הַנְּפָשׁוֹת תְּצוֹדֵדְנָה לְעַמִּי וּנְפָשׁוֹת לָכֶנָה

[7] Bowen asserts, in discussing Hebrew צ-ו-ד, that "in the qal the type of motion indicated is 'to prowl, walk about.'" This assertion may be an attempt to deal with the problem, but it is simply wrong: Hebrew צ-ו-ד is never an intransitive verb of motion.

[8] Kaufman, *Akkadian Influences,* 169.

[9] See at chapter 3, nn. 11–16 above.

תְּחַיֶּינָה. Bowen translates this as "Will you make dizzy my people but preserve your own souls?" However, according to this rendering, the prophet's angry question, meant to point out a contradiction, makes no sense, because there is no contradiction between keeping oneself alive and making other people dizzy. According to the traditional interpretation, the contradiction is quite intelligible because trapping souls leads to their demise.

Ultimately, however, the most damning evidence comes in a verse that Bowen does not translate or discuss. In v. 21 we read, וְקָרַעְתִּי אֶת־מִסְפְּחֹתֵיכֶם וְהִצַּלְתִּי אֶת־עַמִּי מִיֶּדְכֶן וְלֹא־יִהְיוּ עוֹד בְּיֶדְכֶן לִמְצוּדָה "and I shall tear your cloth patches (from your heads) and rescue my people from your clutches [lit., hands], and they will no longer become מצודה in your clutches [lit., hands]." Now, v. 21 continues a sentence that begins in v. 20. In that sentence, the women are described as being מְצֹדְדוֹת and their victims, as being לִמְצוּדָה. The relationship between the two expressions is one of cause and effect. Thus, it is clear that לִמְצוּדָה in v. 21 cannot be separated from מְצֹדְדוֹת in v. 20. But it is also clear that לִמְצוּדָה in v. 21 must refer to something caught in a trap, viz., prey, because it cannot be separated from the phrase וְנִתְפַּשׂ בִּמְצוּדָתִי "and he shall be caught in my trap," used in the previous chapter and a few chapters later (Ezek 12:13; 17:20). In short, the contextual link between לִמְצוּדָה and מְצֹדְדוֹת seriously undermines Bowen's claim that the latter means "are making dizzy" rather than "are trapping." To my mind, this alone is sufficient refutation of a very ill-considered suggestion.

Bibliography

Abou-Assaf, Ali, Pierre Bordreuil, and Alan R. Millard. *La statue de Tell Fekherye et son inscription bilingue assyro-arameénne.* Études assyriologiques. Paris: Recherche sur les civilisations, 1982.

Abravanel, Isaac. פירוש הנביאים לרבינו יצחק אברבנאל. Edited by Yehudah Shaviv. Jerusalem: Chorev, 2009–.

Abusch, Tzvi. "Etemmu." In *Dictionary of Deities and Demons in the Bible,* edited by Karel van der Toorn, Bob Becking, and Pieter W. van der Horst, 309–12. Leiden: Brill, 1999.

———. "Ghost and God: Some Observations on a Babylonian Understanding of Human Nature." In *Self, Soul and Body in Religious Experience,* edited by A. I. Baumgarten, J. Assmann, and G. G. Stroumsa, 363–83. Studies in the History of Religions 78. Leiden: Brill, 1998.

Abusch, Tzvi, and Daniel Schwemer. *Corpus of Mesopotamian Anti-Witchcraft Rituals.* Ancient Magic and Divination 8.1. Leiden: Brill, 2011–.

Adam, Klaus-Peter. "'And he behaved like a prophet among them' (1 Sam 10:11b): The Depreciative Use of נבא and the Comparative Evidence of Ecstatic Prophecy." *Die Welt des Orients* 39 (2009): 3–57.

Aharoni, Yohanan. כתובות ערד. Jerusalem: Bialik, 1975.

Aistleitner, Joseph. *Wörterbuch der ugaritischen Sprache.* Berichte über die Verhandlungen der Sächsischen Akademie der Wissenschaften zu Leipzig, Philologisch-Historische Klasse 106.3. Berlin: Akademie-Verlag, 1963.

Albertz, Rainer, and Rüdiger Schmitt. *Family and Household Religion in Ancient Israel and the Levant.* Winona Lake, Ind.: Eisenbrauns, 2012.

Alexander, Desmond. "The Old Testament View of Life after Death." *Themelios* 11 (1986): 41–46.

Alfrink, Bernard. "L'expression נֶאֱסַף אֶל־עַמָּיו." *Oudtestamentische Studiën* 5 (1948): 118–31.

Allen, James L. "Yeats's Bird-Soul Symbolism." *Twentieth Century Literature* 6 (1960): 117–22.

Allen, James P. "Ba." In *The Oxford Encyclopedia of Ancient Egypt*, 1:161–62. 3 vols. Oxford: Oxford University Press, 2001.

Allen, Leslie C. *Ezekiel 1–19*. Word Biblical Commentary 28. Dallas: Word Books, 1994.

Allen, T. George. "Additions to the Egyptian Book of the Dead." *Journal of Near Eastern Studies* 11 (1952): 177–86.

The American Heritage Dictionary of the English Language. 4th ed. Boston: Houghton Mifflin, 2000.

Aptowitzer, V. "Die Seele als Vogel: Ein Beitrag zu den Anschauungen der Agada." *Monatsschrift für Geschichte und Wissenschaft des Judentums* 69 (1925): 150–68.

Aristotle. *De Anima*. Translated by D. W. Hamlyn. Oxford: Oxford University Press, 1993.

Asher b. Jehiel. פירוש הרא״ש השלם לרבינו אשר ב״ר יחיאל זצ״ל על מסכת כלים. Edited by Y. Goldshtof. Jerusalem: Diqduq Halakhah, 1993.

Asheri, David, Alan Lloyd, and Aldo Corcella. *A Commentary on Herodotus Books I–IV*. Edited by Oswyn Murray and Alfonso Moreno. Oxford: Oxford University Press, 2007.

Assmann, Jan. *Death and Salvation in Ancient Egypt*. Ithaca, N.Y.: Cornell University Press, 2005.

———. "A Dialogue between Self and Soul: Papyrus Berlin 3024." In *Self, Soul and Body in Religious Experience*, edited by A. I. Baumgarten, J. Assmann, and G. G. Stroumsa, 384–403. Studies in the History of Religions 78. Leiden: Brill, 1998.

Avineri, Y. היכל רש״י. 2nd ed. 2 vols. Jerusalem: Mossad Harav Kook, 1985.

Barkay, Gabriel. "The Iron Age II–III." In *The Archaeology of Ancient Israel*, edited by Amnon Ben-Tor, 302–73. Tel-Aviv: Open University of Israel, 1992.

———. קברים וקבורה ביהודה בתקופת המקרא. In קברים ונוהגי קבורה בארץ־ישראל בעת העתיקה, edited by Itamar Singer, 96–164. Jerusalem: Yad Izhak Ben-Zvi, 1994.

Barth, J. "Notiz: Zu dem Zauber des Umnähens der Gelenke." *Monatsschrift für Geschichte und Wissenschaft des Judentums* 57 (1913): 235.

Beall, Todd S. *Josephus' Description of the Essenes Illustrated by the Dead Sea Scrolls*. Society for New Testament Studies Monograph Series 58. Cambridge: Cambridge University Press, 1988.

Becherer, Magnus Anton. *Ueber den Glauben der Juden an Unsterblichkeit der menschlichen Seele vor der babylonischen Gefangenschaft*. Munich: Jakob Giel, 1827.

Becker, Johannes Hendrik. *Het Begrip nefesj in het Oude Testament*. Amsterdam: Maatschappij, 1942.

Beeston, A. F. L., M. A. Ghul, W. W. Müller, and J. Ryckmans. *Sabaic Dictionary*. Louvain-la-Neuve: Peeters, 1982.

Beider, Alexander. *A Dictionary of Ashkenazic Given Names: Their Origins, Structure, Pronunciation, and Migrations*. Teaneck, N.J.: Avoteynu, 1996.

Ben-Ḥayyim, Z. "Traditions in the Hebrew Language, with Special Reference to the Dead Sea Scrolls." *Scripta Hierosolymitana* 4 (1958): 200–214.

———. מסורת השומרונים וזיקתה למסורת הלשון של מגילות ים המלח וללשון חז"ל, *Lešonenu* 22 (1958): 223–45.

Berger, Roger, and Annette Brasseur. *Les séquences de sainte Eulalie*. Publications romanes et françaises 233. Geneva: Droz, 2004.

Berkowitz, Beth A. *Execution and Invention: Death Penalty Discourse in Early Rabbinic and Christian Cultures*. New York: Oxford University Press, 2006.

Berlejung, Angelika. "Falsche Prophetinnen: Zur Dämonisierung der Frauen von Ez 17-21." In *Theologie des AT aus der Perspektive von Frauen*, edited by Manfred Oeming, 179–210. Beiträge zum Verstehen der Bibel 1. Münster: Lit, 2003.

Bertholet, Alfred. *Das Buch Hesekiel*. Kurzer Hand-Commentar zum Alten Testament 12. Freiburg i. B.: J. C. B. Mohr, 1897.

Beyer, Klaus. *Die aramäischen Texte vom Toten Meer*. 2 vols. Göttingen: Vandenhoeck & Ruprecht, 1984–1994.

Biblia sacra iuxta Vulgatam versionem. 5th ed. Edited by Robert Weber and Roger Gryson. Stuttgart: Deutsche Bibelgesellschaft, 2007.

Bieberstein, Klaus. "Jenseits der Todesschwelle: Die Entstehung der Auferweckungshoffnungen in der alttestamentlich-frühjüdischen Literatur." In *Tod und Jenseits im alten Israel und in seiner Umwelt: Theologische, religionsgeschichtliche, archäologische und ikonographische Aspekte*, edited by Angelika Berlejung and Bernd Janowski, 423–46. Forschungen zum Alten Testament 64. Tübingen: Mohr Siebeck, 2009.

Blachère, Régis. "Note sur le substantif *nafs* 'souffle vital,' 'âme' dans le Coran." *Semitica* 1 (1948): 69–77.

Black, Jeremy. "The Imagery of Birds in Sumerian Poetry." In *Mesopotamian Poetic Language: Sumerian and Akkadian,* edited by M. E. Vogelzang and H. L. J. Vanstiphout, 23–46. Cuneiform Monographs 6. Proceedings of the Groningen Group for the Study of Mesopotamian Literature 2. Groningen: Styx, 1996.

Blau, Joshua. *A Handbook of Early Middle Arabic.* Jerusalem: Hebrew University of Jerusalem, 2002.

———. *On Pseudo-Corrections in Some Semitic Languages.* Publications of the Israel Academy of Sciences and Humanities, Section of Humanities. Jerusalem: Israel Academy of Sciences and Humanities, 1970.

———. *Phonology and Morphology of Biblical Hebrew: An Introduction.* Winona Lake, Ind.: Eisenbrauns, 2010.

Blenkinsopp, Joseph. *Ezekiel.* Interpretation. Louisville: John Knox, 1990.

———. *Isaiah 1–39: A New Translation with Introduction and Commentary.* Anchor Bible 19. New York: Doubleday, 2000.

Bloch-Smith, Elizabeth. *Judahite Burial Practices and Beliefs about the Dead.* Journal for the Study of the Old Testament: Supplement Series 123. Sheffield: JSOT Press, 1992.

———. "From Womb to Tomb: The Israelite Family in Death as in Life." In *The Family in Life and in Death: The Family in Ancient Israel. Sociological and Archaeological Perspectives,* edited by Patricia Dutcher-Walls, 122–31. Library of Hebrew Bible/Old Testament Studies 504. New York: T&T Clark International, 2009.

Block, Daniel I. *The Book of Ezekiel.* Vol. 1, *Chapters 1–24.* New International Commentary on the Old Testament. Grand Rapids: Eerdmans, 1997.

Blosser, Benjamin P. *Become like the Angels: Origen's Doctrine of the Soul.* Washington, D.C.: Catholic University of America Press, 2012.

Bohak, Gideon. *Ancient Jewish Magic: A History.* Cambridge: Cambridge University Press, 2008.

Bonatz, Dominik. "Syro-Hittite Funerary Monuments: A Phenomenon of Tradition or Innovation?" In *Essays on Syria in the Iron Age,* edited by Guy Bunnens, 189–210. Ancient Near Eastern Studies, Supplement 7. Louvain: Peeters, 2000.

Bordreuil, Pierre, and Dennis Pardee, "Le rituel funéraire ougaritique RS. 34.126." *Syria* 59 (1982): 121–28.

Bowen, Nancy R. "The Daughters of Your People: Female Prophets in Ezekiel 13:17–23." *Journal of Biblical Literature* 118 (1999): 417–33.

Bremmer, Jan N. "The Soul in Early and Classical Greece." In *Der Begriff der Seele in der Religionswissenschaft*, edited by Johann Figl and Hans-Dieter Klein, 159–69. Der Begriff der Seele 1. Würzburg: Königshausen & Neumann, 2002.

Briggs, Charles A. "The Use of נפש in the Old Testament." *Journal of Biblical Literature* 16 (1897): 17–30.

———. "The Use of רוח in the Old Testament." *Journal of Biblical Literature* 19 (1900): 132–45.

Briggs, Charles A., and Emilie Grace Briggs. *A Critical and Exegetical Commentary on the Book of Psalms.* 2 vols. International Critical Commentary. Edinburgh: T&T Clark, 1906–1907.

Brown, F., S. R. Driver, and C. A. Briggs. *A Hebrew and English Lexicon of the Old Testament.* Oxford: Clarendon, 1907.

Brown, Jonathan A. C. "New Data on the Delateralization of *Ḍād* and Its Merger with *Ẓāʾ* in Classical Arabic: Contributions from Old South Arabic and the Earliest Islamic Texts on *Ḍ* / *Ẓ* Minimal Pairs." *Journal of Semitic Studies* 52 (2007): 335–68.

Brownlee, William H. *Ezekiel 1–19.* Word Biblical Commentary 28. Waco, Tex.: Word Books, 1986.

Broydé, Isaac, and Ludwig Blau. "Soul." In *Jewish Encyclopedia.* New York and London: Funk & Wagnalls, 1907.

Buber, Salomon, ed. מדרש תנחומא. 6 vols. Vilna: Rom, 1913.

———. מדרש תהלים המכונה שוחר טוב. Vilna: n.p., 1891.

Buccellati, Giorgio. *A Structural Grammar of Babylonian.* Wiesbaden: Harrassowitz, 1996.

Buttrick, G. A., ed. *The Interpreter's Dictionary of the Bible.* 4 vols. Nashville: Abingdon, 1962.

Carbon, Jan-Mathieu. "Δάρρων and δαίμον: A New Inscription from Mylasa." *Epigraphica Anatolica* 38 (2005): 1–6.

Carrier, Claude. *Le* Livre des Morts *de l'Égypte ancienne.* Moyen égyptien, le langage et la culture des hiéroglyphes—analyse et traduction 2. Paris: Cybele, 2009.

Cassuto, U. "Baal and Mot in the Ugaritic Texts." *Israel Exploration Journal* 12 (1962): 77–86.

Charles, Robert Henry. *A Critical History of the Doctrine of a Future Life: Or, Hebrew, Jewish, and Christian Eschatology from Pre-prophetic Times till the Close of the New Testament Canon, being Jowett Lectures for 1898–99.* London: Adam & Charles Black, 1899.

———. *Eschatology: The Doctrine of a Future Life in Israel, Judaism and Christianity*. London: Adam & Charles Black, 1913

Clines, David J. A. *Job 1–20*. Word Biblical Commentary 17. Dallas: Word Books, 1989.

Cohen, Harold R. (Chaim). *Biblical Hapax Legomena in the Light of Akkadian and Ugaritic*. Society of Biblical Literature Dissertation Series 37. Missoula, Mont.: Scholars Press, 1978.

Cohen, Menachem, ed. מקראות גדולות הכתר — ספר יחזקאל. Ramat Gan: Bar-Ilan University, 2000.

———. מקראות גדולות הכתר — ספר שמואל. Ramat Gan: Bar-Ilan University, 1993.

———. מקראות גדולות הכתר — ספר תרי עשר. Ramat Gan: Bar-Ilan University, 2021.

Cook, Edward M. "The Orthography of Final Unstressed Long Vowels in Old and Imperial Aramaic." In *Sopher Mahir: Northwest Semitic Studies Presented to Stanislav Segert = Maarav* 5–6 (1990): 53–67.

Cook, Stephen L. "Death, Kinship, and Community: Afterlife and the חסד Ideal in Israel." In *The Family in Life and Death: The Family in Ancient Israel. Sociological and Archaeological Perspectives*, edited by Patricia Dutcher-Walls, 106–21. Library of Hebrew Bible/Old Testament Studies 504. New York: T&T Clark International, 2009.

Cooke, G. A. *A Critical and Exegetical Commentary on the Book of Ezekiel*. International Critical Commentary 21. Edinburgh: T&T Clark, 1936.

Cooley, Robert E. "Gathered to His People: A Study of a Dothan Family Tomb." In *The Living and Active Word of God: Studies in Honor of Samuel J. Schultz*, edited by Morris Inch and Ronald Youngblood, 47–58. Winona Lake, Ind.: Eisenbrauns, 1983.

Cooper, John W. *Body, Soul, and Life Everlasting: Biblical Anthropology and the Monism–Dualism Debate*. Grand Rapids: Eerdmans, 1989.

Cowley, A. *Aramaic Papyri of the Fifth Century B.C.* Oxford: Clarendon, 1923.

Craigie, Peter C. *Ezekiel*. Daily Study Bible Series. Philadelphia: Westminster, 1983.

Cross, Frank Moore. "The Evolution of the Proto-Canaanite Alphabet." *Bulletin of the American Schools of Oriental Research* 134 (1954): 15–24.

———. "The Origin and Early Evolution of the Alphabet." *Eretz-Israel* 8 (1967): 8*–24*.

Dalley, Stephanie. "The Descent of Ishtar to the Underworld." In *The Context of Scripture*, edited by William W. Hallo, 1:381–84. 3 vols. Leiden: Brill, 1997–2002.

Davies, Graham I. "An Archaeological Commentary on Ezekiel 13." In *Scripture and Other Artifacts: Essays on the Bible and Archaeology in Honor of Philip J. King*, edited by Michael D. Coogan, J. Cheryl Exum, and Lawrence E. Stager, 108–25. Louisville: Westminster John Knox, 1994.

Day, John. "The Development of Belief in Life after Death in Ancient Israel." In *After the Exile: Essays in Honor of Rex Mason*, edited by John Barton and David J. Reimer, 231–57. Macon, Ga.: Mercer University Press, 1996.

Delitzsch, Friedrich. *Assyrisches Handwörterbuch*. Leipzig: J. C. Hinrichs, 1896.

———. "Glossario Ezechielico-Babylonico." In *Liber Ezechielis*, edited by S. Baer, x–xviii. Leipzig: B. Tauchnitz, 1884.

DeVries, LaMoine F. "Cult Stands: A Bewildering Variety of Shapes and Sizes." *Biblical Archaeology Review* 13.4 (July/August 1987): 26–37.

Dhorme, E. *A Commentary on the Book of Job*. Translated by Harold Knight. Nashville: Thomas Nelson, 1984.

Dietrich, M. *The Neo-Babylonian Correspondence of Sargon and Sennacherib*. State Archives of Assyria 17. Helsinki: Helsinki University Press, 2003.

Dietrich, M., O. Loretz, and J. Sanmartín, eds. *Die keilalphabetischen Texte aus Ugarit*. Alter Orient und Altes Testament 24.1. Neukirchen-Vluyn: Neukirchener Verlag, 1976.

Dion, Paul-Eugène. *La langue de Ya'udi: Description et classement de l'ancien parler de Zencirli dans le cadre de langues sémitiques du nord-ouest*. Waterloo, ON: Editions SR, 1974.

Donner, H., and W. Röllig, eds. *Kanaanäische und aramäische Inschriften*. 3 vols. in 1. Wiesbaden: Harrassowitz, 1966–1969.

Driver, Godfrey Rolles. "Linguistic and Textual Problems: Ezekiel," *Biblica* 19 (1938): 60–69, 175–87.

———. "Plurima Mortis Imago." In *Studies and Essays in Honor of Abraham A. Neuman, President, Dropsie College for Hebrew and Cognate Learning, Philadelphia*, edited by Meir Ben-Horin, Bernard D. Weinryb, and Solomon Zeitlin, 128–43. Leiden: Brill, 1962.

Driver, Samuel Rolles. *A Treatise on the Use of the Tenses in Hebrew and Some Other Syntactical Questions.* 3rd ed. London: Oxford University Press, 1892. Reprinted, with an introductory essay by W. Randall Garr, Grand Rapids: Eerdmans, 1998.

Dumermuth, Fritz. "Zu Ez. XIII 18–21." *Vetus Testamentum* 13 (1963): 228–29.

Dussaud, René. "La notion d'âme chez les israélites et les phéniciens." *Syria* 16 (1935): 267–77.

Edgerton, William F., and John A. Wilson. *Historical Records of Ramses III: The Texts in* Medinet Habu *Volumes I and II.* Studies in Ancient Oriental Civilizations 36. Chicago: University of Chicago Press, 1936.

Ehrenkrook, Jason von. "The Afterlife in Philo and Josephus." In *Heaven, Hell, and the Afterlife: Eternity in Judaism, Christianity, and Islam,* edited by J. Harold Ellens, 1:97–118. 3 vols. Psychology, Religion, and Spirituality. Santa Barbara: Praeger, 2013.

Eichrodt, Walther. *Ezekiel: A Commentary.* Translated by Cosslett Quin. Old Testament Library. Philadelphia: Westminster, 1970.

Eisemann, Moshe. *Yechezkel/The Book of Ezekiel.* New York: Mesorah, 1977.

Eissfeldt, Otto. *Der Beutel der Lebendigen: Alttestamentliche Erzählungs- und Dichtungsmotive im Lichte neuer Nuzi-Texte.* Berichte über die Verhandlungen der Sächsischen Akademie der Wissenschaften zu Leipzig, Philologisch-Historische Klasse 105.6. Berlin: Akademie-Verlag, 1960.

Elitzur, Yoel. *Ancient Place Names in the Holy Land: Preservation and History.* Jerusalem: Magnes, 2004.

Elledge, C. D. *Life after Death in Early Judaism: The Evidence of Josephus.* Wissenschaftliche Untersuchungen zum Neuen Testament 2/208. Tübingen: Mohr Siebeck, 2006.

Entenman, George Lynn. *The Development of Nasal Vowels.* Texas Linguistic Forum 7. Austin: Department of Linguistics, University of Texas at Austin, 1977.

Epstein, J. N. מבוא לנוסח המשנה: נוסח המשנה וגלגוליו למימי האמוראים הראשונים ועד דפוסי ר׳ יו״ט ליפמן הלר (בעל תוי״ט). 3rd ed. Jerusalem: Magnes, 2000.

Erman, Adolf, and Hermann Grapow. *Wörterbuch der aegyptischen Sprache.* 7 vols. Leipzig: J. C. Hinrichs, 1926–1963.

Ewald, Heinrich. *Die Propheten des Alten Bundes.* 2nd ed. 3 vols. Göttingen: Vandenhoeck & Ruprecht, 1867–1868.

Faivre, Daniel. *Vivre et mourir dans l'ancien Israël: Anthropologie biblique de la Vie et de la Mort.* Paris: L'Harmattan, 1998.

Farber, Walter. "Witchcraft, Magic, and Divination in Ancient Mesopotamia." In *Civilizations of the Ancient Near East,* edited by Jack M. Sasson, 3:1895–1909. 4 vols. New York: Scribner, 1995.

Faulkner, R. O. *Ancient Egyptian Book of the Dead.* New York: Barnes & Noble, 2005.

———. *The Ancient Egyptian Coffin Texts.* 3 vols. Modern Egyptology Series. Warminster: Aris & Phillips, 1973–1978.

Fischer, Irmtraud. *Gotteskünderinnen: Zu einer geschlechterfairen Deutung des Phänomens der Prophetie und der Prophetinnen in der Hebräischen Bibel.* Stuttgart: Kohlhammer, 2002.

Fohrer, Georg. *Ezechiel.* Handbuch zum Alten Testament 1/13. Tübingen: Mohr-Siebeck, 1955.

Folmer, Margaretha. "Rare Demonstrative Pronouns in Targum Onqelos: דנן and דיכי." In *In the Shadow of Bezalel: Aramaic, Biblical and Ancient Near Eastern Studies in Honor of Bezalel Porten,* edited by Alejandro F. Botta, 89–124. Culture and History of the Ancient Near East 60. Leiden: Brill, 2013.

Frazer, James G. *Folk-lore in the Old Testament: Studies in Comparative Religion, Legend and Law.* 3 vols. London: Macmillan, 1918–1919.

———. *The Golden Bough: A Study in Comparative Religion.* 1st ed. 2 vols. London: Macmillan, 1890.

———. *The Golden Bough: A Study in Magic and Religion.* 13 vols. New York: Macmillan, 1935–1937.

———. "Hunting for Souls." *Archiv für Religionswissenschaft* 11 (1908): 197–99.

Frege, Gottlob. "Über Sinn und Bedeutung." *Zeitschrift für Philosophie und philosophische Kritik* n.F. 100 (1892): 25–50.

Frey, Johannes. *Tod, Seelenglaube und Seelenkult im alten Israel.* Leipzig: A. Deicher, 1898.

Friedman, Richard Elliott, and Shawna Dolansky Overton. "Death and Afterlife: The Biblical Silence." In *Judaism in Late Antiquity,* edited by Jacob Neusner, 4:35–60. 5 vols. Handbook of Oriental Studies. The Near and Middle East. Leiden: Brill, 1995–2001.

Gafney, Wilda. *Daughters of Miriam: Women Prophets in Ancient Israel.* Minneapolis: Fortress, 2008.

Gardiner, Alan H. *Egyptian Grammar.* 3rd ed. London: Oxford University Press, 1957.

Garfinkel, Stephen P. "Studies in Akkadian Influences in the Book of Ezekiel." Ph.D. diss., Columbia University, 1983.

Garr, W. Randall. "On Voicing and Devoicing in Ugaritic." *Journal of Near Eastern Studies* 45 (1986): 45–52.

Gaster, Theodor H. *Myth, Legend and Custom in the Old Testament: A Comparative Study with Chapters from Sir James G. Frazer's* Folklore in the Old Testament. New York: Harper & Row, 1969.

Geller, M. J. *Evil Demons: Canonical* Utukkū lemnūtu *Incantations.* State Archives of Assyrian Cuneiform Texts 5. Helsinki: Neo-Assyrian Text Corpus Project, 2007.

Geller, Stephen A. *Parallelism in Early Biblical Poetry.* Harvard Semitic Monographs 20. Missoula, Mont.: Scholars Press, 1979.

George, Andrew. "Babylonian and Assyrian: A History of Akkadian." In *Languages of Iraq, Ancient and Modern,* edited by J. N. Postgate, 31–71. London: British School of Archaeology in Iraq, 2007.

Gesenius, Wilhelm. *Thesaurus philologicus linguae Hebraeae et Chaldaeae Veteris Testamenti.* 3 vols. in 1. Leipzig: F. C. W. Vogel, 1835–1853.

Gibson, John C. L. *Textbook of Syrian Semitic Inscriptions.* 4 vols. Oxford: Clarendon, 1971–2009.

Ginsberg, H. L. "The Northwest Semitic Languages." In *Patriarchs,* edited by Benjamin Mazar, 102–24. World History of the Jewish People 2. New Brunswick, N.J.: Rutgers University Press, 1966.

———. "Ugaritic Myths, Epics, and Legends." In *Ancient Near Eastern Texts Relating to the Old Testament,* edited by J. B. Pritchard, 129–55. 3rd ed. Princeton: Princeton University Press, 1969.

Ginzberg, Louis. "Beiträge zur Lexikographie des Jüdisch-Aramäischen." *Monatsschrift für Geschichte und Wissenschaft des Judentums* 78 (1934): 9–33.

———. *The Legends of the Jews.* Translated by Henrietta Szold. 7 vols. Philadelphia: Jewish Publication Society, 1909–1938.

Gluska, Isaac. "Akkadian Influences on the Book of Ezekiel." In *"An Experienced Scribe Who Neglects Nothing": Ancient Near Eastern Studies in Honor of Jacob Klein,* edited by Yitschak Sefati et al., 718–37. Bethesda, Md.: CDL, 2005.

Goshen-Gottstein, Moshe H., ed. ספר ישעיהו. 3 vols. Jerusalem: Magnes, 1973–1981.

Green, Joel B. "Soul." In *The New Interpreter's Dictionary of the Bible,* edited by Katharine Doob Sakenfeld, 5:358–59. 5 vols. Nashville: Abingdon, 2006–2009.

Greenberg, Moshe. *Ezekiel 1–20: A New Translation with Introduction and Commentary*. Anchor Bible 22. Garden City, N.Y.: Doubleday, 1983.

———. *Ezekiel 21–37: A New Translation with Introduction and Commentary*. Anchor Bible 22A. Garden City, N.Y.: Doubleday, 1997.

Greenfield, Jonas C. "The Dialects of Early Aramaic." *Journal of Near Eastern Studies* 37 (1978): 93–99.

———. "Un rite religieux araméen et ses parallèles." *Revue biblique* 80 (1973): 46–52.

Greenstein, Edward L. "A Phoenician Inscription in Ugaritic Script?" *Journal of the Ancient Near Eastern Society* 8 (1976): 50–57.

Grüneisen, Karl. *Der Ahnenkultus und die Urreligion Israels*. Halle a.S.: Max Niemeyer, 1900.

Haas, Volkert. "Death and the Afterlife in Hittite Thought." In *Civilizations of the Ancient Near East*, edited by Jack M. Sasson, 3:2021–30. 4 vols. New York: Scribner, 1995.

Hackl, Johannes. "Language Death and Dying Reconsidered: The Rôle of Late Babylonian as a Vernacular Language." *Imperium and Officium Working Papers*, July 2011, http://iowp.univie.ac.at/sites/default/files/IOWP_RAI_Hackl.pdf.

Hajek, John. *Universals of Sound Change in Nasalization*. Oxford: Blackwell, 1997.

Hallo, William W., and K. Lawson Younger, eds. *The Context of Scripture*. 3 vols. Leiden: Brill, 1997–2002.

Hasenfratz, Hans-Peter. "Religionswissenschaftliches zur Seelenkonzeption: Am Beispiel Altägyptens." In *Der Begriff der Seele in der Religionswissenschaft*, edited by Johann Figl and Hans-Dieter Klein, 121–30. Der Begriff der Seele 1. Würzburg: Königshausen & Neumann, 2002.

Hays, Christopher B. *Death in the Iron Age II and in First Isaiah*. Forschungen zum Alten Testament 79. Tübingen: Mohr Siebeck, 2011.

Heard, John Bickford. *The Tripartite Nature of Man*. Edinburgh: T. &T. Clark, 1866.

Heidel, Alexander. *The Gilgamesh Epic and Old Testament Parallels*. Chicago: University of Chicago Press, 1946.

Held, Moshe. "Pits and Pitfalls in Akkadian and Biblical Hebrew." *Journal of the Ancient Near Eastern Society* 5 (1973): 173–90.

Herrmann, Johannes. *Ezechiel.* Kommentar zum Alten Testament 11. Leipzig: A. Deichert, 1924.

Herrmann, Virginia R. "Introduction: The Katumuwa Stele and the Commemoration of the Dead in the Ancient Middle East," In *In Remembrance of Me: Feasting with the Dead in the Ancient Middle East,* edited by Virginia Rimmer Herrmann and J. David Schloen, 17–23. Chicago: Oriental Institute of the University of Chicago, 2014.

———. "The Katumuwa Stele in Archaeological Context." In *In Remembrance of Me: Feasting with the Dead in the Ancient Middle East,* edited by Virginia Rimmer Herrmann and J. David Schloen, 49–56. Chicago: Oriental Institute of the University of Chicago, 2014.

Hitzig, Ferdinand. *Der Prophet Ezechiel.* Kurzgefasstes exegetisches Handbuch zum Alten Testament 8. Leipzig: Weidmann, 1847.

Hobbes, Thomas. *Leviathan or the Matter, Forme, and Power of a Common-wealth Ecclesiasticall and Civil.* London: Andrew Crooke, 1651. Reprinted as *Hobbes's Leviathan: Reprinted from the Edition of 1651 with an Essay by the Late W. G. Pogson Smith.* Oxford: Oxford University Press, 1909.

Hochegger, Hermann. "Die Vorstellungen von 'Seele' und Totengeist bei afrikanischen Völkern." *Anthropos* 60 (1965): 273–339.

Hoenigswald, Henry M. *Language Change and Linguistic Reconstruction.* Chicago: University of Chicago Press, 1960.

Hoftijzer, J., and K. Jongeling, *Dictionary of the North-West Semitic Inscriptions.* 2 vols. Handbook of Oriental Studies, The Near and Middle East 21. Leiden: Brill, 1995.

Honeyman, A. M. "*Merismus* in Biblical Hebrew." *Journal of Biblical Literature* 71 (1952): 11–18.

Horovitz, H. S., ed. ספרי על ספר במדבר. Leipzig: Gustav Fock, 1917.

Horovitz, H. S., and I. A. Rabin, eds. מכילתא דרבי ישמעאל. Frankfurt am Main: J. Kauffmann, 1931.

Huehnergard, John, "What Is Aramaic?" *Aram* 7 (1995): 261–82.

Hutter, Manfred. "Kultstelen und Baityloi: Die Ausstrahlung eines syrischen religiösen Phänomens nach Kleinasien und Israel." In *Religiongeschichtliche Beziehungen zwischen Kleinasien, Nordsyrien, und dem Alten Testament: Internationales Symposion Hamburg, 17.–21. März 1990,* edited by Bernd Janowski, Klaus Koch, and Gernot Wilhelm, 87–108. Orbis biblicus et orientalis 129. Göttingen: Vandenhoeck & Ruprecht, 1993.

Ibn Balʿam, Judah. פירוש ר' יהודה אבן בלעם לספר יחזקאל. Edited by Maʿaravi Perez. Ramat Gan: Bar-Ilan University Press, 2000.

Ibn Ezra, Abraham. יסוד מורא וסוד תורה: מהדורה מדעית מבוארת. Edited by Joseph Cohen in collaboration with Uriel Simon. Ramat Gan: Bar-Ilan University Press 2002.

Illés, Orsolya. "Single Spell Book of the Dead Papyri as Amulets." In *Totenbuch-Forschungen: Gesammelte Beiträge des 2. Internationalen Totenbuch-Symposiums Bonn, 25. bis 29. September 2005*, edited by Burkhard Backes, Irmtraut Munro, and Simone Stöhr, 121–33. Studien zum Altägyptischen Totenbuch 11. Wiesbaden: Harrassowitz, 2006.

Illman, Karl-Johan. *Old Testament Formulas about Death*. Publications of the Research Institute of the Åbo Akademi Foundation 48. Åbo: Åbo Akademi, 1979.

Jacob, Edmond, Albert Dihle, et al. "ψυχή κτλ." In *Theological Dictionary of the New Testament*, edited by G. Kittel and G. Friedrich, 9:608–60. Translated by G. W. Bromiley. 10 vols. Grand Rapids: Eerdmans, 1964–1976.

Jacob of Serug. *Homiliae Selectae Mar-Jacobi Sarugensis*. Edited by Paul Bedjan. 5 vols. Leipzig: Harrassowitz, 1905–1910. Reprinted, Piscataway, N.J.: Gorgias Press, 2006.

Jastrow, Marcus. *A Dictionary of the Targumim, the Talmud Babli and Yerushalmi, and the Midrashic Literature*. London: Luzac, 1903.

Jean, Charles-F., and Jacob Hoftijzer. *Dictionnaire des inscriptions sémitiques de l'ouest*. New ed. Leiden: Brill, 1965.

Jeffers, Ann. *Magic and Divination in Ancient Palestine and Syria*. Studies in the History and Culture of the Ancient Near East 8. Leiden: Brill, 1996.

Johnson, Aubrey R. *The Vitality of the Individual in the Thought of Ancient Israel*. Cardiff: University of Wales Press, 1964.

Johnston, Philip S. *Shades of Sheol: Death and Afterlife in the Old Testament*. Downers Grove, Ill.: InterVarsity, 2002.

Johnstone, T. M. *Ḥarsūsi Lexicon*. London: Oxford University Press, 1977.

———. *Mehri Lexicon and English-Mehri Word-List*. London: School of Oriental and African Studies, University of London, 1987.

Josephus. *Josephus in Nine Volumes*. Translated by H. St. J. Thackeray et al. 9 vols. Loeb Classical Library. London: William Heinemann, 1927–1976.

Jost, Renate. "Die Töchter deines Volkes prophezeien." In *Für*

Gerechtigkeit streiten: Theologie im Alltag einer bedrohten Welt. Für Luise Schottroff zum 60. Geburtstag, edited by Dorothee Sölle, 59–65. Gütersloh: Kaiser, 1994.

Joüon, Paul. *A Grammar of Biblical Hebrew.* Translated and revised by T. Muraoka. 2 vols. Subsidia Biblica 14.1–2. Rome: Pontificio Istituto Biblico, 1991.

Kahana, Menahem I. המכילתות לפרשת עמלק: לראשוניותה של המסורת במכילתא דרבי ישמעאל בהשוואה למקבילתה במכילתא דרבי שמעון בן יוחי. Jerusalem: Magnes, 1999.

Kammenhuber, A. "Die hethitischen Vorstellungen von Seele und Leib, Herz und Leibesinnerem, Kopf und Person (I. Teil)." *Zeitschrift für Assyriologie* 56 (1964): 150–212.

Kasher, Rimon. יחזקאל. 2 vols. Tel Aviv: Am Oved, 2004.

Kaufman, Stephen A. *The Akkadian Influences on Aramaic.* Assyriological Studies 19. Chicago: University of Chicago Press, 1974.

Kazimirski, A. de Biberstein. *Dictionnaire arabe-français.* Beirut: Librairie du Liban, 1860.

Keel, Othmar. *The Symbolism of the Biblical World: Ancient Near Eastern Iconography and the Book of Psalms.* Translated by Timothy J. Hallett. New York: Seabury, 1978.

Keil, Carl F. *Biblical Commentary on the Prophecies of Ezekiel.* Translated by James Martin. 2 vols. Edinburgh: T&T Clark, 1876.

Kilwing, Norbert. "נֶפֶשׁ und ΨΥΧΗ: Gemeinsames und Unterscheidendes im hebräischen und griechischen Seelenverständnis." In *Studien zu Psalmen und Propheten: Festschrift für Hubert Irsigler,* 377–401. Herders Biblische Studien 64. Freiburg: Herder, 2010.

Kingsley, Mary H. "Black Ghosts." *The Cornhill Magazine* n.s. 1 (July–December 1896): 79–92.

———. *Travels in West Africa: Congo Français, Corsico and Cameroons.* London: Macmillan, 1897.

Kirshenbaum, Karen. ריהוט הבית במשנה. Ramat Gan: Bar-Ilan University Press, 2013.

Kitchen, K. A. *Ramesside Inscriptions Translated & Annotated.* 5 vols. Oxford: Blackwell, 1993–.

Klawans, Jonathan. *Josephus and the Theologies of Ancient Judaism.* New York: Oxford University Press, 2012.

Kleinknecht, Hermann, Friedrich Baumgärtel, et al. "πνεῦμα, πνευματικός." In *Theological Dictionary of the New Testament,* edited by G. Kittel and G. Friedrich, 6:332–455. Translated by G. W. Bromiley. 15 vols. Grand Rapids: Eerdmans, 1964–1976.

Koehler, L., W. Baumgartner, and J. J. Stamm. *Hebräisches und aramäisches Lexikon zum Alten Testament.* Leiden: Brill, 1967–1996.

Koehler, L., W. Baumgartner, and J. J. Stamm. *The Hebrew and Aramaic Lexicon of the Old Testament.* Translated and edited under the supervision of M. E. J. Richardson. 5 vols. Leiden: Brill, 1994–2000.

Kogan, Leonid. "Proto-Semitic Lexicon." In *The Semitic Languages: An International Handbook,* edited by Stefan Weninger, 179–258. Handbücher zur Sprach- und Kommunikationswissenschaft 36. Berlin: De Gruyter Mouton, 2012.

Koller, Aaron. לבוא ולהיכנס: היבטים סינכרוניים ודיאכרוניים בסמנטיקה של הפועל "לבוא" בעברית העתיקה. *Lešonenu* 75 (2013): 149–64.

Kooten, George H. van. "The Anthropological Trichotomy of Spirit, Soul, and Body in Philo of Alexandria and Paul of Tarsus." In *Anthropology in the New Testament and Its Ancient Context: Papers from the EABS-Meeting in Piliscsaba/Budapest,* edited by Michael Labahn and Outi Lehtipuu, 87–119. Contributions to Biblical Exegesis and Theology 54. Leuven: Peeters, 2010.

Korpel, Marjo C. A. "Avian Spirits in Ugarit and in Ezekiel 13." In *Ugarit, Religion and Culture: Proceedings of the International Colloquium on Ugarit, Religion and Culture, Edinburgh, July 1994. Essays Presented in Honour of Professor John C. L. Gibson,* edited by N. Wyatt, W. G. E. Watson, and J. B. Lloyd, 99–113. Ugaritisch-biblische Literatur 12. Münster: Ugarit-Verlag, 1996.

Krašovec, Jože. *Der Merismus in Biblisch-Hebräischen und Nordwestsemitischen.* Biblica et Orientalia 33. Rome: Biblical Institute Press, 1977.

Krebernik, Manfred. "Ein aramäischer Text in griechischer Schrift?" in *"Sprich doch mit deinen Knechten aramäisch, wir verstehen es!" … Festschrift für Otto Jastrow zum 60. Geburtstag,* edited by Werner Arnold and Hartmut Bobzin, 425–28. Wiesbaden: Harrassowitz, 2002.

Kretzschmar, Richard. *Das Buch Ezechiel.* Handkommentar zum Alten Testament. Göttingen: Vandenhoeck & Ruprecht, 1900.

Krüger, Annette. "Auf dem Weg 'zu den Vätern': Zur Tradition der alttestamentlichen Sterbenotizen." In *Tod und Jenseits im alten Israel und in seiner Umwelt: Theologische, religionsgeschichtliche, archäologische und ikonographische Aspekte,* edited by Angelika Berlejung and Bernd Janowski, 137–150. Forschungen zum Alten Testament 64. Tübingen: Mohr Siebeck, 2009.

Kutscher, Eduard Yechezkel. "The Language of the 'Genesis Apocryphon': A Preliminary Study," *Scripta Hierosolymitana* 4 (1958): 1–34. Reprinted in מחקרים בעברית ובארמית, edited by Zeev Ben-Ḥayyim, Aron Dotan, and Gad Sarfatti, 3–36. Jerusalem: Magnes, 1977.

———. הלשון והרקע הלשוני של מגילת ישעיהו השלמה ממגילות ים המלח. Jerusalem: Magnes, 1959.

———. מחקרים בארמית הגלילית. Jerusalem, 1952. Eng. trans. in idem, *Studies in Galilean Aramaic*. Translated by Michael Sokoloff. Ramat Gan: Bar-Ilan University Press, 1976.

———. מלים ותולדותיהן. Jerusalem: Kiryath Sefer, 1965.

———. "Mittelhebräisch und Jüdisch-Aramäisch im neuen Köhler-Baumgartner." In *Hebräische Wortforschung: Festschrift zum 80. Geburtstag von Walter Baumgartner*, 158–75. Supplements to Vetus Testamentum 16. Leiden: Brill, 1967. Reprinted in Kutscher, *Hebrew and Aramaic Studies*, 156–73. Jerusalem: Magnes, 1977.

Lane, Edward W. *Arabic-English Lexicon*. London: Williams & Norgate, 1863–1877.

Lange, Armin. *Vom prophetischen Wort zur prophetischen Tradition: Studien zur Traditions- und Redaktionsgeschichte innerprophetischer Konflikte in der Hebräischen Bibel*. Forschungen zum Alten Testament 34. Tübingen: Mohr Siebeck, 2002.

Lange, Nicholas de. *Greek Jewish Texts from the Cairo Genizah*. Texte und Studien zum antiken Judentum 51. Tübingen: Mohr Siebeck, 1996.

Lauha, Risto. *Psychophysischer Sprachgebrauch im Alten Testament: Eine struktursemantische Analyse von* לב*,* נפש *und* רוח. Annales Academiae Scientiarum Fennicae, Dissertationes Humanarum Litterarum 35. Helsinki: Suomalainen tiedeakatemia: 1983.

Laum, Bernhard. *Stiftungen in der griechischen und römischen Antike: Ein Beitrag zur antiken Kulturgeschichte*. 2 vols. Leipzig: B. G. Teubner, 1914.

Laurin, Robert. "The Concept of Man as a Soul." *Expository Times* 72 (1960–1961): 131–34.

Leary, Mark R., and Nicole R. Buttermore. "The Evolution of the Human Self: Tracing the Natural History of Self-Awareness." *Journal for the Theory of Social Behaviour* 33 (2003): 365–403.

Leiman, S. Z. "Abarbanel and the Censor." *Journal of Jewish Studies* 19 (1968): 49–61.

Leitz, Christian. *Tagewählerei: Das Buch* ḥ3t nḥḥ pḥ.wy ḏt *und ver-*

wandte Texte. 2 vols. Ägyptologische Abhandlungen 55. Wiesbaden: Harrassowitz, 1994.

Lemaire, André. "Le dialecte araméen de l'inscription de Kuttamuwa (Zencirli, VIIIe s. av. n. è)." In *In the Shadow of Bezalel: Aramaic, Biblical and Ancient Near Eastern Studies in Honor of Bezalel Porten*, edited by Alejandro F. Botta, 145–50. Culture and History of the Ancient Near East 60. Leiden: Brill, 2013.

———. "Rites des vivants pour les morts dans le royaume de Sam'al (VIIIe siècle av. n. è.)." In *Les vivants et leurs morts: Actes du colloque organisé par le Collège de France, Paris, le 14–15 avril 2010*, 129–37. Orbis biblicus et orientalis 257. Fribourg: Academic Press, 2012.

Lemaire, André, and Benjamin Sass. "The Mortuary Stele with Samʾalian Inscription from Ördekburnu near Zincirli." *Bulletin of the American Schools of Oriental Research* 369 (2013): 57–136.

Lesko, Leonard H. "Death and the Afterlife in Ancient Egyptian Thought." In *Civilizations of the Ancient Near East*, edited by Jack M. Sasson, 3:1763–74. 4 vols. New York: Scribner, 1995.

Leslau, W. *Comparative Dictionary of Geʿez*. Wiesbaden: Harrassowitz, 1987.

Levine, Baruch A., Jean-Michel de Tarragon, and Anne Robertson. "The Patrons of the Ugaritic Dynasty (KTU 1.161)." In *The Context of Scripture*, edited by William W. Hallo, 357–58. 3 vols. Leiden: Brill, 1997–2002.

Levita, Elijah. ספר התשבי. Basel: Conrad Waldkirch, 1601.

Lewis, Theodore J. *Cults of the Dead in Ancient Israel and Ugarit*. Harvard Semitic Monographs 39. Atlanta: Scholars Press, 1989.

Licht, Jacob. מגילת ההודיות ממגילות מדבר יהודה. Jerusalem: Bialik, 1957.

Lichtenstein, Max. *Das Wort* נפש *in der Bibel: Eine Untersuchung über die historischen Grundlagen der Anschauung von der Seele und die Entwickelung der Bedeutung des Wortes* נפש. Schriften der Lehranstalt für die Wissenschaft des Judentums 4.5–6. Berlin: Mayer & Müller, 1920.

Lieberman, Saul. "Some Aspects of After Life in Early Rabbinic Literature." In *Harry Austryn Wolfson Jubilee Volume on the Occasion of His Seventy-Fifth Birthday*, edited by Saul Lieberman, 2:495–532. 2 vols. Jerusalem, 1965. Reprinted in Saul Lieberman, *Texts and Studies*, 235–72. New York: Ktav, 1974.

———, ed. מדרש דברים רבה. 2nd ed. Jerusalem: Shalem, 1992.

———. תוספתא כפשוטה: באור ארוך לתוספתא. 10 vols. New York: Jewish Theological Seminary of America, 1955–.

———. תוספת ראשונים. 4 vols. Jerusalem: Bamberger & Wahrmann, 1937–1939.

Lods, Adolphe. *La croyance à la vie future et le culte des morts dans l'antiquité israélite.* 2 vols. Paris: Fischbacher, 1906.

———. "Magie hébraïque et magie cananéenne." *Revue d'histoire et de philosophie religieuses* 7 (1927): 1–16.

Loretz, Oswald. "Nekromantie und Totenvokation in Mesopotamien, Ugarit und Israel." In *Religiongeschichtliche Beziehungen zwischen Kleinasien, Nordsyrien, und dem Alten Testament,* edited by Bernd Janowski, Klaus Koch, and Gernot Wilhelm, 285–318. Orbis biblicus et orientalis 129. Göttingen: Vandenhoeck & Ruprecht, 1993.

Lowth, William. *A Commentary upon the Prophet Ezekiel.* London: W. Mears, 1723.

Lyons, John. *Semantics.* 2 vols. Cambridge: Cambridge University Press, 1977.

Lys, Daniel. *Nèphèsh: Histoire de l'âme dans la révélation d'Israël au sein des religions proche-orientales.* Études d'histoire et de philosophie religieuses 50. Paris: Presses Universitaires de France, 1959.

Ma'agarim. Electronic Resource. *The Historical Dictionary Project of the Academy of the Hebrew Language.* Jerusalem: Academy of the Hebrew Language. Online, http://maagarim.hebrew-academy.org.il/.

Maimonides (Rambam). משנה עם פירוש רבינו משה בן מימון. Edited by Yosef Qafiḥ. 7 vols. Jerusalem: Mossad Harav Kook, 1963–1968.

Mandelbaum, Bernard, ed. פסיקתא דרב כהנא. 2 vols. New York: Jewish Theological Seminary of America, 1962.

Mankowski, Paul V. *Akkadian Loanwords in Biblical Hebrew.* Harvard Semitic Studies 47. Winona Lake, Ind.: Eisenbrauns, 2000.

Margulies, Mordecai, ed. מדרש ויקרא רבה. New York: Jewish Theological Seminary of America, 1993.

Martinet, André. "Remarques sur le consonantisme sémitique." *Bulletin de la Société Linguistique de Paris* 49 (1953): 67–78. Reprinted in idem, *Évolution des langues et reconstruction,* 248–61. Paris: Presses Universitaires de France, 1975.

Masson, Emilia. "La stèle mortuaire de Kuttamuwa (Zincirli): Comment l'appréhender." *Semitica et Classica* 3 (2010): 47–58.

Matthes, J. C. "De doodenvereering bij Israël." *Theologisch Tijdschrift* 35 (1901): 320–49.

Mazzini, Giovanni. "On the Problematic Term *syr/d* in the New Old

Aramaic Inscription from Zincirli." *Ugarit-Forschungen* 41 (2009): 505–7.

McKane, William. *A Critical and Exegetical Commentary on Jeremiah*. International Critical Commentary. Edinburgh: T&T Clark, 1996.

Midrash rabbah. מדרש רבה על חמשה חומשי תורה וחמש מגילות. 2 vols. Vilna: Rom, 1884.

Meier, Gerhard. *Die assyrische Beschwörungssammlung Maqlû*. Archiv für Orientforschung 2. Berlin: privately published, 1937.

Melchert, H. Craig. "Remarks on the Kuttamuwa Inscription." *Kubaba* 1 (2010): 4–11, http://www.fcsh.unl.pt/kubaba/KUBABA/Melchert_2010__Remarks_on_the_Kuttamuwa_Stele.pdf.

Menaḥem b. Saruq. *Maḥberet*. Edited by Angel Sáenz-Badillos. Granada: Universidad de Granada, 1986.

Meyers, Eric M. *Jewish Ossuaries: Reburial and Rebirth. Secondary Burials in Their Ancient Near Eastern Setting*. Biblica et Orientalia 24. Rome: Biblical Institute Press, 1971.

———. "Secondary Burials in Palestine." *Biblical Archaeologist* 33 (1970): 2–29.

———. "The Theological Implications of an Ancient Jewish Burial Custom." *Jewish Quarterly Review* 62 (1971): 97–119.

Milgrom, Jacob. *Leviticus 1–16: A New Translation with Introduction and Commentary*. Anchor Bible 3. New York: Doubleday, 1991.

Militarev, Alexander, and Leonid Kogan. *Semitic Etymological Dictionary*. Münster: Ugarit-Verlag, 2000.

Mishna Codex Parma (De Rossi 138): An Early Vowelized Manuscript of the Complete Mishna Text. Jerusalem: Kedem, 1970.

Moore, George Foot. *A Critical and Exegetical Commentary on Judges*. International Critical Commentary 7. New York: Charles Scribner's Sons, 1895.

Moran, William L. "The Hebrew Language in Its Northwest Semitic Background." In *The Bible and the Ancient Near East: Essays in Honor of William Foxwell Albright*, edited by G. Ernest Wright, 59–84. Garden City, N.Y.: Doubleday, 1961.

Morenz, Siegfried. *Egyptian Religion*. Translated by Ann E. Keep. Ithaca, N.Y.: Cornell University Press, 1973.

Moreshet, Menahem. לקסיקון הפועַל שנתחדש בלשון התנאים. Ramat Gan: Bar-Ilan University Press, 1980.

Morgenstern, Matthew. הארמית הבבלית היהודית בתשובות הגאונים — עיונים בתורת ההגה, בתצורת הפועל, בכינויים ובסגנון. Ph.D. dissertation, Hebrew University, 2002. English abstract, 13–15.

Moshavi, Adina. *Word Order in the Biblical Hebrew Finite Clause: A Syntactic and Pragmatic Analysis of Preposing.* Linguistic Studies in Ancient West Semitic 4. Winona Lake, Ind.: Eisenbrauns, 2010.

Mowinckel, Sigmund. *Psalmenstudien.* Videnskapsselskapets Skrifter. II. Hist.-Filos. Klasse. 1921, no. 4. 6 vols. Kristiania: J. Dybwad, 1921–1924.

Muchiki, Yoshiyuki. *Egyptian Proper Names and Loanwords in North-West Semitic.* Society of Biblical Literature Dissertation Series 173. Atlanta: Society of Biblical Literature, 1999.

Muraoka, Takamitsu. "The Tell-Fekherye Bilingual Inscription and Early Aramaic." *Abr-Nahrain* 22 (1983–1984): 79–117.

Muraoka, Takamitsu, and Bezalel Porten. *A Grammar of Egyptian Aramaic.* Handbook of Oriental Studies, The Near and Middle East 32. Leiden: Brill, 1998.

Murtonen, A. *The Living Soul: A Study of the Meaning of the Word næfæš in the Old Testament Hebrew Language.* Studia Orientalia 23.1. Helsinki: Societas Orientalis Fennica, 1958.

Naḥmanides (Ramban). *Commentary on the Torah.* Translated by Charles B. Chavel. 5 vols. New York: Shilo, 1971–1976.

Nathan b. Jehiel. ספר ערוך השלם. Edited by Alexander Kohut. 8 vols. Vienna: n.p., 1878–1892.

Naveh, Joseph. כתובות ארמיות קדומות. *Lešonenu* 29 (1965): 183–97.

Nebe, Wilhelm. "Eine neue Inschrift aus Zincirli auf der Stele des Kutamuwa und die hebräische Sprachwissenschaft." In *Jüdische Studien als Disziplin—die Disziplinen der Jüdischen Studien: Festschrift der Hochschule für Jüdische Studien Heidelberg 1979–2009,* edited by Johannes Heil and Daniel Krochmalnik, 311–32. Schriften der Hochschule für Jüdische Studien Heidelberg 13. Heidelberg: Winter, 2010.

Niehr, Herbert. "Zum Totenkult der Könige von Samʾal im 9. und 8. Jh. v. Chr." *Studi epigrafici e linguistici* 11 [1994]: 57–73.

Noorlander, Paul. "Samʾalian in Its Northwest Semitic Setting: A Historical-Comparative Approach." *Orientalia* 81 (2012): 202–38.

Notarius, T. "*ʔq(n)* 'wood' in the Aramaic Ostraca from Idumea: A Note on the Reflex of Proto-Semitic /*ṣ̂/ in Imperial Aramaic," *Aramaic Studies* 4 (2006): 101–9.

Nutkowicz, Hélène. *L'homme face à la mort au royaume de Juda: Rites, pratiques, et représentations.* Patrimoines. Judaïsme. Paris: Cerf, 2006.

Oesterley, W. O. E. *Immortality and the Unseen World: A Study in Old Testament Religion.* London: Society for Promoting Christian Knowledge, 1921.

Olmo Lete, Gregorio del. "KTMW and His 'Funerary Chapel.'" *Aula Orientalis* 29 (2011): 308–10.

Olmo Lete, Gregorio del, and Joaquín Sanmartín. *A Dictionary of the Ugaritic Language in the Alphabetic Tradition.* Handbook of Oriental Studies 67. Leiden: Brill, 2003.

Olyan, Saul M. "Some Neglected Aspects of Israelite Interment Ideology." *Journal of Biblical Literature* 124 (2005): 601–16.

Oppenheim, A. Leo. *Ancient Mesopotamia: Portrait of a Dead Civilization.* Chicago: University of Chicago Press, 1964.

Orel, Vladimir. "Textological Notes." *Zeitschrift für die alttestamentliche Wissenschaft* 109 (1997): 408–13.

Oriental Institute of the University of Chicago. *The Assyrian Dictionary of the Oriental Institute of the University of Chicago.* Chicago: Oriental Institute, 1956–.

Origen. *Homélies sur Ézéchiel.* Translated by Marcel Borret. Sources chrétiennes 352. Paris: Cerf.

———. *Origenis Hexaplorum.* Edited by Frederick Field. Oxford: Clarendon, 1875.

Osborne, James F. "Secondary Mortuary Practice and the Bench Tomb: Structure and Practice in Iron Age Judah." *Journal of Near Eastern Studies* 70 (2011): 35–53.

Padgham, Joan. *A New Interpretation of the Cone on the Head in New Kingdom Egyptian Tomb Scenes.* BAR International Series 2431. Oxford: Archaeopress, 2012.

Pardee, Dennis. "The Katumuwa Inscription." In *In Remembrance of Me: Feasting with the Dead in the Ancient Middle East,* edited by Virginia Rimmer Herrmann and J. David Schloen, 45–48. Chicago: Oriental Institute of the University of Chicago, 2014.

———. "A New Aramaic Inscription from Zincirli." *Bulletin of the American Schools of Oriental Research* 356 (2009): 51–71.

Parker, Robert. "A Funerary Foundation from Hellenistic Lycia." *Chiron* 40 (2010): 103–21.

Parkhurst, John. *An Hebrew and English Lexicon without Points.* London: W. Faden, 1762.

Parpola, S. "National and Ethnic Identity in the New-Assyrian Empire and Assyrian Identity in Post-Empire Times." *Journal of Assyrian Academic Studies* 18 (2004): 5–49.

Parry, Donald W., and Elisha Qimron, eds. *The Great Isaiah Scroll (1QIsa[a]): A New Edition*. Studies on the Texts of the Desert of Judah 32. Leiden: Brill, 1999.

Paton, Lewis B. "The Hebrew Idea of the Future Life: I, Earliest Conceptions of the Soul." *Biblical World* 35 (1910): 8–20.

Patrich, Joseph. קבורה ראשונה על־פי מקורות חז״ל — לביאורם של מונחים. In קברים ונוהגי קבורה בארץ־ישראל בעת העתיקה, edited by Itamar Singer, 190–211. Jerusalem: Yad Izhak Ben-Zvi, 1994.

Pedersen, Johannes. *Israel: Its Life and Culture*. 2 vols. London: Oxford University Press, 1926–1940.

Perez, Ma'aravi, ed. פירוש ר׳ יהודה אבן בלעם לספר יחזקאל. Ramat Gan: Bar-Ilan University Press, 2000.

Peshiṭta Institute. *The Old Testament in Syriac according to the Peshiṭta Version*. Leiden: Brill, 1972–.

Philo. *Philo in Ten Volumes*. Translated by F. H. Colson and G. H. Whitaker. Loeb Classical Library. London: William Heinemann, 1929–1962.

Pinch, Geraldine. *Magic in Ancient Egypt*. Austin: University of Texas Press, 1994.

Pitard, Wayne T. "Care of the Dead at Emar." In *Emar: The History, Religion, and Culture of a Syrian Town in the Late Bronze Age*, edited by Mark W. Chavalas, 123–40. Bethesda, Md.: CDL, 1996.

Pohlmann, Karl-Friedrich. *Das Buch des Propheten Hesekiel (Ezechiel)*. 2 vols. Das Alte Testament deutsch 22. Göttingen: Vandenhoeck & Ruprecht, 1996–2001.

Porten, Bezalel, and Ada Yardeni. *Textbook of Aramaic Documents from Ancient Egypt*. 4 vols. Texts and Studies for Students. Jerusalem: Hebrew University of Jerusalem, 1986–1999.

Porteous, N. W. "Soul." In *The Interpreter's Dictionary of the Bible*, edited by G. A. Buttrick, 4:428–29. 4 vols. Nashville: Abingdon, 1962.

Pritchard, J. B., ed. *Ancient Near Eastern Texts Relating to the Old Testament*. 3rd ed. Princeton: Princeton University Press, 1969.

Qimron, Elisha. ארמית מקראית. 2nd ed. Jerusalem: Bialik, 2002.

———. *The Hebrew of the Dead Sea Scrolls*. Harvard Semitic Studies 29. Atlanta: Scholars Press, 1986.

Quirke, Stephen. *Egyptian Literature 1800 BC: Questions and Readings*. Egyptology 2. London: Golden House, 2004.

———. *Going Out in Daylight – prt m hrw: The Ancient Egyptian Book of the Dead – Translation, Sources, Meanings*. GHP Egyptology 20. London: Golden House Publications, 2013.

Rahmani, L. Y. *A Catalogue of Jewish Ossuaries in the Collections of the State of Israel*. Jerusalem: Israel Antiquities Authority, 1994.

Ricks, Stephen D. *Lexicon of Inscriptional Qatabanian*. Studia Pohl 14. Rome: Pontificio Istituto Biblico, 1989.

Rignell, Gösta. *The Peshitta to the Book of Job: Critically Investigated with Introduction, Translation, Commentary and Summary*. Edited by Karl-Eric Rignell. Kristianstad: Monitor, 1994.

Ritner, Robert K. "The Cult of the Dead." In *Ancient Egypt*, edited by David P. Silverman, 132–47. New York: Oxford University Press, 1997.

Robinson, H. Wheeler. *The Christian Doctrine of Man*. 2nd ed. Edinburgh: T&T Clark, 1913.

Rubin, Nissan. הקבורה השנייה בארץ־ישראל בתקופת המשנה והתלמוד — הצעה למודל שיטתי לקשר שבין המבנה החברתי לדרכי הטיפול במת. In קברים ונוהגי קבורה בארץ־ישראל בעת העתיקה, edited by Itamar Singer, 248–69. Jerusalem: Yad Izhak Ben-Zvi, 1994.

———. *Time and Life Cycle in Talmud and Midrash: Socio-anthropological Perspectives*. Judaism and Jewish Life. Boston: Academic Studies Press, 2008.

Saadia Gaon. *The Book of Beliefs and Opinions*. Translated by Samuel Rosenblatt. Yale Judaica Series 1. New Haven: Yale University Press, 1948.

———. משלי עם תרגום ופירוש הגאון רבנו סעדיה בן יוסף בן יוסף פיומי. Edited by Yosef Qafiḥ. Jerusalem: Va'ad le-Hotsa'at Sifre Rasag, 1976.

———. ספר הנבחר באמונות ובדעות. Edited by Yosef Qafiḥ. Jerusalem: Sura; New York: Yeshiva University, 1969.

———. תהלים עם תרגום ופירוש הגאון רבינו סעדיה בן יוסף פיומי. Edited by Yosef Qafiḥ. New York: American Academy for Jewish Research 1966.

Safrai, Shmuel, and Ze'ev Safrai. משנת ארץ ישראל: מסכתות מועד קטן וחגיגה עם מבוא ופירוש היסטורי חברתי. Ramat Gan: Bar-Ilan University Press, 2012.

Saggs, H. W. F. "'External Souls' in the Old Testament." *Journal of Semitic Studies* 19 (1974): 1–12.

Sakenfeld, Katharine Doob, ed. *The New Interpreter's Dictionary of the Bible*. 5 vols. Nashville: Abingdon, 2006–2009.

Salonen, Armas. *Vögel und Vogelfang im alten Mesopotamien*. Suomalaisen Tiedeakatemian toimituksia B 180. Helsinki: Suomalainen Tiedeakatemia, 1973.

Sander, Otto. "Leib-Seele-Dualismus im Alten Testament?" *Zeitschrift für die alttestamentliche Wissenschaft* 77 (1965): 329–32.

Sanders, Seth L. "The Appetites of the Dead: West Semitic Linguistic and Ritual Aspects of the Katumuwa Stele." *Bulletin of the American Schools of Oriental Research* 369 (2013): 35–55.

Scharbert, Josef. *Fleish, Geist und Seele im Pentateuch: Ein Beitrag zur Anthropologie der Pentateuchquellen.* Stuttgarter Bibelstudien 19. Stuttgart: Katholisches Bibelwerk, 1967.

Schechter, Salomon, ed. אבות דרבי נתן. Vienna: Ch. D. Lippe, 1887.

Schloen, J. David. "The City of Katumuwa: The Iron Age Kingdom of Sam'al and the Excavation of Zincirli." In *In Remembrance of Me: Feasting with the Dead in the Ancient Middle East,* edited by Virginia Rimmer Herrmann and J. David Schloen, 27–38. Chicago: Oriental Institute of the University of Chicago, 2014.

Schloen, J. David, and Amir S. Fink. "New Excavations at Zincirli Höyük in Turkey (Ancient Samʾal) and the Discovery of an Inscribed Mortuary Stele." *Bulletin of the American Schools of Oriental Research* 356 (2009): 1–13.

Schmidt, Brian B. "The Gods and the Dead of the Domestic Cult at Emar: A Reassessment." In *Emar: The History, Religion, and Culture of a Syrian Town in the Late Bronze Age,* edited by Mark W. Chavalas, 141–63. Bethesda, Md.: CDL, 1996.

———. *Israel's Beneficent Dead: Ancestor Cult and Necromancy in Ancient Israelite Religion and Tradition.* Forschungen zum Alten Testament 11. Tübingen: J. C. B. Mohr, 1994.

———. "Memory as Immortality: Countering the Dreaded 'Death after Death' in Ancient Israelite Society." In *Judaism in Late Antiquity,* edited by Jacob Neusner, 4:87–100. 5 vols. Handbook of Oriental Studies. The Near and Middle East. Leiden: Brill, 1995–2001.

Schmitt, Rüdiger. *Magie im Alten Testament.* Alter Orient und Altes Testament 313. Münster, Ugarit-Verlag, 2004.

Schneider, Hans D. "Bringing the *Ba* to the Body: A Glorification Spell for Padinekhtnebef." In *Hommages à Jean Leclant,* edited by Catherine Berger, Gisèle Clerc, and Nicolas Grimal, 355–62. 4 vols. Bibliothèque d'étude 106/4. Cairo: Institut français d'archéologie orientale, 1994.

Schröter, R. "Gedicht des Jacob von Sarug über den Palast, den der

Apostel Thomas in Indien baute." *Zeitschrift der deutschen morgenländischen Gesellschaft* 25 (1871): 321–77.

———. "Nachträge zu dem … Gedicht des Jacob von Sarug: 'über den Palast, den der Apostel Thomas in Indien baute.'" *Zeitschrift der deutschen morgenländischen Gesellschaft* 28 (1874): 584–626.

Schwab, Johann. *Der Begriff der nefeš in den heiligen Schriften des Alten Testamentes: Ein Beitrag zur altjüdischen Religionsgeschichte.* Borna-Leipzig: R. Noske, 1913.

Schwally, Friedrich. *Das Leben nach dem Tode: Nach den Vorstellungen des alten Israel und des Judentums einschliesslich des Volksglaubens im Zeitalter Christi, eine biblisch-theologische Untersuchung.* Giessen: J. Ricker, 1892.

Scurlock, JoAnn. "Death and the Afterlife in Ancient Mesopotamian Thought." In *Civilizations of the Ancient Near East,* edited by Jack M. Sasson, 3:1883–93. 4 vols. New York: Scribner, 1995.

———. "Soul Emplacements in Ancient Mesopotamian Funerary Rituals." In *Magic and Divination in the Ancient World,* edited by Leda Ciraolo and Jonathan Seidel, 1–6. Ancient Magic and Divination 2. Leiden: Brill, 2002.

Seebass, Horst. "נֶפֶשׁ *nep̱eš.*" In *Theological Dictionary of the Old Testament,* edited by G. Johannes Botterweck and H. Ringgren, 9:496–519. Translated by J. T. Willis, G. W. Bromiley, and D. E. Green. 15 vols. Grand Rapids: Eerdmans, 1974–.

Selbie, J. A. "Ezekiel xiii. 18-21." *Expository Times* 15 (1903–1904): 75.

Seow, C. L. "Am עם." In *Dictionary of Deities and Demons in the Bible,* edited by Karel van der Toorn, Bob Becking, and Pieter W. van der Horst, 24–26. 2nd rev. ed. Grand Rapids: Eerdmans, 1999.

Shoemaker, William Ross. "The Use of רוּחַ in the Old Testament, and of πνεῦμα in the New Testament: A Lexicographical Study." *Journal of Biblical Literature* 23 (1904): 13–67.

Simpson, William Kelley, Robert K. Ritner, and Vincent A. Tobin. *Literature of Ancient Egypt: An Anthology of Stories, Instructions, Stelae, Autobiographies, and Poetry.* 3rd ed. New Haven: Yale University Press, 2003.

Smend, Rudolf. *Der Prophet Ezechiel.* 2nd ed. Kurzgefasstes exegetisches Handbuch zum Alten Testament 8. Leipzig: S. Hirzel, 1880.

Smith, Henry P. "Frazer's 'Folk-Lore in the Old Testament.'" *Harvard Theological Review* 17 (1924): 63–82.

Smith, Mark S., and Elizabeth Bloch-Smith. "Death and the Afterlife in Ugarit and Israel." *Journal of the American Oriental Society* 108 (1988): 277–84.

Soden, Wolfram von. *Akkadisches Handwörterbuch.* 3 vols. Wiesbaden: Harrassowitz, 1965–1981.

———. *Grundriss der akkadischen Grammatik.* 3rd ed. Analecta Orientalia 33. Rome: Pontificium Institutum Biblicum, 1995.

Sokoloff, Michael. *A Dictionary of Jewish Babylonian Aramaic of the Talmudic and Geonic Periods.* Ramat Gan: Bar-Ilan University Press, 2002.

———. *A Dictionary of Jewish Palestinian Aramaic of the Byzantine Period.* Ramat Gan: Bar-Ilan University, 1990.

———. קטעי בראשית רבה מן הגניזה. Jerusalem: Israel Academy of Sciences and Humanities, 1982.

———. *A Syriac Lexicon: A Translation from the Latin, Correction, Expansion, and Update of C. Brockelmann's* Lexicon Syriacum. Winona Lake, Ind.: Eisenbrauns, 2009.

Spronk, Klaas. *Beatific Afterlife in Ancient Israel and in the Ancient Near East.* Alter Orient und Altes Testament 219. Neukirchen-Vluyn: Neukirchener Verlag, 1986.

Stavrakopoulou, Francesca. *Land of Our Fathers: The Roles of Ancestor Veneration in Biblical Land Claims.* Library of Hebrew Bible/Old Testament Studies 473. New York: T&T Clark, 2010.

Stec, David M. *The Text of the Targum of Job: An Introduction and Critical Edition.* Arbeiten zur Geschichte des antiken Judentums und des Urchristentums 20. Leiden: Brill, 1994.

Stein, Gil J. "Foreword." In *In Remembrance of Me: Feasting with the Dead in the Ancient Middle East,* edited by Virginia Rimmer Herrmann and J. David Schloen, 9. Chicago: Oriental Institute of the University of Chicago, 2014.

Steiner, Richard C. "Addenda to *The Case for Fricative-Laterals in Proto-Semitic.*" In *Semitic Studies in Honor of Wolf Leslau on the Occasion of His Eighty-fifth Birthday, November 14th, 1991,* edited by Alan S. Kaye, 1499–1513. Wiesbaden: Harrassowitz, 1991.

———. "The Aramaic Text in Demotic Script." In *The Context of Scripture,* edited by William W. Hallo and K. Lawson Younger, Jr., 1:309-27. 3 vols. Leiden: Brill, 1997.

———. *A Biblical Translation in the Making: The Evolution and Impact of Saadia Gaon's* Tafsīr. Cambridge, Mass.: Harvard University Center for Jewish Studies, 2010.

———. *The Case for Fricative-Laterals in Proto-Semitic.* American Oriental Series 59. New Haven: American Oriental Society, 1977.

———. "Does the Biblical Hebrew Conjunction -ו Have Many Meanings, One Meaning, or No Meaning at All?" *Journal of Biblical Literature* 119 (2000): 249–67.

———. *Early Northwest Semitic Serpent Spells in the Pyramid Texts.* Harvard Semitic Studies 61. Winona Lake, Ind.: Eisenbrauns, 2011.

———. "Hebrew: Ancient Hebrew." In *International Encyclopedia of Linguistics,* 2:110–18. 4 vols. New York: Oxford University Press, 1992.

———. "*Mattan* and *Shay* in the Lachish Ewer Inscription." *Eretz-Israel* (Joseph Naveh Memorial Volume, forthcoming).

———. "The *Mbqr* at Qumran, the *Episkopos* in the Athenian Empire, and the Meaning of *lbqrʾ* in Ezra 7:14: On the Relation of Ezra's Mission to the Persian Legal Project." *Journal of Biblical Literature* 120 (2001): 623–46.

———. "*Muqdam u-Meʾuḥar* and *Muqaddam wa-Muʾaḫḫar:* On the History of Some Hebrew and Arabic Terms for *Hysteron Proteron* and *Anastrophe.*" *Journal of Near Eastern Studies* 66 (2007): 33–45.

———. "On the Dating of Hebrew Sound Changes (*Ḫ > Ḥ and *Ġ > ʿ) and Greek Translations (2 Esdras and Judith)." *Journal of Biblical Literature* 124 (2005): 229-67.

———. "On the Rise and Fall of Canaanite Religion at Baalbek: A Tale of Five Toponyms." *Journal of Biblical Literature* 128 (2009): 507–25.

———. "Papyrus Amherst 63: A New Source for the Language, Literature, Religion, and History of the Arameans." In *Studia Aramaica: New Sources and New Approaches,* edited by M. J. Geller, J. C. Greenfield, and M. P. Weitzman, 199–207. Journal of Semitic Studies Supplement 4. Oxford: Oxford University Press, 1995.

———. "Poetic Forms in the Masoretic Vocalization and Three Difficult Phrases in Jacob's Blessing: יֶתֶר שְׂאֵת (Gen 49:3), יְצוּעִי עָלָה (Gen 49:4), and יָבֹא שִׁילֹה (Gen 49:10)." *Journal of Biblical Literature* 129 (2010): 209-35.

———. "Saadia vs. Rashi: On the Shift from Meaning-Maximalism to Meaning-Minimalism in Medieval Biblical Lexicology." *Jewish Quarterly Review* 88 (1998): 213–58.

———. "Variation, Simplifying Assumptions and the History of Spirantization in Aramaic and Hebrew." In שערי לשון: מחקרים

בלשון העברית, בארמית ובלשונות היהודים מוגשים למשה בר־אשר, edited by A. Maman, S. E. Fassberg, and Y. Breuer, *52–*65. 3 vols. Jerusalem: Bialik, 2007.

———. "Vowel Syncope and Syllable Repair Processes in Proto-Semitic Construct Forms: A New Reconstruction Based on the Law of Diminishing Conditioning." In *Language and Nature: Papers Presented to John Huehnergard on the Occasion of His 60th Birthday*, edited by Rebecca Hasselbach and Naʿama Pat-El, 365–90. Studies in Ancient Oriental Civilizations 67. Chicago: Oriental Institute, 2012.

Steiner, Richard C., and Adina Moshavi. "A Selective Glossary of Northwest Semitic Texts in Egyptian Script." In J. Hoftijzer and K. Jongeling, *Dictionary of the North-West Semitic Inscriptions*, 2:1249–66. 2 vols. Handbook of Oriental Studies, The Near and Middle East 21. Leiden: Brill, 1995.

Steiner, Richard C., and Charles F. Nims, "Ashurbanipal and Shamash-shum-ukin: A Tale of Two Brothers from the Aramaic Text in Demotic Script." *Revue Biblique* 92 (1985): 60–81.

———. "You Can't Offer Your Sacrifice and Eat It Too: A Polemical Poem from the Aramaic Text in Demotic Script." *Journal of Near Eastern Studies* 43 (1984): 89–114.

Stevenson, Kenneth, and Michael Glerup, eds. *Ezekiel, Daniel*. Vol. 13 of *Ancient Christian Commentary on Scripture, Old Testament*, edited by Andrew Louth et al. Downers Grove, Ill.: InterVarsity, 2008.

Stökl, Jonathan. "The מתנבאות in Ezekiel 13 Reconsidered." *Journal of Biblical Literature* 132 (2013): 61–76.

Streck, Michael P. "Akkadian and Aramaic Language Contact." In *The Semitic Languages: An International Handbook*, edited by Stefan Weninger, 416–24. Handbücher zur Sprach- und Kommunikationswissenschaft 36. Berlin: De Gruyter Mouton, 2012.

———. "Amorite." In *The Semitic Languages: An International Handbook*, edited by Stefan Weninger, 452–59. Handbücher zur Sprach- und Kommunikationswissenschaft 36. Berlin: De Gruyter Mouton, 2012.

Struble, Eudora J., and Virginia Rimmer Herrmann. "An Eternal Feast at Samʾal: The New Iron Age Mortuary Stele from Zincirli in Context." *Bulletin of the American Schools of Oriental Research* 356 (2009): 15–49.

Suriano, Matthew J. "Breaking Bread with the Dead: Katumuwa's

Stele, Hosea 9:4, and the Early History of the Soul." *Journal of the American Oriental Society* 134 (2014): 385–405.

———. "Death, Disinheritance, and Job's Kinsman-Redeemer." *Journal of Biblical Literature* 129 (2010): 49–66.

Tal (Rosenthal), Abraham. לשון התרגום לנביאים ראשונים ומעמדה בכלל ניבי הארמית. Tel Aviv: Tel Aviv University, 1975.

———. מילון הארמית של השומרונים. Leiden: Brill, 2000.

———. *The Samaritan Targum of the Pentateuch: A Critical Edition*. 3 vols. Tel-Aviv: Tel-Aviv University, 1980–1983.

Tarashchansky, N. N. מִסְפָּחוֹת. *Talpiyyot* 1 (1895): 15-17 (in אוצר הספרות section).

Taylor, John H. *Death and the Afterlife in Ancient Egypt*. London: British Museum Press, 2001.

———, ed. *Journey through the Afterlife: Ancient Egyptian Book of the Dead*. Cambridge, Mass.: Harvard University Press, 2010.

Teixidor, Javier. *The Pagan God: Popular Religion in the Greco-Roman Near East*. Princeton: Princeton University Press, 1977.

Tengström, Sven, et al. "רוּחַ *rûaḥ*." In *Theological Dictionary of the Old Testament*, edited by Johannes Botterweck and H. Ringgren, 13:365–402. Translated by J. T. Willis, G. W. Bromiley, and D. E. Green. 8 vols. Grand Rapids: Eerdmans, 1974–.

Tertullian. *Quinti Septimi Florentis Tertulliani De Anima*. Edited by J. H. Waszink. Supplements to Vigiliae Christianae 100. Leiden: Brill, 2010.

Theodor, J., and C. Albeck, eds. מדרש בראשית רבא. Berlin: M. Poppeloyer, 1927.

Thompson, Stith. *Motif-Index of Folk-Literature: A Classification of Narrative Elements in Folktales, Ballads, Myths, Fables, Mediaeval Romances, Exempla, Fabliaux, Jest-Books, and Local Legends*. 6 vols. Bloomington: Indiana University Press, 1975.

Tigay, Jeffrey H. *Deuteronomy* דברים: *The Traditional Hebrew Text with the New JPS Translation*. JPS Torah Commentary. Philadelphia: Jewish Publication Society, 1996.

Toorn, Karel van der. "Dead That Are Slow to Depart: Evidence for Ancestor Rituals in Mesopotamia. In *In Remembrance of Me: Feasting with the Dead in the Ancient Middle East*, edited by Virginia Rimmer Herrmann and J. David Schloen, 81–84. Chicago: Oriental Institute of the University of Chicago, 2014.

———. *Family Religion in Babylonia, Syria, and Israel: Continuity and*

Change in the Forms of Religious Life. Studies in the History and Culture of the Ancient Near East 7. Leiden: Brill, 1996.

———. *From Her Cradle to Her Grave: The Role of Religion in the Life of the Israelite and the Babylonian Woman*. Translated by Sara J. Denning-Bolle. Biblical Seminar 23. Sheffield: JSOT Press, 1994.

Toorn, Karel van der, Bob Becking, and Pieter W. van der Horst, eds. *Dictionary of Deities and Demons in the Bible*. 2nd ed. Leiden: Brill, 1999.

Torge, Paul. *Seelenglaube und Unsterblichkeitshoffnung im Alten Testament*. Leipzig: J. C. Hinrichs, 1909.

Triebel, Lothar. *Jenseitshoffnung in Wort und Stein: Nefesch und pyramidales Grabmal als Phänomene antiken jüdischen Bestattungswesens im Kontext der Nachbarkulturen*. Arbeiten zur Geschichte des antiken Judentums und des Urchristentums 56. Leiden: Brill, 2004.

Tromp, Nicholas J. *Primitive Conceptions of Death and the Nether World in the Old Testament*. Biblica et Orientalis 21. Rome: Pontifical Biblical Institute, 1969.

Tropper, Josef. *Die Inschriften von Zincirli: Neue Edition und vergleichende Grammatik des phönizischen, sam'alischen und aramäischen Textkorpus*. Abhandlungen zur Literatur Alt-Syrien-Palästinas 6. Münster: Ugarit-Verlag, 1993.

———. *Nekromantie: Totenbefragung im Alten Orient and im Alten Testament*. Alter Orient und Altes Testament 223. Neukirchen-Vluyn: Neukirchener Verlag, 1989.

Tsukimoto Akio. *Untersuchungen zur Totenpflege (*kispum*) im alten Mesopotamien*. Alter Orient und Altes Testament 216. Neukirchen-Vluyn: Neukirchener Verlag, 1985.

Ulrich, Eugene, and Peter W. Flint, eds. *Qumran Cave 1.II: The Isaiah Scrolls*. Discoveries in the Judaean Desert 32. Oxford: Clarendon, 2010.

Vernant, Jean Pierre. "Psuche: Simulacrum of the Body or Image of the Divine?" In idem, *Mortals and Immortals: Collected Essays*, edited by Froma I. Zeitlin, 186–92. Princeton: Princeton University Press, 1991.

Versteegh, Kees. "Loanwords from Arabic and the Merger of *ḍ/ḏ*." *Israel Oriental Studies* 19 (1999): 273–86.

Vleeming, S. P., and J. W. Wesselius. *Studies in Papyrus Amherst 63: Essays on the Aramaic Texts in Aramaic-Demotic Papyrus Amherst 63*. 2 vols. Amsterdam: Juda Palache Instituut, 1985–1990.

Voigt, Rainer M. "Die Laterale im Semitischen, *Die Welt des Orients* 10 (1979): 93–114.

Weicker, Georg. *Der Seelenvogel in der alten Litteratur und Kunst: Eine mythologisch-archaeologische Untersuchung*. Leipzig: B. G. Teubner, 1902.

Wenning, Robert. "'Medien' in der Bestattungskultur im eisenzeitlichen Juda?" In *Medien im antiken Palästina: Materielle Kommunikation und Medialität als Thema der Palästinaarchäologie*, edited by Christian Frevel, 109–50. Forschungen zum Alten Testament 2/11. Tübingen: Mohr Siebeck, 2005.

Wernhart, Karl R. "Ethnische Seelenkonzepte." In *Der Begriff der Seele in der Religionswissenschaft*, edited by Johann Figl and Hans-Dieter Klein, 45–60. Würzburg: Königshausen & Neumann, 2002.

Wevers, John William. *Ezekiel*. Century Bible, New Series. London: Nelson, 1969.

Wilkinson, Toby A. H. *Early Dynastic Egypt*. London: Routledge, 1999.

Wilson, John A. "The Story of Sinuhe." In *Ancient Near Eastern Texts Relating to the Old Testament*, edited by J. B. Pritchard, 18–22. 3rd ed. Princeton: Princeton University Press, 1969.

Wolff, Hans Walter. *Anthropology of the Old Testament*. Philadelphia: Fortress, 1974.

Wood, W. Carleton. "The Religion of Canaan: From the Earliest Times to the Hebrew Conquest." *Journal of Biblical Literature* 35 (1916): 1–133.

Woodward, John B. *Man as Spirit, Soul, and Body: A Study of Biblical Psychology*. Pigeon Forge, Tenn.: Grace Fellowship International, 2007.

Xella, Paolo. "Death and the Afterlife in Canaanite and Hebrew Thought." In *Civilizations of the Ancient Near East*, edited by Jack M. Sasson, 3:2059–70. 4 vols. New York: Scribner, 1995.

Yakubovich, Ilya. "The West Semitic God El in Anatolian Hieroglyphic Transmission." In *Pax Hethitica: Studies on the Hittites and Their Neighbours in Honour of Itamar Singer*, edited by Yoram Cohen, Amir Gilan, and Jared L. Miller, 385–98. Studien zu den Boğazköy-Texten Herausgegeben von der Kommission für den Alten Orient der Akademie der Wissenschaften und der Literatur, Mainz, 51. Wiesbaden: Harrassowitz, 2010.

Yalon, Henoch. פרקי לשון. Jerusalem: Bialik, 1971.

———. Review of Yehudah Grazovski (Goor), מלון השפה העברית. In קונטרסים לעניני הלשון העברית, edited by Henoch Yalon, part 2 (= שנה שניה), 21–22. Jerusalem: Wahrmann Books, 1963.

Yardeni, Ada. אוסף תעודות ארמיות, עבריות ונבטיות ממדבר יהודה וחומר קרוב. Jerusalem: Hebrew University, 2000.

———. שטר מכר ממדבר יהודה: נחל צאלים 9, *Tarbiz* 63 (1994): 299–320.

Young, Ian. "The Languages of Ancient Samʾal." *Maarav* 9 (2002): 93–105.

Younger, K. Lawson. "Two Epigraphic Notes on the New Katumuwa Inscription from Zincirli." *Maarav* 16 (2009): 159–79.

Žabkar, Louis V. *A Study of the Ba Concept in Ancient Egyptian Texts.* Studies in Ancient Oriental Civilization 34. Chicago: University of Chicago Press, 1968.

Zadok, Ran. "On the Amorite Material from Mesopotamia." In *The Tablet and the Scroll: Near Eastern Studies in Honor of William W. Hallo,* edited by Mark E. Cohen, Daniel C. Snell, and David B. Weisberg, 315–33. Bethesda, Md.: CDL, 1993.

Zevit, Ziony. "Phoenician NBŠ/NPŠ and Its Hebrew Semantic Equivalents." *Maarav* 5–6, special issue, *Sopher Mahir: Northwest Semitic Studies Presented to Stanislav Segert,* edited by Edward M. Cook, 337–44. Winona Lake, Ind.: Eisenbrauns, 1990.

———. *The Religions of Ancient Israel: A Synthesis of Parallactic Approaches.* London: Continuum, 2001.

Zilber, David. נפש, נשמה ורוח, וזיקתן לבשר ורוח — במקרא ולאחריו, *Beth Mikra* 16 (1971): 312–25.

Zimmerli, Walther. *Ezekiel 1: A Commentary on the Book of the Prophet Ezekiel, Chapters 1–24.* Translated by Ronald E. Clements. Hermeneia. Philadelphia: Fortress, 1979.

———. *Ezekiel 2: A Commentary on the Book of the Prophet Ezekiel, Chapters 25–48.* Translated by James D. Martin. Hermeneia. Philadelphia: Fortress, 1983.

Index of Ancient Texts

Hebrew and Jewish Aramaic Texts

Hebrew Bible

Genesis
1:24, 83, 125
1:30, 69, 83, 125
2:7, 84, 85, 85n17, 86, 86n18, 125
2:23, 74
3:15, 78, 125
6:17, 69, 83, 125
7:15, 69, 83
7:22, 84, 125
8:21, 79n44
9:4, 82n3
12:13, 74
15:15, 92, 95
17:14, 125
18:2, 104
19:20, 74
23:4, 94n6
23:9, 144
24:45, 79n44
24:55, 146
25:8–9, 94, 101–2
27:44, 146n85
32:11, 76
35:18, 3, 63, 69, 71–72, 125
35:29, 94, 96, 101–2
37:21, 77, 125
37:21–22, 78n40
37:35, 102
40:4, 146
43:18, 64
44:9, 144
49:6, 73–74
49:17, 36
49:29, 94
49:33, 91, 94
49:33–50:13, 101
50:13, 65, 94

Exodus
5:21, 75
9:21, 144
12:33, 120
13:10, 146n85
20:2, 62
21:23, 144
21:26, 63
23:16, 95
33:21–22, 134n20

Leviticus
7:20, 4
13:6, 26n14, 40
13:8, 26n14
17:11, 78, 82, 83, 83n10, 84, 118, 125
17:14b, 82n3
18:29, 98–99
19:8, 125
22:3, 99
23:39, 95
25:29, 146n85

Numbers
6:6, 4, 83
9:13, 125
9:22, 146n85
11:30, 91, 96
12:14, 91, 96
12:15, 91
15:30, 99
16:22, 87, 90, 92, 109, 125
16:28, 24
17:27, 120
19:13, 83
20:24, 94, 96
23:9, 134n20
23:10, 107
27:13, 94
27:16, 87, 90, 92
31:2, 94, 96

Deuteronomy
2:28, 144
12:9, 70n6
12:23, 76, 82n3

Deuteronomy (*cont.*)
13:10, 103n10
14:25, 144
19:6, 77, 125
19:11, 77, 125
21:23, 94n6
22:2, 91, 95
22:6, 76n30
25:1, 26n14
27:25, 78
28:35, 75n29
28:68, 64
32:1, 76
32:50, 94
33:11, 78
34:6, 94n6

Joshua
15:60, 134
18:14, 134
20:4, 91

Judges
2:10, 91, 95
5:22, 36
12:3, 11n6
15:19, 81, 90, 117
16:30, 107
19:18, 91, 95

1 Samuel
1:3, 146
2:6, 120
14:19, 91
14:52, 91
16:5, 58
19:5, 11n6
24:3, 134n20
24:11 (12), 72, 164
25:29, 4, 45, 62, 68
27:1, 79n44
28:13, 59n24, 120
28:14, 119, 121
28:21, 11n6
28:24, 88n24
30:12, 81, 90, 117

2 Samuel
1:9, 69, 125
6:1, 88n24
11:27, 91
14:25, 75n29
17:13, 91

1 Kings
12:33, 24
17:21–22, 82
17:22, 69–70, 81, 117, 125
19:10, 72
19:14, 72
20:32, 74
21:6, 144
21:15, 144
22:10, 25
22:24, 78

2 Kings
4:1, 64
9:34, 94n6
13:21, 94n6
22:20, 91, 95, 96–97

Isaiah
1:6, 75n29
2:4, 29
3:22, 38, 41
5:14, 104
5:28, 36
8:19, 59–60
10:18, 75, 83n7, 112n42, 125
14:9–11, 119, 120n4
15:1, 36n48
19:3, 120
22:13, 147
26:9, 69, 81, 117
29:4, 60
36:11, 29
38:14, 60
38:17, 104, 106, 126
55:3, 74
60:20, 91
66:24, 112n42

Jeremiah
2:16, 78
4:19, 79
14:14, 25
18:16, 26
29:26, 25
34:11, 64
34:16, 64
38:16, 78, 125
38:17, 74
38:20, 74
40:14, 77
40:15, 77
47:6, 91
51:56, 36

Ezekiel
12:13, 166
13, 68
13:2, 24–25
13:17, 24–26
13:17–21, 5–8, 65–67, 124–25
13:18, 9, 24, 29, 40, 41, 44, 163–66
13:18–20, 8n27, 28
13:19, 26
13:20, 9, 29, 43, 44, 45, 65, 68, 165–66
13:21, 166
13:22, 26
13:23, 26
16:16, 40n16
17:20, 166

18:4, 79
23:14, 31n16
32:30, 119
36:26, 81
42:5, 88n24

Hosea
10:14, 76n30

Joel
4:10, 110–11

Jonah
2:7, 73

Micah
3:5, 26
4:4, 78
4:14, 78n39

Habakkuk
2:5, 104n11

Zephaniah
1:7, 58

Zechariah
12:1, 81–82, 87, 90
14:4, 136

Malachi
2:3, 130

Psalms
3:8, 78, 125
6:3–4, 77
7:6, 72n21, 73–74
11:1, 58
16:10, 3
21:6, 148
26:9, 73, 96–97
27:5, 134n20
27:10, 91
30:4, 120
31:6, 47, 48
37:15, 36
42:1, 79
42:6, 79
42:12, 79, 125
43:5, 79
49:15, 104n12, 126
49:19–20, 97–98, 109, 126
49:20, 92, 95
62:6, 79
63:2, 76, 83n7
66:8, 80
66:14, 118
78:39, 87–88, 90
86:13, 120
88:4, 73
88:11–13, 109, 126
89:52, 36
90:10, 58
94:17, 121
95:11, 70
103:1, 70, 79, 80
103:1–5, 79, 125
103:2, 79, 80
103:2–4, 74, 125
103:22, 79, 80
104:1, 79, 80
104:29, 88, 89, 90, 91–92, 95, 97, 109, 126
104:35, 79, 80
105:17, 64
115:17, 121
116:7, 69–70, 79, 125
118:27, 130
119:175, 74
124:7, 58
140:11, 103, 126
141:8, 82n3
143:3, 72n21, 73
144:1, 118
146:1, 79
146:4, 88, 89, 90
147:3, 36

Job
2:5–6, 74, 77, 125
2:7, 75n29
3:17–19, 119
4:19, 88n26
7:9, 120
7:11, 81, 117
9:5, 136
10:1, 74, 125
10:12, 79n42
12:10, 47, 79, 81, 87, 90, 117
13:14, 11n6, 77, 83n7, 97
13:28, 104n12, 110
14:10, 110, 126
14:20–22, 111–14, 126
14:22, 77, 83n7, 112n47, 113–14, 121
17:13, 109, 126
19:26–27, 107
33:21–22, 75
34:14, 89, 90, 101, 102, 109, 126
34:14–15, 88, 91–92, 95
36:14, 107

Proverbs
1:10, 88n24
4:22, 75, 83n7
6:26, 43
15:24, 120n4
16:24, 75, 77
21:16, 109, 126

Ruth
3:15, 41

Song of Songs
5:6, 62, 69, 70–71, 125

Qohelet
2:7, 88
3:20–21, 88
3:21, 62, 89
12:4, 60, 62
12:5, 130
12:7, 73, 88, 89, 90–92, 101, 102, 109, 112n47, 125, 126

Lamentations
1:19, 81, 117
3:4, 104n12
3:52, 63
4:20, 29

Esther
7:4, 64

Daniel
2:13, 163n3
2:14, 163n3
2:34, 142
2:35, 142
3:22, 142

Nehemiah
4:7, 36
5:5, 64
6:8, 24

2 Chronicles
28:10, 64

Apocryphal Books

Ben Sira
12:6, 103

Texts from the Judean Desert

1QIsa[a]
38:17, 104n12

Murabbaʿāt
72:10, 142

Targumim

Targum Onqelos, 140

Targum Jonathan (Tg. Neb.), 140
1 Sam 25:29, 62
Isa 15:1, 36n48
Ezek 13:18, 40
Ezek 16:16, 40n16

Midrashim

Mekilta, 32n28, 146n85

Sipre Numbers, 31n18

Genesis Rabbah, 47–48, 112n45, 121n8

Leviticus Rabbah, 62, 63, 112nn43, 45; 118n18

Deuteronomy Rabbah, 48

Canticles Rabbah, 62–63

Pesiqta de Rab Kahana, 62

Tanḥuma, 48

Midrash Tehillim, 48

Mishnah (*m.*)

Kilʾayim
9:2, 31n19

Šabbat
4:2, 32n29
23:5, 72

Šeqalim
6:2, 72n19

Yebamot
16:3, 72, 112n43
16:4, 72

Sanhedrin
6:6, 103, 126

Middot
1:8, 35

Kelim, 36, 68
16:4, 32nn20, 24; 36
20:1, 34
25:1, 34, 45n9
26:2, 45n9
26:9, 32n23
28–29, 32n26
28:5, 32nn23, 26; 36
28:9, 32n28
29:2, 32nn21, 26

Oholot
1:6, 72

Negaʿim
11:12, 40

Miqwaʾot
7:6, 32n20
10:2, 32nn20, 22

Niddah
10:4, 110n37

Tosefta (*t.*)

Ḥagigah
1:4, 130

Baba Qamma
11:12, 32n27, 40

Sanhedrin
13:4, 100n22, 106

Zebaḥim
8:17, 83n10

Kelim BM
10:2/3, 34

Oholot
12:2, 32n27

Jerusalem Talmud (*y.*)

Kilʾayim
8.4.31c, 118n18

Moʿed Qaṭan
1.5.80c, 103, 126
3.5.82b, 112

Yebamot
16.3.15c, 112n45

Sanhedrin
6.10.23d, 103, 126

Babylonian Talmud (*b.*)

Berakot
18b, 112n42

Šabbat
13b, 112n42
152b, 108–9, 112n42, 113, 121, 126
152b–153a, 105, 126

Roš Haššanah
17a, 106

Ketubbot
57b, 146n85

Baba Qamma
119b, *40*

Sanhedrin
91a, 62, 63

ʿAbodah Zarah
65a, 32n26

Minor Tractates

ʾAbot de Rabbi Nathan, 62

Kalla Rabbati, 40

Greek and Latin Texts

Classical Texts and Inscriptions

Plato
Phaedo
81e, 54

Aristotle
De Anima, 82n3
2.1.12 413a, 4n17
2.2.14 414a, 4n18

Virgil
Aeneid, 82n3

Posidonius Inscription (Halikarnassos), 14, 149

Hellenistic Jewish Texts

Septuagint
Gen 2:7, 85n17, 86
Deut 32:22, 120n4
Ezek 13:18, 20, 33, 38

Aquila
Ezek 13:20, 55

Philo, 125
Who Is the Heir
§55, 84–85

Josephus, 125
Antiquities
1.1.2 §34, 85–86

Jewish War
2.8.11 §154, 53
2.8.12 §159, 54n36
2.8.14 §165, 109n30
3.8.5 §§372–74, 101n2
7.8.7 §349, 48–49
7.8.7 §§344–45, 53n33

Early Christian Texts

Peshiṭta
1 Sam 24:11 (12), 164
Ezek 13:18, 33
Job 14:10, 110

Tertullian
De Anima
44.2–3, 47

Vulgate
Ezek 13:18, 41, 42n23
Ezek 13:20, 55

Jacob of Serug
poem based on *Acts of Thomas*, 60–61

Egyptian Texts

Pyramid Texts, 107

Coffin Texts, 50, 107

Book of the Dead, 45, 50, 56, 107, 112n45, 122
Book of the Dead (*cont.*)
chap. 89, 51–52
chap. 92, 21
chap. 169, 89

Theban Tomb no. 65, Hatshepsut, 89

Theban Tomb no. 82, Thutmose III, 89

Medinet Habu Inscriptions, 56

Calendar (Papyrus Cairo 86637), 56

"Dialogue of a Man with his *Ba*," 80

"Story of Sinuhe," 70

Sumerian and Akkadian Texts

"Descent of Ishtar to the Underworld," 57n10

"Dumuzi and Geštinana," 57n10

Maqlû III 8, 50–51

Utukkū lemnūtu
5:2, 60n25
5:6, 60n25
6:1–2, 60n25

Ugaritic Texts

CAT/*KTU*
1.5 I 6–8, 103, 126
1.18 IV, 71–72
1.161, 57–58

Northwest Semitic Inscriptions

Arad no. 24
line 18, 137, 138n43,

KAI
no. 24, 150, 154
no. 24 line 8, 144
no. 25, 150, 154
no. 117 line 1, 109n32
no. 214 lines 15–18, 20–24, 12–13, 15
no. 214 line 18, 147nn91–92
no. 214 line 19, 133
no. 215 line 9, 145
no. 215 line 18, 147n90
no. 216 line 8, 147n90
no. 222B line 40, 137

Katumuwa
Inscription, 11–12, 13–14, 16n27, 124, 128–62

Ördekburnu
Inscription, 137n33, 146

Papyrus Amherst
63, 133, 135n26, 143n66, 158–59

TADAE A 6.2 lines 4 and 8, 135

Tell Fekherye
Inscription, 137, 155

Arabian and Arabic Texts

Abū l-Ḥasan
Inscriptions, 131n9

Quran
39:42, 21, 47

Index of Subjects
(including scholars up to 1900)

Abravanel, Isaac, 25n8
abstract meaning/referent, 72–73, 78–79
Achaemenid period, 16n24, 135, 143n66
accident, 73n24. *See also* abstract meaning/referent
accusative
  cognate, 132
  of limitation, 77–78
  of product, 36–37n53
  pronoun, omission of, 147
Akkadian, 29–31
  baštu (aspect of the self), 50–51
  dūtu (aspect of the self), 50–51
  eṭemmu ("ghost, spirit of the dead"), 17, 60n25, 120, 122–23
    nature of, 18, 85n15, 116–17, 122, 122n14
    transformation of, after death, 109–10
    treatment of, 17
  kasītu ("binding magic, state of being bound"), 28–29, 31
  ṣuddu ("to cause to turn, to make dizzy"), 163–66
  zaqīqu (free soul, dream-soul), 18, 47, 56–57, 85n14
alphabet
  adaptation of, 154–56
  Arabic, 143n65,
  Judeo-Arabic, 156n130
  Nabatean, 156n130
  Old Aramaic, 154–56
  Phoenician, 154–56
  Urdu, 143n65
Amorite(s), 19, 100n23, 157, 161–62
ancestors
  circle of, 92, 95
  of the living, 17n30, 18, 19
  of the newly deceased, 91–100, 109–10
annihilation: of soul, 87, 100, 106, 109, 122
Aquila. *See* Index of Ancient Texts
Arabic, 133, 134n22, 143n65, 156n130, 157
  hamara ("pour"), 104n11
  nafas ("breath"), 65n47
  nafs ("blood," "soul," "self," "person"), 21, 65n47, 82n3, 115, 127
  safīḥ ("large sack"), 39
  tanabbaʾa ("arrogate to oneself the gift of prophecy"), 25n8
Aramaic
  dialects, 133, 150–54, 160–62
  in Greek script, 147
  in Judah, Babylonia, and Assyria, 29–30
  morphology, 146, 151, 153–54

Aramaic (*continued*)
origins of, 160–62
provincial variety of , 150, 153
Aristotle. *See* Index of Ancient Texts
Asher b. Jehiel, 34n39
Authorized Version, 44
automeronymy, 116

bags, 34–35, 34n39, 45
Bar-Rakib, 152–53
Becherer, Magnus Anton, 94n4
Bertholet, Alfred, 7–8, 23n1, 28n3
bilingual(ism), 29–30, 109n32, 136, 154–56
bipartite soul, 83, 85n14, 86, 102, 125
bird-soul, 6, 20, 46n1, 47, 52, 55–67, 116, 122, 125. *See also* Hebrew: פרחות
body. *See also* synecdoche
burial and decomposition of, 101–14, 126
and Egyptian *ba*, 20, 52–53, 123
and Greek ψυχή, 122, 123
and נפש, 2, 4–5, 10–12, 14, 53n33, 68–70, 74–77, 82–83, 97, 102, 106, 115, 117, 119, 125–26
as nest of soul, 61, 70
as prison of soul, 53n33, 54
and soul, as merism, 75–77
soul hovering above,
in Israel, 112
in Egypt, 112n45
body soul, 10n4, 47, 50, 82–83, 116. *See also* Hebrew: נפש הבשר
bones, 14, 75, 94, 103, 105, 108, 109, 113
Briggs, Charles A., 69nn3, 5, 87–90
burial, primary and secondary, 93, 94n6, 95n10, 96n13, 103, 105, 107, 108n25, 109, 126–27. *See also* funerary: practice

casus pendens, 144–45
Charles, Robert Henry, 84n11, 86–87
Codex Kaufmann (Mishnah), 34n37, 36n52, 40n14
Codex Parma (Mishnah), 34n37, 35n45, 103
cremation, 14, 16, 122n14

declarative: nuance of causatives, 26
decomposition pit, 103–5, 106, 126
Deir ʿAllā, 160–61
Delitzsch, Friedrich, 23n1, 28–29, 38–39
dentalization: of Old French *m*, 142n63
diachronic interpretation, 102
disembodied: meaning of, 10–11, 12n11, 123
doublets, 138, 157
dream-souls (נפשים), 18, 22, 46–54, 56, 65–66, 71, 124–25, 164
Driver, Samuel Rolles, 144
dualism: soul-body, 3n14, 74–77, 88, 122–23, 126. *See also* monism: soul-body

Egypt/Egyptian
akh (spirit), 20
ba (soul), 15n23, 20, 44, 44–45n8, 46n1, 51–53, 56, 65, 70, 80, 89, 100n22, 107, 112n45, 122–23, 126
ka (spiritual component of person), 21, 99
shabti figures, 44, 44–45n8
šuyt (shadow, shade), 21
Eliezer of Beaugency (twelfth century), 26n12, 64n44
elision
of glottal stop, 133
of final nasals, 142–43

elliptical expression, 84, 97
Epigraphic South Arabian, 16n24, 124, 130. *See also* Sabaic
epithet, divine, 90, 132n13, 133, 135–36
Esarhaddon, 157
Essenes, 53–54
Ethiopic, Ethiopian Semitic, 115, 139, 158
Ewald, Heinrich, 23n2, 55n2
external soul, 10, 50, 66

fading: of body soul, 107
folk etymology, 120n2, 133n16
Frazer, James G., 6–7, 6n19, 33, 43, 45, 46n1, 49–50, 51, 58–59, 59n21, 68
free soul, 10n4, 21, 46, 47, 63n36, 71, 115, 121, 127. *See also* separable soul
Frege, Gottlob, 71n13
Frey, Johannes, 84n11
funerary
- cult/offerings, 12, 14, 17, 17n30, 18, 19–20, 139, 148, 149
- foundations/endowments, 148–49
- monuments, 11, 13, 15, 16, 19, 124
- practice, 9, 103

Galilean Aramaic, 72, 134, 135, 142n63, 143
Geez. *See* Ethiopic, Ethiopian Semitic
Geonim, Babylonian, 153n120. *See also* Saadia Gaon
Gesenius, Wilhelm, 32–33, 35nn44, 46, 36, 94n4
ghosts, spirits of the dead, 7, 16–18, 57–60, 121
grave goods, 21–22, 114
Greek
- δαίμων (immortal guiding spirit), 14, 149–50
- πνεῦμα (= רוח), 85–86
- ψυχή (soul), 4, 48, 53, 55, 63n36, 84–86, 109, 115, 122–23

Gregory the Great, 33n34

Hadad, 12–13, 129, 132–33, 136, 148
Heard, John Bickford, 86n19
Hebrew
- אסף ("bring in"), 91–92, 94–98
- חיים ("life"), 68, 69, 72–75
- כר ("large cushion, mattress"), 32–34
- כסת ("pillow, pillow casing"), ix, 7, 9, 22, 28–37, 39–45, 51, 66, 68, 124. *See also* pillows; pillow-traps
- -ל (preposition). *See* ingressive -ל
- מצדדות ("are trapping"),163–66
- מהמרות ("decomposition pits"), 104, 126
- מספחות ("patches"), 9, 21, 22, 38–42, 124
- נפש הבשר ("body soul, bodily component of נפש"), 74n27, 78, 82–83, 86, 87, 106–7, 109, 111, 118, 121, 125, 126
- נפש חיה ("vitalized soul; living creature"), 83, 85–87, 125
- נפשים ("dream-souls"), 9, 65
- עמים ("kinsmen"), 100n23, 126
- פרחות ("bird-souls"), 5–6, 9, 55–56, 61–63, 64–65, 125. *See also* bird-soul(s)
- רוח ("spiritual component of נפש"), 47–48, 69, 73n24, 81–92, 97, 101, 106–7, 109, 117–18, 121, 125–26
- רפאים ("Rephaim, denizens of Sheol"), 109, 119, 121, 126

Herodotus, 157
hitpaʿel: depreciative/pretensive use of, 25–26
Hittite(s), 14, 19–20, 57, 115, 116n8. *See also* Luwian

Hitzig, Ferdinand, 44
Hobbes, Thomas, 3
holographic images, 121n8
hyperbole, 120–21
hysteron proteron, 111

Ibn Ezra, Abraham, 73n24, 85n14, 146n85
Ibn Kaspi, Joseph, 25n8
immaterial, 44, 122
immortal, 14, 18n32, 53–54, 97–98, 115, 116–17, 149–50
ingressive -לְ, 63–64
inscriptions. *See* Index of Ancient Texts
intensive action, 163–64
Isaiah of Trani, 4, 24n5, 64n44, 83n8
iterative action, 163

Jacob of Serug. *See* Index of Ancient Texts
Jerome, 33n33. *See also* Index of Ancient Texts
Jewish Babylonian Aramaic, 41, 108n28, 153n120
Joseph Ḥayyun, 64n44
Josephus. *See* Index of Ancient Texts
Judeo-Arabic, 34, 40n15, 76, 77, 104n12, 106n17, 156n130

Katumuwa
  Aramaic inscription of. *See* Index of Ancient Texts
  etymology and vocalization of, 11n7
Kazimirski, A. de Biberstein, 39n11
Keil, Carl F., 37n53, 63–64
Kingsley, Mary H., 49, 51
kispu ritual, 17–20, 59–60n24
Kraetzschmar, Richard, 7, 28n3
Kubaba, 137

Lane, Edward W., 25n8, 39n11, 82n3, 115n1
Levita, Elijah, 32
literary license, 73n23
Lowth, William, 43–44
Luwian, 14, 132, 136, 161–62. *See also* Hittite(s)

magic, 6–8, 23–24, 26–27, 28, 29n4, 39, 43, 51–54, 140 *See also* witchcraft/witch(es)
Maimonides, 34, 100n22
mater lectionis, 135, 151
meaning
  abstract, 78–79
  archaic, 100, 126
  paradigmatic evidence for, 117–18
  and reference, 71
  syntagmatic evidence for, 117–18
Menaḥem b. Saruq, 34–35
Menaḥem b. Simeon, 35, 36, 64n44
merism, 75–77
meronymy, 118
  automeronymy, 116
  co-meronyms, 75n29
Mesopotamia, 16–21, 29–31, 47, 50, 56–57, 85n14, 99, 109–10, 116–17, 122, 124, *See also* Akkadian
metanalysis, 36. *See also* reanalysis
metonymy, 15–16
monism: soul-body, 87, 123. *See also* dualism: soul-body
Moore, George Foot, 119n1

nasal(ized) vowels: in Aramaic and Hebrew, 142–43
Nathan b. Jehiel of Rome, 32
Neanderthals, 21
necromancy, 7, 59–60, 108–9, 121
netherworld. *See* underworld
neutralization: of voicing, 138

North/Northwest Arabian, 131n9, 157

Origen, 33n33, 85n14
oscillation. *See* soul oscillation
ossilegium. *See* funerary: practice
ossuary, 105, 107, 108

Panamuwa I (king), 12–13, 17
Panamuwa II (king), 11, 129, 152–53
Parkhurst, John, 2–3, 5
pars pro toto. *See* synecdoche
Paul of Tarsus, 2, 85, 86
Peshiṭta. *See* Index of Ancient Texts
pillows, 22, 28–37
  filling of, 38–42, 54, 66
  function of, 32, 33–35,
  manufacture of, 31–32, 36, 42, 65–66, 124
  as metaphor, 33n34
pillow-traps: for dream-souls, 5–6, 22, 28–37, 42, 44–45, 51–52, 54, 64, 66, 124–25, 164
Plato. *See* Index of Ancient Texts
plural ending, masculine
  Common Aramaic, 146
  Jewish Babylonian Aramaic, 153n121
  Samalian, 151–52
poetic epithet, 73
poetic parallelism, 42, 70, 73–74, 76–77, 81, 91, 117, 118
polel: archaic verb stem, 164–65
polyphony: in Aramaic alphabet, 154
Posidonius: funerary inscription of. *See* Index of Ancient Texts
prophetesses: women posing as, 5, 7, 23–26, 33n34, 59, 124
Proto-Aramaic, 158, 160–61
Proto-Northwest Semitic, 133n17, 160
Proto-Semitic, Proto-West Semitic, 21, 35n47, 100n23, 115, 127, 130n4, 139, 154, 156, 157, 165
punishment: in afterlife, 62, 99–100, 106, 125, 126

Qara, Joseph, 35
Qimḥi, David, 43, 64n44, 103, 104n12, 120n4
Quran. *See* Index of Ancient Texts

Ramban (Naḥmanides; Moses b. Naḥman Gerondi), 82n3, 98–99
Rashbam (Samuel b. Meir), 146n85
Rashi (Solomon b. Isaac), 4n16, 60, 64n44, 94–96, 111n39, 113, 146n85
reanalysis, 120n2. *See also* metanalysis
recursion/recursiveness, 145
Rephaim, 109, 119, 121, 126
restrictive/non-restrictive modifier, 120n4
Reuel (Jewish exegete from Byzantium), 26–27, 35

Saadia Gaon, 72–73n23, 76–77, 104n12, 105–6n17, 118n18
Sabaic, 16n24, 115, 134. *See also* Epigraphic South Arabian
Samal
  inscriptions from. *See* Index of Ancient Texts
  languages and dialects of, 150–62
Samaritan(s), 78n39, 134, 141n57
Sargon II, 29–30
Schröter, R., 61nn27–29
Schwally, Friedrich, 84n11, 112n47
semantic bleaching, 75n28
separable soul, 1, 2n9, 10n4, 12n11, 72, 102. *See also* free soul
Septuagint. *See* Index of Ancient Texts

Sequence of St. Eulalie, 142n63
Shanidar Cave, 20–22, 127
Sheol, 7, 73, 98n18, 99, 101–2, 104nn11–12, 106–7, 109, 111, 119–21, 123, 126
Smend, Rudolf, 23n1, 28, 63n39
Smith, William Robinson, 6, 7
sociolect: of Samalian, 154
sociolinguistic
  change, 152
  marker, 153
  situation
    in Judah, 29
    in Mesopotamia, 29–31
    in Samal, 150–54
soul oscillation
  eternal, in Egypt, 107, 108
  transitional, in Israel, 106–7, 108
spatial location, 69, 71, 78–79, 82, 125
spells: for soul, 24n5, 50, 51–54
spelling
  fluctuation of, 159n149
  folk-etymological, 133n16
  historical, 133
  inverse, 137–38
  reform of, 155
spelling pronunciation, 159n149
spirits of the dead. *See* ghosts, spirits of the dead
standard Old Aramaic, 150–55, 160–61
style shifting, 153n120, 154
Symmachus, 33, 41–42
synchronic interpretation, 102n8, 103
synecdoche, 130
  and בשר meaning "body," 75, 82–83, 116n8
  and נפש meaning "corpse," 83, 116
  and נפש meaning "funerary monument," 15–16
  and נפש meaning "person," 83, 116n8
  and נפש חיה meaning "living creature," 83. 125
  and עצם meaning "body," 75
Syriac, 60–61, 110, 138nn42–43, 164

Tarashchansky, N. N., 40–42
targumim, official: oldest layer of, 143n66
Taurus mountains: Aramaic etymology of name, 134–35
Tertullian, 47
transitional period: after death, 106, 109, 114, 126
traps: for soul, 6, 49, 50, 51,
tripartite soul, 85n14, 118n18
tripartite human being, 86–87

Ugarit/Ugaritic, 20, 21, 57–58, 71–72, 95n11, 103–4, 106–7n19, 127, 133, 134, 137, 138n43
underworld, 7, 52, 57, 89, 98, 100n23, 101, 102, 106, 109. *See also* Sheol
Urdu: *nūn* of nasalization, 143n65

vegetative soul, 82
vocative, 79

witchcraft/witch(es), 1, 23–24, 26, 27, 49, 50–51, 66, 121
wordplay, 73n23

Yeats, William Butler, 59, 80

Zincirli (ancient Samal), 9, 10–14, 19, 124, 128

www.ingramcontent.com/pod-product-compliance
Lightning Source LLC
Chambersburg PA
CBHW021840220426
43663CB00005B/337
* 9 7 8 1 6 2 8 3 7 0 7 6 8 *